The Spaces of Mental Capacity Law

This book explores the conceptual spaces and socio-legal context which mental capacity laws inhabit. It will be seen that these norms are created and reproduced through the binaries that pervade mental capacity laws in liberal legal jurisdictions – such as capacity/incapacity, autonomy/paternalism, empowerment/protection, carer/cared-for, disabled/non-disabled, public/private. Whilst on one level the book demonstrates the pervasive reach of laws questioning individuals' mental capacity, within and beyond the medical context with which it is most commonly associated, at a deeper and perhaps more important level it challenges the underlying norms and assumptions underpinning the very idea of mental capacity, and reflects outwards on the transformative potential of these realisations for other areas of law. In doing so, whilst the book offers lessons for mental capacity law scholarship in terms of reform efforts at both domestic and international levels, it also offers ways to develop our understandings of a range of linked legal, policy, and theoretical concepts. In so doing, it offers new critical vantage points for both legal critique and conceptual change beyond mental capacity law.

The book will be of interest to researchers in mental capacity law, disability law, and socio-legal studies, as well as critical geographers and disability studies scholars.

Beverley Clough is based in the Centre for Law & Social Justice, School of Law at the University of Leeds, UK.

Part of the
SOCIAL JUSTICE
series

series editors
Sarah Keenan, *Birkbeck College, University of London, UK*
Davina Cooper, *University of Kent, UK*
Sarah Lamble, *Birkbeck College, University of London, UK*

for information about the series and details of previous and forthcoming titles,
see https://www.routledge.com/Social-Justice/book-series/RCSOCJ

A GlassHouse book

The Spaces of Mental Capacity Law

Moving Beyond Binaries

Beverley Clough

Routledge
Taylor & Francis Group
a GlassHouse Book

First published 2022
by Routledge
2 Park Square, Milton Park, Abingdon, Oxon OX14 4RN

and by Routledge
605 Third Avenue, New York, NY 10158

a GlassHouse book

Routledge is an imprint of the Taylor & Francis Group, an informa business

British Library Cataloguing-in-Publication Data
A catalogue record for this book is available from the British Library

Library of Congress Cataloging-in-Publication Data
A catalog record has been requested for this book

ISBN: 9781138478695 (hbk)
ISBN: 9781032115771 (pbk)
ISBN: 9781351067881 (ebk)

DOI: 10.4324/9781351067881

Typeset in Bembo
by Deanta Global Publishing Services, Chennai, India

Contents

Acknowledgements

Writing this book has been a challenging process, spanning three lockdowns, two pregnancies, and a global pandemic. It has been a fraught time in which many of us have been starkly reminded of the importance of relationality and connection. Whilst physically distant from friends, colleagues, and support networks, they have all helped to sustain this project.

Firstly, I must thank the Independent Social Research Foundation (ISRF) who funded my early career fellowship in 2017. This provided the time and space to enable me to explore and challenge ideas underpinning mental capacity law through a variety of disciplinary perspectives. Attending conferences from other disciplines and fully immersing myself in the debates and research agendas within these has offered me rich and deep insights to take back to mental capacity scholarship. Without the support of the ISRF, this book simply would not have happened.

I have been privileged to be part of the Centre for Law & Social Justice at the University of Leeds since 2015, and this has exposed me to various socio-legal and theoretical approaches, piquing my curiosity as to how these can be utilised as tools to tap into some of the stubborn and pervasive frameworks that seem to surround mental capacity law. Huge thanks go to Michael Thomson and Julie Wallbank for providing this exciting space which helped shape my early career and theoretical journey. Thanks also to colleagues within the Centre over the years who have been constantly supportive and inspiring: Katie Cruz, Mitchell Travis, Jen Hendry, Chris Dietz, Jess Mant, Luke Clements, Hilary Sommerlad, Rebecca Moosavian, Craig Purshouse, and Illias Trispiotis. Particular thanks go to Amanda Keeling for all of those conversations back in our shared office, where some of the ideas for the book started to form. Also to Anna Lawson, who has been a constant source of support throughout the book and beyond, and whose leadership within the Centre for Disability Studies has helped to expose me to the importance of disability studies to my work. Beyond Leeds, I am indebted to a number of colleagues who have helped shape my ideas, or provided invaluable support and good humour along the way, including Kirsty Keywood, Neil Allen, Peter Bartlett, Laura Pritchard-Jones, Jaime Lindsey, Paul Skowron, Rosie Harding, Lucy Series, Linda Steele, and Camilla Sabroe Jydebjerg.

I owe immense thanks to people who have listened to and provided feedback on various iterations of these ideas at conferences over the past few years. I must also thank those who have provided careful feedback on drafts of the book, particularly the series editors Davina Cooper, Sarah Keenan, and Sarah Lamble. Thank you to Craig Purshouse, Camilla Sabroe Jydebjerg, Jonathan Herring, Margaret Davies, Mitchell Travis, Camillia Kong, and Nick Gill.

Finally, and most importantly, to my family and friends who have kept me going and provided much-needed care, support, walks, laughs, drinks, cake, and opportunities for dancing.

Introduction

A 34-year-old man with autism, significant learning disabilities, and physical and sensory impairments is residing in a wholly unsuitable flat. He cannot stand independently, uses a wheelchair, and requires one-to-one and sometimes two-to-one support. His flat is too small to accommodate a wheelchair, however, so he often must pull himself along the floor, resulting in painful bursitis of the knees and callouses to his knees and ankles. The flat has no outside space. He was placed in this accommodation as part of a care package funded by his Clinical Commissioning Group and County Council.

The legal response to this, through the mental capacity framework, was to recognise that whilst this amounted to a deprivation of liberty, it could be justified as being in his best interests (*North Yorkshire County Council v MAG & Ors* [2016] EWCOP 5). The man was deemed to lack mental capacity in relation to his residence decisions, which effectively placed the power to make these in the hands of social care professionals and, in turn, the judiciary. Arguments that more appropriate accommodation ought to be found were dismissed through the Court of Protection distancing themselves from public law decision making. As such, they were purportedly bound to endorse the situation as being in his best interests.

There are a number of angles from which this case can be critiqued, and it will be returned to later in the book. For now, it serves as an important illustration of the range of issues that the mental capacity legal framework engages, and the resonance of these with broader debates across law, the humanities, and social sciences. It invites us to reflect on the removal of legal agency through a legal framework distinguishing disabled and non-disabled individuals on the basis of rationality, a framework which is ostensibly built on Enlightenment ideals of autonomy and empowerment. In doing so, questions as to legal subjectivity, and longstanding critiques of the liberal legal subject, are engaged. It calls into question the role of the state and institutions in the shaping of individual choice, and the divide between the public and the private realms which has served to exclude problems from the legal and political gaze and to distance the state from responsibility. Care, and the role and place of care in our society, becomes a very tangible and urgent concern through this case. Feminist legal theorists, social policy scholars, care ethicists, and geographers

DOI: 10.4324/9781351067881-101

have been grappling with care as a practice and a political theory, and here we have the laying bare of a legal, social, and political framework which can create and endorse such *un*caring conditions. Liberty, and the justifications for the deprivation of liberty through this legal framework, are similarly called into question here, testing the boundaries of theoretical debates as to what is meant by liberty, and the role of the state and individuals within these debates.

In this regard, mental capacity law offers a compelling framework for critical socio-legal scholarship to engage with, yet it has been a relatively self-contained area of research. It occupies a curious position in the legal and academic field, often taught as part of medical or health care law modules, cementing an idea of it as simply being about medical decision making. Indeed, many of the 'headline' cases do involve medical issues and given the very human and personal nature of these sorts of decisions, it is not surprising that many feel drawn to them. Cases involving refusal of life-saving treatment by a socialite who has "lost their sparkle" (*Kings College NHS Foundation Trust v C and V* [2015] EWCOP 59), or the refusal of the amputation of gangrenous or infected limbs (*Re C* (adult: refusal of medical treatment) [1994] 1 All ER 819 (QBD); *Wye Valley NHS Trust v B* [2015] EWCOP 60), or those involving the force-feeding of patients with anorexia (*A Local Authority v E* [2012] EWHC 1639 (COP)) predictably capture public attention. But mental capacity law is situated within a complex web of legal, policy, and ethical frameworks. Cases reaching the Court of Protection engage questions of community care/social welfare, residence, wills, marriage, sexual relations, relationships, financial decision making, and social media use. As noted above, as well as the breadth of legal issues it pertains to, and overlaps with other areas of law, it engages questions of disability, legal subjectivity, care, empowerment, the role of the state and institutions, liberty, and the public/private divide. The reach of the logics of the Mental Capacity Act 2005 and policy in this area is currently under-recognised.

This book aims to rectify this by bringing awareness of mental capacity law to the wider attention of both socio-legal scholarship and scholarship in other disciplines, as well as seeking to advance critical conceptual debates taking place in these areas through bringing them into conversation with mental capacity law. In this way, whilst the book offers lessons for mental capacity law scholarship in terms of reform efforts at both domestic and international levels, it also offers ways to develop our understandings of a range of linked legal, policy, and theoretical concepts. In so doing, it can offer new critical vantage points for both legal critique and conceptual change beyond mental capacity law.

Whilst the interrogation of the current legal framework for mental capacity law necessarily focuses on the domestic legal context and the Mental Capacity Act 2005, the insights offered have a broader international relevance. Many jurisdictions, particularly Commonwealth jurisdictions, contain decision making regimes within which legal agency can be denied to individuals with cognitive impairments on the basis of 'incapacity' or 'incompetence'. Such jurisdictions, as in England and Wales, tend to foreground autonomy and consent as part of their personal legal decision making frameworks, disavow paternalism, and situate responses to those with cognitive impairments within an empowerment/protection dichotomy. The arguments contained within these chapters will, as such, resonate across these jurisdictions at a conceptual, if not doctrinal, level.

Overview of the legal framework and context

The Mental Capacity Act 2005 (MCA) governs decision making on behalf of a person who is deemed to lack capacity. It came into force in 2007 after a long and contentious period of discussion and drafting. In the 1995 Law Commission Report on *Mental Incapacity* (Law Commission, 1995) various reasons were given for the need for reform. They pointed to the way in which the law governing this area was "unsystematic and full of glaring gaps" (para 1.1) and has "failed to keep up with developments in our understanding of the rights and needs of those with mental disability" (para 1.1). Furthermore, there was perceived to be a lack of an effective framework for resolving disputes about the care of people without capacity or for legitimating or regulating the substitute decision making that regularly took place in practice (para 1.5). The social context was also deemed to be an important factor in pushing for legal reform, with the Law Commission pointing to the moves to community care, the ageing population, medical advances, and a rights-focused law and policy agenda as being key social and political drivers for change in this area (para 2.31).

In many ways, the resulting legislation consolidated and codified the existing common law principles which had developed through various cases. One of the central claims that heralded the MCA, and which regularly appears in discussions of the MCA in academic and policy literature, is the idea that the legislation is 'empowering' for those with disabilities – see, for example, Lord Falconer's foreword to the Code of Practice where he states that "it will empower people to make decisions for themselves wherever possible" (Department for Constitutional Affairs, 2007). The Act sets out five statutory principles which underpin the statute in s1. These are: a presumption of capacity; a need to take all practicable steps to help someone make a decision; that a person is not to be treated as unable to make a decision merely because it is unwise; acts or decisions on behalf of an incapacitous person must be in their best interests; and the need to have regard to the least restrictive alternative.

Section 2 outlines the diagnostic element of mental capacity, outlining how "a person lacks capacity in relation to a matter if at the material time he is unable to make a decision for himself in relation to the matter because of an impairment of, or a disturbance in the functioning of, the mind or brain" (s2(1)). Section 3 of the Act goes on to define what is meant by "unable to make a decision" (s3(1)) and, if a finding of incapacity is made, the Act further lays out that decisions must be made on the basis of a 'best interests' test (s1(5) and s4).

Ostensibly then, the MCA presents a simplistic framework for making decisions on behalf of those who are deemed to lack mental capacity, but as will be seen, this belies the complexity of issues that fail to be considered in this context. Much of the literature in this area also tends to under-theorise or under-appreciate the political underpinnings of the legislation and policy in this area. As will be seen, mental capacity law does not exist in a vacuum. The Act itself is premised upon particular ideals of subjectivity and the role of professionals and other institutions. It sets up a framework of legal and spatial relations, drawing boundaries around and within these relations as it does so. These boundaries are inflected with an interwoven network of binaries which help to shape and form the logics of the legislation as well as broader legal frameworks. We will encounter these throughout the book, but to name a few here: autonomy/paternalism; capacity/incapacity; empower/protect; and public/private. It will be seen that these are not neutral, and contrary to the simplistic and abstracted vision of the legislation, the workings of the Act and its logics play an active role in shaping and buttressing ideas of legal subjectivity and the role of the state. Delving into the spatial boundaries that are drawn in the jurisprudence (around individuals, around professional obligations, around state institutions) enables a challenge to the perceived neutrality and inevitability of this legal framework.

This book explores the underpinnings of the Act and the relations it creates in order to highlight both the processes which create and solidify these relations, and the effects of these in terms of the rendering of the legal subject and the role of institutions. This close analysis and excavation of the mental capacity framework helps to expose the problematic norms which are rooted in it. A legal subject built on Enlightenment ideals of autonomy and rationality, and a desire to facilitate professional decision making without recourse to the judiciary, are stark features. Yet it will be seen that these ideals are dangerous and damaging and have far-reaching repercussions across the legal landscape.

It is an important moment to be undertaking such analysis, given the state of flux that the legislative framework is currently in. The UN Convention on the Rights of Persons with Disabilities 2006 (CRPD), ratified by the UK government in 2009, has often been hailed as signalling a 'paradigm shift' in relation to disability rights (Mittler, 2015). Such optimistic statements are often accompanied by assertions that at the heart of the CRPD is the empowerment of disabled people. However, disability law scholar Gerard Quinn has suggested that whilst on one level, the CRPD is clearly about disability, he invites the approach that this is not all that it does, and that it can be viewed as part of an ongoing, broader debate about theories of justice (Quinn, 2011). This book takes up this theme and considers the routes to transformative approaches to social justice, not just in the context of disability but for our broader understandings of the legal subject and the role and responsibilities of various actors, including the state and institutions.

Several articles of the Convention pose a direct challenge to the Mental Capacity Act and its organising framework – the very logics which will be exposed through the book. Scholars, activists, and professionals (legal, medical, psychiatric, social work) have been at loggerheads trying to stake a claim for particular interpretations of the key articles, many of which could take us in challenging new directions in this area. The Committee on the CRPD has been drip-feeding General Comments and reports on State Parties from which it is possible to variously glean the ethos of the Convention (although these too have a mixed reception). In the wake of this there has been a revived interest in theories of relational autonomy, particularly given the emphasis on supported decision making in Art 12 of the CRPD, which states that persons with disabilities have the right to legal capacity on an equal basis with others. This has the potential to pull the rug from underneath the mental capacity framework. There are also emerging, reignited debates about the Social Model of Disability, the extent to which this is 'too material' and whether it ignores embodied experience. In the legal and political context, growing interest in ideas of universal vulnerability has triggered new thinking about the role of the state and institutions. There are also parallel debates in fields such as geography and cultural studies, where there is increasing engagement with spatial approaches to disability. It is an exciting and vital time to be engaged with mental capacity law.

A spatial lens: boundaries in mental capacity law

And yet, this book has been borne of a frustration with the direction and parameters of the debates around the CRPD and its legal implementation in the UK legal context, which are similarly taking place across other (particularly Commonwealth) jurisdictions. In many ways, they map onto the pre-existing boundaries of our debates at a domestic level about the MCA, about the grand 'clashes' between autonomy and paternalism, about empowering *or* protecting, and about the legitimate moment at which the state ought to 'step in' to an otherwise private realm populated by free individuals. These play out in cases around the refusal of medical treatments where others (the clinical team or families) disagree, in situations where individuals are involved in abusive or coercive relationships that others are concerned about, in instances where there is potential financial exploitation, or where there is conflict around the suitability of a particular care plan. These parameters – these boundaries in our thinking, drawn by stark binaries – have led us to a static and stagnant legal landscape within which attempts to challenge the legal framework hit up against the other side of the binary and then retreat. Through exposing the spaces carved by, and strongly guarded by, these boundaries – perceived as natural, immovable and given – this book offers the opportunity to dismantle them.

A core part of the problem for this field so far, and perhaps one that is linked to the narrow vision that has developed of what mental capacity law is about, is that it has been perceived as simply about *law*. Legal scholars engaging with the Act (myself included) have not fully integrated other disciplinary insights into their analysis; likewise, it has not attracted sufficient or sustained critical attention from other disciplines. When presenting some early ideas for this book at a medical humanities conference, one of the conference delegates commented during the discussion that "these changes can't be achieved, it is about law and law is..." (punctuated by a shrug). The shrug here spoke volumes. Far from putting me off the project, it reminded me that a core problem in this area (as with many other areas of legal academic discipline) is that law itself is being viewed as a static, authoritative, and positivist 'thing', rather than the politically infused, shifting, and active beast that socio-legal scholars have long been illuminating.

As such, this project has been about bringing these missing voices into concert in order to demonstrate the constructed nature of the boundaries drawn (and importantly *how* they have been constructed), their productive effects, and ways in which they can begin to be unravelled. An important and particularly pertinent strand of socio-legal thought for this endeavour is legal geography. Given the importance of boundaries and binaries (with their inside/outside and organising role) to mental capacity law, there is a need for conceptual tools to deeply and carefully engage with their spatial nature. David Delaney in particular has written about the importance of the spatial imaginary engaging not just with the material but also the social, discursive, and performative aspects of space (Delaney, 2010). Indeed, the very distinction between the material and discursive here would be questioned. Delaney suggests the need to consider that "social space is continuously reproduced and transformed through *how* it is performed" (Delaney, 2010, 15) and that this encompasses the performative aspects of material-discursive spaces. It is crucial for this project, and for broader socio-legal scholarship, to rethink both the legal and the spatial. In terms of the spatial, this rethink entails a concern with discursive organising and performance, but also "spatialisation of difference and the pragmatic effacement, denial or recalibration of difference" (Delaney, 2010, 18). As well as reconceptualising space,

> the legal must also be treated as consisting of and implicating the dynamic, reciprocal intertwinements of social imaginaries, with performative and material aspects of sociality ... The legal is continuously performed, re-enacted. The legal is continuously and creatively done and redone. The legal is always happening.
>
> (Delaney, 2010, 19)

Others writing on the importance of law and space, such as Sarah Keenan (2015) and Andreas Philippopoulos-Mihalopoulos (2018), have drawn attention to the need to carefully avoid framing law and space in a binary way and to approach the relationship between them as dynamic. As Keenan suggests, "[t]hat is, to not only add space as a factor to be taken into account in socio-legal issues, but to also embrace the uncertainty of space" (2015, 39). Arguing that we need to take seriously Doreen Massey's approach to space as dynamic (Massey, 2005), Keenan suggests that this allows us to more usefully explore "how different spaces are produced, how particular subjects come to belong in those spaces and what constitutes the complex relation between space and the subject" (Keenan, 2015, 39). This provides a useful framework for challenging the static and given boundaries of mental capacity law, interrogating the connections between this space and the subject, and exposing the effects of the spaces these produce.

Interestingly, the Court of Protection has acknowledged the importance of space to mental capacity law. As McFarlane LJ put it in *PC & Anor v City of York Council* [2013] EWCA Civ 478,

> there is a space between an unwise decision and one which an individual does not have the mental capacity to take and ... it is important to respect that space, and to ensure that it is preserved, for it is within that space that an individual's autonomy operates.
>
> (para 54)

Here, however, space is seen as a pre-given and natural or observable phenomenon – one which ought to be preserved. Moreover, it is a space which bounds the individual and their autonomy as a realm of non-interference.

As will be seen in this book, this individual realm is central to the underpinnings and logics of mental capacity law and liberal legal frameworks more broadly. Instead of presupposing this natural realm of non-interference, the engagement with spatial dynamics offered in the chapters that follow will disrupt and expose the ways that such spaces are created and maintained through legal processes, and the wider spaces and boundaries that they are mutually imbricated with. Such boundaries will be seen to be both material and discursive, and are drawn around and between individuals, the state and institutions. The differential legal spaces that disabled people inhabit through these legal processes – ones which linger despite claims that disabled people have been *physically* moved from institutions into communities – and the "definitional walls" (Jarrett, 2020) that are created will be explored. This has particular relevance for legal understandings of and approaches to disability, but importantly thinking about law *through* disability in this way reveals the persistence of liberal ideals of legal subjectivity and the role of institutions which have problematic effects for many in society.

Such ideas resonate with emerging feminist new materialist theory (Coole and Frost, 2010) as well as critical disability studies approaches which seek to rethink broader concepts *through* disability (Goodley et al., 2019). A number of important themes will emerge from bringing law, disability, and space into conversation, which build upon but also offer new insights for existing debates across a number of disciplines, including philosophy, political science, geography, and legal theory. Together, these provide a rich and nuanced backdrop for critiquing the development of the boundaries of mental capacity law, as well as the tools to dismantle them. For mental capacity law, this entails a shift from progressive literatures which are focused on the individual agent (such as through the lens of their autonomy and choice) and instead suggests the need to consider the conceptual and material networks that mental capacity law inhabits. This is not to say that the legal subject is not important; instead, it is the recursive relationship between the legal subject and the material and discursive spaces that they are situated within which matters.

In particular, the importance of relationality and attentiveness to the dynamic processes which work to inscribe the current contours of approaches to law will be a central theme. This will be demonstrated through foregrounding the prevalence of mutually reinforcing binaries, which act to draw the parameters of debate in this context currently. Such binaries are reinforced and reproduced through various mechanisms in the context of mental capacity law and, as already suggested, are increasingly reiterated without question in debates surrounding the implementation of the CRPD. As will be seen, such uncritical reiteration is a tangible barrier to the achievement of the 'paradigm shift' envisaged in the Convention. Whilst this 'paradigm shift' may have been politically progressive for disability rights, its actualisation has remarkably been heavily under-theorised and under-explored. The current moment for mental capacity law is thus important. The existential crisis visited upon it by the CRPD provides an opportune moment to reconsider – and reconfigure – these boundaries.

Bringing these disciplines into conversation through a sustained interrogation of legal processes in mental capacity law also offers new critical insights to these debates through drawing attention to the more complex role of law within the spatial imaginaries they work with. Moreover, it offers new conceptual tools for recognising and confronting some of the barriers to emancipatory legal and policy projects in other contexts. The approach of carefully mapping conceptual connections and processes of boundary drawing through such processes, tracing their becoming and reinscription, and their material and discursive effects will have utility for activist and progressive discourses in socio-legal studies which have similarly tended to centre efforts on the legal subject and their agency/choice.

Structure of the book

The book begins with an overview of the roots, objectives, and convergences of relational and spatial thinking across law and other disciplines. This provides the conceptual tools for examining the legal landscape, its underpinning ideas, processes, and effects. It offers new ways of approaching and thinking about law, disentangling it from a traditionally positivist and often abstract focus. These conceptual tools are utilised in a more sustained way in relation to mental capacity law in Chapter 2. This chapter takes the opportunity posed by the CRPD as an important moment to question and challenge the organising binaries in this context and to foreground their problematic effects in terms of shaping the (disabled) legal subject and demarcating the role and responsibilities of the state and other institutions. Building on critiques of the

Social Model of Disability, spatial and relational dynamics, and a focus on the assemblage offers new ways to conceptualise disability and mental capacity, without getting stuck in static and linear ideas of subjectivity and the role of the state. The chapter also provides an overview of the conceptual underpinnings and binaries which frame this area of law, demonstrating their boundary drawing role. Chapter 3 examines in more depth the construction and deployment of the capacity/incapacity binary, and its effects in terms of sorting individuals into different legal spaces. Chapter 4 similarly looks at the sorting of individuals into fixed and static identities in the legislative framework, this time through the care/disability binary. It responds to some potential difficulties that might be experienced in bringing together relational theories (which, as will be seen, share some affinities with care ethics approaches) and critical disability studies, given the historical debates in these fields. Here, I challenge this stark dichotomy between care and disability by focusing on the relational and spatial challenge to static and fixed identities, as well as bringing attention to contextual and structural factors which shape them. Through the discussion in Chapters 3 and 4, we get a sense of the separate spaces of the individual and the state that are created through these legal processes. These spaces are interrogated in more depth in Chapter 5, where the reach and role of the state, and ideas of the boundaries of state responsibility in relation to legal subjects, are challenged. Chapter 6 takes up this discussion in the context of liberty and its role in mental capacity jurisprudence, highlighting the purported spaces of freedom that underpin these logics. Finally, Chapter 7 then considers the way that the public/private divide is deployed in mental capacity jurisprudence, and the stark effects that this has both at a theoretical and a practical level. In tracing and exposing these boundaries, it will be seen that they need constant maintenance and reiteration through policy and jurisprudence, and that they will persist unless their techniques are better understood, and their logics are challenged as part of rethinking law in the wake of the CRPD.

References

Coole, D. and Frost, S. 2010. *New Materialisms: Ontology, Agency, and Politics*. Durham, NC: Duke University Press.

Delaney, D. 2010. *Nomospheric Investigations: The Spatial, the Legal and the Pragmatics of World-Making*. Oxfordshire: Routledge.

Department for Constitutional Affairs. 2007. *Mental Capacity Act 2005 Code of Practice*. London: The Stationery Office.

Goodley, D, Lawthom, R., Liddiard, K. and Runswick-Cole, K. 2019. 'Provocations for Critical Disability Studies' *Disability & Society* 34(6), 972–97.

Jarrett, S. 2020. *Those They Called Idiots: The Idea of the Disabled Mind from 1700 to the Present Day*. London: Reaktion Books.

Keenan, S. 2015. *Subversive Property: Law and the Production of Spaces of Belonging*. Oxfordshire: Routledge.

Law Commission. 1995. *Mental Incapacity*. London: HMSO.

Massey, D. 2005. *For Space*. London: Sage.

Mittler, P. 2015. 'The UN Convention on the Rights of Persons with Disabilities: Implementing a Paradigm Shift' *Journal of Policy and Practice in Intellectual Disabilities* 12(2), 79–89.

Philippopoulos-Mihalopoulos, A. 2018. 'And For Law: Why Space Cannot Be Understood Without Law' *Law, Culture and the Humanities*. OnlineFirst, 1–20.

Quinn, G. 2011. 'Rethinking Personhood: New Questions in Legal Capacity Law and Policy' in *Lecture*, Vancouver: University of British Columbia. http://citizenship.sites.olt.ubc.ca/files/2014/07/Gerard_Quinn_s_Keynote_-_April_29__2011.pdf last accessed 18/6/2021.

1 The conceptual terrain

Spatial dynamics and law

As suggested in the Introduction, relations (between actors, institutions, and the state, but also between the organising binaries and boundaries of law) are a core but often unrecognised part of mental capacity law. Relational theory has already played an important role in challenging the perceived liberal legal subject who inhabits legal frameworks. This has been a central concern for a number of feminist theorists who have illuminated how liberal legal frameworks have been built around and shaped an ideal of an individualistic, rationalistic, and masculine legal subject; one who is seen to be ubiquitous in law yet reflective of no one. Enlightenment ideas associated with this subject – of rationality, self-determination, and human progress – have been steadily challenged through feminist legal critique. The relational autonomy literature has been crucial in challenging this individualistic legal subject and foregrounding interpersonal relationships as being a more reflective starting point, taking into account the relational constraints upon choice, as well as the ways that choices are made in relation to and with others (Mackenzie and Stoljar, 2000). This has also provided an important and powerful critique of law and its individualistic underpinnings in the context of mental capacity (Harding, 2017; Kong, 2017). Yet, as will be seen throughout the book, many who adopt a relational approach in the context of law and legal critique still struggle against the boundaries drawn by the binaries underpinning the legal logics. As Davies suggests, "concepts are proving to be rather pliable, though the substrate, the background of Western philosophical and cultural knowledge, is rather more difficult to shift" (Davies, 2017, 13).

Whilst relational approaches often pose significant challenges to the methodological and/or normative individualism at the heart of (particularly Western) liberal legal approaches, a spatial turn in the humanities and social sciences provides additional tools to deepen the critique offered by relationality, and to avoid falling back into this binary thinking. Such approaches tend to share a focus on the importance of the relations between institutions and systems, but also draw attention to the spaces and the consequent power relations that are enabled by these dynamic processes. Using space as a locus of critique enables attention to the historicity and development of particular frameworks (both conceptual and material), the production of boundaries, and their role in sedimenting particular ideals and material effects around difference. Importantly,

DOI: 10.4324/9781351067881-1

the challenge to the perceived naturalness and given-ness of these boundaries avoids the tendency to reinforce them that often occurs in relational literature. In conversation with new materialism, through a shared concern with relational dynamics, such approaches move beyond critique and instead focus on *change*; on the ways in which such spatial arrangements can be reconfigured. It is here that scope for rethinking approaches to social justice will emerge. As legal geographers have been increasingly suggesting, it is only through seeing institutions as complicit in the material context impacting on relational connections and intra-actions that such a shift may occur.

At a general (and necessarily simplistic) level, new materialism follows a period of the rise and then demise of materialist approaches to law and social theory, which were subsumed by a post-structuralist and constructivist turn. Materialism in this sense can be understood variously (physicality, objects, social, and economic conditions), however, in terms of social theory, it was understood through historical materialist traditions, rooted in the writing of Marx, which focused on social relations and structures. Following a cultural turn which instead shifted to ideas of social and linguistic constructionism and post-structuralism, there was a scepticism of the essentialising and abstract 'grand' theorisation of society, and materialist approaches broadly fell out of favour. In a sense, new materialist theories seek to both revive and rethink materiality and its role as part of, and in relation to, discursive processes. As Conaghan puts it, new materialism,

> seeks to counter the tendency to erase materiality from theoretical discourse while at the same time highlighting new understandings of the material in light of scientific and technological advances. Revisiting materialism, it is argued, offers new radical potentialities – ethical, conceptual, theoretical and political – in the wake of the postmodernist failure to provide an adequate theoretical base for an activist, politically transformative and materially grounded feminism.
>
> (Conaghan, 2013, 37)

Matter and the material is understood through a more dynamic lens. Barad suggests that "[w]hat is at stake in this dynamic conception of matter is an unsettling of nature's presumed fixity and hence an opening up of the possibilities of change" (Barad, 2007, 64). It is impossible to do justice to the richness and nuance of these eclectic new materialist approaches and the distinctions and connections between them. What will be done, however, is to provide a brief overview of some of the relevant core insights that emerge when these approaches are considered together. The discussion will then turn to consider how these insights can transform (but also be transformed by) critical approaches to law, before outlining in more detail the particular socio-legal lens for the argument in the book, which will provide the conceptual backdrop for further engagement with mental capacity law throughout the book.

Space as a process

Spatialising the analysis takes a much more process-driven approach to relations – seeing them as constantly changing and shifting, with a variety of entangled agencies involved. Moreover, relations and subject positions will differ depending on the spatial contexts in which entities are situated. Indeed, a difficulty with previous relational approaches, and vulnerability theory, as discussed earlier, is that the relations engaged with were often seen in a static and linear way, with little engagement with the context, temporality, or historicity of such relations. Instead, bringing spatial approaches into conversation with relationality plays an important role in drawing attention to these processes, and to the various interacting relations which play a role in creating particular material and discursive spaces.

Aligned to this focus on the processes through which particular spaces are created and configured is an appreciation of the historicity of such processes – the path-dependency of well-worn ideas and the ways that alternative junctures could have produced alternative spatial arrangements. This poses an important challenge to the given-ness of certain 'common-sense' ideas about the organisation of particular spaces – both material and discursive. Instead, we can utilise these tools to analyse *why* these spaces have been organised in this way, *when* and *where* were alternative trajectories considered and/or discounted, *how* could arrangements have been otherwise, and *what* might the impacts of this be. This draws in important elements of historicity and socio-political critique. As Soja suggests, there is "growing awareness of the simultaneity and interwoven complexity of the social, the historical and the spatial" (Soja, 1999, 262). Such questions of the spatial, the temporal, and social must be thought together – they are interdependent. This is a distinct shift from seeing space as a static or objective entity. Such an analysis holds not just for material understandings of space and how the boundaries of particular spaces, and relations within such spaces, have come to be drawn, but also for more conceptual and discursive ideas of the spatiality of particular frameworks and societal orderings. There are echoes here of the new materialism discussed above and the relational dynamics of space. Barad's attention to the assemblage, for example, helps to visualise the various actors and forces (again, both human and non-human) which intra-act and are constantly shifting. By being attentive to these, we can see the various processes and intra-actions which have led to the prominence of particular ideals and the relational dynamics which have been central to this. This takes us beyond linear understandings of progress and change, complicating the picture to enable an understanding of alternative sites and moments for disruption and reconfiguration. This has particular relevance for legal change, challenging approaches which seek to alter one aspect of the legal framework without being attentive to the complex legal and conceptual networks that this is entangled with, and the roots of this entanglement.

Space as an assemblage

As geographers such as Massey et al. suggest, relational thinking, aligned to space, challenges the idea of space as static blocks – instead we see spaces as interconnected (Massey et al., 1999, 12). Whatmore further submits that,

> This means not ignoring the effects of established contours and boundaries that mark the social landscape but, rather, recognising that these spatial parameters inhere in a host of socio-technical practices – such as property, sovereignty and identity – that are always in the making, not in some a priori order of things.
>
> (Whatmore, 1999, 31)

This echoes the assemblage analysis that has been advanced by Karen Barad, a physicist and feminist theorist who has been influential in the development of new materialisms. In this, assemblages are seen not as static entities, but as constantly shifting through intra-action with other assemblages – changing the configurations of such assemblages as this process continues. Barad utilises the idea of an entanglement – an "entangled state of agencies" – and argues that the focus needs to be on how these stand in relation to each other. Rather than presuming separate individual agencies that precede their interaction, instead focusing on intra-action shows that distinct agencies rather emerge through *intra-action* with others – encompassing humans, non-humans, cultural, material, techno-scientific, environmental, and institutional forces. This is an ongoing process, impacted by different dynamic intra-actions, which then shift and shape experience. The term 'interaction' is commonly used in relational theories to discuss how elements are working together, whereas intra-action for Barad moves away from seeing pre-established, finite individual entities as interacting, and towards recognising the dynamic, shifting inseparability of agents, and constant processes of making, remaking, and unmaking that occur through these intra-actions. Geographers such as Anderson et al. point to the utility of assemblage thinking for seeing how "spatial forms and processes are held together and might have been assembled otherwise" (Anderson et al., 2012, 7) as well as providing insights into how they can change and be reworked (9).

Through looking at relations as part of assemblages, they become "dynamic, unfolding processes, rather than static ties between inert substances" (Sunley, 2008, 5), and the lens moves from simply interpersonal relations towards more complex networks of a variety of different human and non-human actors. Such relations are not necessarily linear, and disrupt the teleological notion of progress which has underpinned post-Enlightenment political theory as well as ideas of scientific discovery. Reconfiguring understandings of agency and interaction leaves little space for the idea of individual free-will or self-determination as the central goal of political theory and avoids reinforcing the givenness of debates as being about, for example, balancing competing ideals of autonomy and paternalism, or state intervention versus freedom. The current, familiar boundaries of debate are not reiterated – instead, these very boundaries are the source of challenge through this lens.

Space as networks of power

A significant element of this analysis which will be seen throughout the book is the importance of power relations. Whilst the ontological flattening and non-hierarchical approach to various agents within relational and spatial approaches may give the impression that power differentials may be overlooked – i.e. are theorists really saying that a plant has the same agency as a human? – this is not the thrust of the theories discussed here. The issue of agency will be examined more throughout the book. Suffice it to say here though, that broadening the agentic analysis of various forces in relation to each other does and must recognise the importance of power. Indeed, this is something that such approaches can address more fully than more abstract theories, given the central focus on interrogating the various processes and intra-actions (human, non-human, material, discursive, technological, cultural) through which particular norms become cemented and dominant. This focus on process and relation moves away from the idea that power is an attribute or property of particular individuals or entities (as is often the case in more humanistic approaches, particularly those based on agency as autonomy) and instead sees it as a relational process. Coole and Frost, writing in the context of new materialisms and their importance for politics, humanities, and social sciences (2010), highlight the way in which subjectivity becomes seen as embedded in "dense networks of power" (2). As Allen argues, through this analysis, "power is modified and transformed as it passes from hand to hand … [and is] actively constituted *through* space" (Allen, 1999, 198). Power is thus seen as a "creative capacity, rather than as a form of instrumental 'power over'" (Blomley, 2004, 90). Massey et al. similarly posit that "spatialising power through a geographical imagination … reveals that such power is not always the same across space-time, and its exercise is not a continual process" (Massey et al., 1999, 172). What we see then is that power is reproduced in various ways through these relational intra-actions, and the various agents within this allow attention to be drawn to the ways in which these agential relations can be reconfigured if the aim is to disrupt particular flows of power. In many ways this focus on power aligns with Foucauldian analysis of governmentality, biopolitics, and power (Lemke, 2015), although the new materialist focus has the potential to further granularise the understanding of power, engaging with the interaction of the material and discursive, unbound from what Barad has termed the "humanist orbit" (Barad, 2007, 668). Moreover, building on (and perhaps departing from[1]) Foucault, the subject within this

1 There is ongoing debate as to the extent to which the 'death of the subject' charge against Foucault is overstated (see e.g. Allen (2002)).

analysis is itself an important agential element of the assemblage. As Conaghan suggests, ascribing this agency to the very materiality of bodies allows attention to be drawn to the role of bodies in conferring and configuring meaning (Conaghan, 2013). As will be seen in engaging this approach with mental capacity law, this challenges the idea of linearity in calls to 'empower' individuals or institutions, instead seeing the response as necessarily more complex and variously located.

Space as a differentiating practice

Aligned to the importance of the processes through which particular spaces are made is the recognition of space as a differentiating practice. Here we see the ways that processes work to inscribe difference upon areas, landscapes, humans, and non-human groups. As Smith suggests, we need to engage with the idea of social difference as a process of categorisation, as opposed to seeing (and reproducing) difference as a static representation: "This modern idea of difference casts social and spatial categories, divisions between places and people, as a natural and therefore unproblematic fact of life" (Smith, 1999, 129). Being attentive to processes as differentiating practices helps to draw attention to the points raised above – the historicity of these; the various (socio-political, technological, discursive, material) forces that feed into categories and their materialisation; power relations (and points of resistance) occurring through these processes; and the ways that particular categories of difference become cemented. Barad similarly talks about this in terms of boundary making practices which work to determine what 'matters' and what gets excluded from mattering.

This focus on the processes through which sedimentation of categories of differentiation occurs resonates through the non-representational approach taken by many spatial theorists, particularly in human geography. Essentially, non-representational theory seeks to emphasise the processes involved in assigning and producing matter and meaning and the way in which knowledge is part of this process, rather than being an objective 'discovery' of a pre-existing 'thing'. This is part of a challenge to the way in which "representationalism would have us focus on what seems to be evidentially given, hiding the very practices that produce the illusion of givenness" (Barad, 2007, 359). This is not about overlooking difference and differential embodiment or situatedness, but rather thinking about how these differences come to matter: how does a particular representation (of a problem, of an object) configure our responses? Again, there are strong convergences here with the ethos of new materialist theorists and feminist theorists who draw attention to the importance of situated knowledge (Haraway, 1991; Coole and Frost, 2010) and the exclusion of particular (alternative) approaches in the processes of creating and assigning meaning. Barad, similarly and not surprisingly sharing a non-representational starting point, highlights a key problem with representational approaches:

> Like the frustrated would-be-runner in Zeno's paradox, representationalism never seems to get any closer to solving the problem it poses because it is caught in the impossibility of stepping outward from its metaphysical starting place. What is needed is a new starting place.
>
> (Barad, 2007, 137)

Rather than presuming the correctness of the current, received representation (of space in both the material and ideological sense), such approaches, through considering the processes that have cohered in creating the particular representation, enable the space to consider how it could be different.

A core part of this, and an aspect which may be more strongly elucidated in Barad's work in comparison to some non-representational approaches, is the importance of what is *excluded* by representations and differentiating processes. Considering Barad's agential realist approach and the practice of 'agential cuts', Hollin et al. suggest that,

> Barad's emphasis is not on the possibility of multiple ontologies, but on the relative stability afforded to matter after it has intra-actively emerged, due to the same apparatuses producing the same outcome. The ethical significance of agential realism, therefore, is not just in extending the idea that things 'could have been otherwise' to the ontological realm but in conceptualizing the precise moments at which things congeal 'as they are', by understanding the processes through which particular material properties emerge and other realities are excluded from being. Any given phenomenon, for Barad, is understood as being composed of specific intra-actions, with discreet identities (such as 'subject' and 'object') only emerging after an agential cut has taken place.
>
> (Hollin et al., 2017, 938)

The agential cut, in Barad's work, refers to the ways in which agencies are entangled, yet via particular apparatus, agential cuts are made in order to confer meaning. These cuts (as boundary drawing practices) importantly, can be made in different ways and will always necessarily exclude. This process of exclusion does not make these agencies or their entangled effects disappear – merely they are excluded from the particular materialisation of meaning. At the same time, what is excluded can often play an important role in shaping 'the inside'. As Gill et al. discuss in the context of law's exclusions, it is important and productive to think "not only about law's omnipresence but also the absences that shape the way law is experienced and practiced" (2020, 2). What is interesting about this is that Barad is clear that agential cuts are active choices for which we need to take responsibility. They are not neutral, pre-political, or objective. This stance provides an important way to challenge the creation and the effects of cuts or boundary drawing practices in the context of law, in order to demonstrate their material and discursive effects and to trace responsibility for these.

Space as a challenge to binary approaches

Furthermore, one of the common threads linking spatial approaches is the challenge to binary thinking and dualisms. In drawing attention to the historicity of these binary frames, it allows us to see that they are not 'natural' or presumed in advance. As will be seen in later chapters, this has important repercussions in a field such as mental capacity law which is rigidly framed by a number of interlinked binaries such as autonomy/paternalism, empowerment/protection, public/private, disabled/non-disabled.

Building on the attentiveness to processes of boundary drawing, and space as a differentiating practice, Massey et al. discuss the paradox central to binary approaches in that the two terms placed in opposition are presumed to be unrelated, yet depend upon the existence of the other. (Massey et al., 1999, 111). As they discuss, this invites discussion of their distance, closeness, *and* separation – two sides of the binary are simultaneously brought together *and* kept apart. Binaries here then play an important role in creating space, as well as helping to draw the conceptual terrain and boundaries within it.

The naturalness of these binaries is, as such, challenged through awareness of their creation and reinforcement. Whatmore has critiqued the nature/society binary which has been central to more everyday understandings of geography, as well as the human/non-human binary, which is often connected to this (Whatmore, 1999, 25). Similarly, she challenges the either/or strand in social and political theory around realism/constructionism, which itself reifies such separation (Whatmore, 1999, 24). Instead, following Haraway's call to build theories "whose geometries, paradigms and logics break out of binaries … and nature/culture modes of any kind" (Haraway, 1991, 129), Whatmore suggests the need to start instead from a focus on the *living* as opposed to abstract areas of life and the interconnected agents within this (Whatmore, 1999, 25). Again there are strong resonances with the new materialist project as well as the work of post-humanist scholars, and Haraway and Barad (among other feminist science and technology studies scholars), whose critical starting point, and vantage point, is not constrained by such binaries at the outset and instead flattens the ontological hierarchies and the given-ness of the binary frames and their production.

For example, thinking back to the discussion of space as a differentiating practice above, and the way that Baradian agential cuts create an "external", it might be thought there that the internal/external or inside/outside binary is being endorsed. However, this is not the case – agential cuts instead draw attention to the fact that there *is no external*, only the illusion of such by the act of intervening or attempting to measure. The point which is being made is that these cuts are not neutral. Moreover, what occurs outside of the lens of the binary frame still persists and still reproduces – it simply occurs outside the realm of socio-political recognition or responsibility. Similarly, the human/non-human dualism which undergirds post-Enlightenment humanist (and liberal) theory is variously challenged by new materialists and post-humanists whose dynamic agential approach instead draws attention to entangled agencies of various actors (including animals, plants, material objects) in particular assemblages. This has significant repercussions for the binary frames, which are mutually dependent on the human/non-human dualism and the socio-political claims that develop from this.

Implications for approaches to social justice and law

So far, we have seen that considering relational and spatial insights in conversation can, and has, been productive in the social sciences and humanities for moving debates beyond the static parameters that had come to frame the disciplines. Yet the relevance of this for law and the critical study of law has yet to be fully explored. The remaining sections in this chapter will outline how bringing law into a spatial analysis can both allow us to radically rethink the concept of law and the structures which currently frame critical legal studies, but how spatial and relational theory can similarly benefit from a more rigorous and nuanced understanding of legal processes as a key part of the dynamics which are central to the production and effects of space. It will begin by outlining how spatialising the analysis allows us to challenge the current conceptual, doctrinal, and material boundaries of law. It will then turn to consider the insights which flow from this for central concepts in legal theory, namely the legal subject and the role of the state. Rethinking these concepts will lay the groundwork for the critical approach taken throughout the book in relation to mental capacity law and disability; however, the impact of this critical reconfiguration will resonate more broadly.

Rethinking legal boundaries

The focus on issues such as processes, relational dynamics, and the subsequent challenge to the boundaries of particular (material and discursive) arrangements resonates and provides additional critical tools for a longstanding argument from some feminist legal theorists and critical legal scholars about the concept of law. In mainstream legal theory, law tends to be seen in a positivist manner in that it is often seen as a project of the state (Braverman et al., 2004, 7), and also that the determinacy of law is often presupposed in the view that "social problems can be reached by applying legal rules in a principled, disinterested and rational way" (Munro, 2007, 43). Law is often portrayed as a closed system, particularly in liberal legal approaches, with static and solid boundaries drawn around legal institutions and mechanisms – such as the state, government, parliament, the courts, legal actors (judiciary, barristers, solicitors), and legal subjects. In this view, such institutions have clearly defined roles and relations to other institutions, defined by legal and professional boundaries. These tend to be overlaid by an omnipresent public/private divide, which aids in the delineation of the realms of the state and citizens. Only via legal mechanisms can these be changed.

Through considering the spatial analysis of boundaries and processes of boundary drawing, and drawing attention to the porosity of these boundaries, we can begin to acknowledge the power relations which inhere in them, their constructed nature, and the techniques of their reproduction. Rather than being pre-political, common sense, or neutral descriptions of the essence of the role of the state or the legal subject, such boundaries can be critiqued as being deliberate, constructed, and fundamentally political materialisations of particular ideals. Scholars such as Margaret Davies have sought to 'unlimit' law, "to suspend the conceptual, doctrinal and institutional boundaries to imagine different modalities for understanding law" (Davies, 2017, i). In doing so, she challenges the theoretical, political, doctrinal, and geographical boundaries which are drawn, and which are perceived by both mainstream legal scholars and those 'outside' of this as static and fixed. As she goes on to suggest, this vision sees law not as a static entity, but as a "material-social dialogue in process" (Davies, 2017, 7) whose "boundaries and limits do not work in isolation, but create a web of insides and outsides, together with all of the exclusory and identity-forming characteristics of such spaces" (137). The institutional relations, and particular domains of law including the public and the private, become seen as more porous, and subject to constant maintenance (and potential disruption).

As with Barad's work, we see here the idea of living, active, and ongoing processes which play a part in the creation of a phenomenon – here, law. Considering critical geography and new materialisms alongside law enables us to see the "unacknowledged assumptions about space that work to stabilize the validity of seemingly obvious propositions, identities, and the very meaning of 'law' (Blomley, Delaney, and Ford, 2001, xv; also see Hogg, 2002). Law, through this analysis, "is not just poured into pre-existing 'spaces' but, rather, is constitutive of spatialities, spatial relationships, spatial performances, and experiences as these, in turn, condition the lived character of the legal" (Delaney, 2004, 240).

This critique of boundaries offers a compelling approach for mental capacity scholarship, which has been heavily framed and frustrated by seemingly fixed and pre-given boundaries. Moreover, it offers important tools for other social justice projects which hit up against the hard edges of critical debate and reform possibilities. Moreover, this reconceptualisation of law must also have repercussions for 'external' views of law. The positivist understanding of law tends to permeate the vision of law that exists in other disciplines, such as social sciences and humanities, including geography itself. The critical moves here are not just about law taking on spatial metaphors but also how spatial analyses can be similarly enriched by engaging with legal processes. Critiquing the absence and distancing from law in Massey's spatial analyses, Philippopoulos-Mihalopoulos argues that, "[s]pace and law are co-constituting … The omission to deal with the law has this remarkable effect: we are presented with the outcomes of the law's presence in space, but not the causes" (Philippopoulos-Mihalopolos,

2018, 8). He goes on to explore how in Massey's work, and more generally in spatial literature,

> law often appears to be irrelevant (abstract, closed, textual, hegemonic, orderly, apolitical) when compared to the immediacy of political struggles. It seems too slow for the urgency of geopolitical and ecological issues, and too co-opted for anti-hegemonic thinking.
>
> (Philippopoulos-Mihalopolos, 2018, 2)

Once law is seen as part of the ongoing inter- (or intra-) relations in the processes of boundary creation and spatial organising, its critical role in reconfiguring such relations and dynamics becomes more apparent. In the remaining sections, the particular impact that such analyses can have in terms of spatialising the legal subject and the role of the state will be discussed, before exploring these ideas in more depth throughout the book.

The legal subject

The approaches discussed above build on and add a new dimension to a long-rehearsed argument challenging the idea of the liberal legal subject. The issue of separation and boundedness is core to the liberal legal subject, with legal norms such as autonomy, bodily integrity, and self-determination drenched in these commitments. Blomley draws attention to the "art of separation" (Walzer, 1984), which is reflected in the legal "maintenance and policing of the public-private divide" (Blomley, 2005, 283–4). Nedelsky similarly refers to property and the boundedness of property as a central organising principle of liberal legal systems, which also underlies the ideal of autonomy and protection from the intrusion of others (Nedelsky, 2006). As Ford argues,

> These walls of liberalism do in fact define liberty, but they do much more than this – they create the very entity that is to enjoy liberty. Both individual rights and the formal rules of jurisdiction are 'technologies of the self', they are discourses and concrete acts that define political selfhood and provide the model for biological individuals to 'perform themselves' as (autonomous, rational, profit-maximising, god-fearing, desiring, wilful, raced, sexed) selves.
>
> (Ford, 2000, 208)

This normative ideal of the liberal legal subject can thus be seen as being produced through a number of practices and what Blomley terms "spatialized performances" (Blomley, 2005, 282). Drawing attention to such practices helps to illuminate the "constructions of legality that take place in everyday settings; material performances that cite and reproduce normativity" (Davies, 2017, 7). In law, there are a "multiplicity of discursive fields" (Leckey, 2008, 5) through which these norms can be produced and reproduced, including through the legislature, through judicial interpretation and precedent, through legal scholarship, and, importantly, through laws inter- (and intra-, following Barad) actions with other discursive fields and institutional relations. As Leckey proposes, looking at the legal subject produced through a particular juridical regime "captures the manner in which the legal system structures identity and reconfigures the field of social possibilities in ways over which individuals do not exert full agency" (Leckey, 2008, 6). The shifting nature of the spatial and relational context in which we are situated is in direct contrast to the static and temporally linear idea of the liberal subject and identity categories used to organise the liberal legal framework. As Davies points out, the legal subject thus becomes not singular and self-determining, but fragmented, hybrid, relational, and plural (Davies, 2017, 6). Static categories or legal descriptors thus become further blurred, with legal subjects potentially occupying any number of these concurrently as their context shifts. This relationship between the subject and discursive and material context is thus recursive and ongoing.

Such relations are not necessarily linear, and disrupt the teleological notion of progress which has underpinned post-Enlightenment political theory as well as ideas of scientific discovery. Unlike the potentially linear understanding of autonomy or resilience employed by relational autonomists and vulnerability theorists, agency in the context of new materialism is seen in a much more diffuse manner. Moreover, the concept of agency here does not repeat the normative centrality of autonomy (and, as such, reproduce the broader institutional and political frameworks) that some relational theorists do. Reconfiguring understandings of agency and intra-action leave little space for the idea of individual free-will or self-determination as the central goal of political theory and avoid reinforcing the given-ness of debates as being about, for example, balancing competing ideals of autonomy and paternalism, or state intervention versus freedom. The comfortable boundaries of debate are not reiterated – instead, these very boundaries are the source of challenge for new materialist theorists. This understanding enables a more in-depth exploration of the material and discursive spaces – the practices and processes – which we not only inhabit but, importantly, are an active part of.

This structuring of identity can further be seen in the processes of differentiation which take place through these legal practices. Often, such practices take place without scrutiny, given the dominant idea that political boundaries are neutral or pre-political. Yet the engagement with spatial and relational dynamics brings these practices into sharper focus and enables us to challenge this neutrality. As Barad suggests,

> liberal social and political theories and theories of scientific knowledge alike owe much to the idea that the world is composed of individuals – presumed to exist before the law, or the discovery of the law-awaiting or inviting representation.
>
> (Barad, 2007, 46)

Instead, new materialist and spatial approaches emphasise the processes involved in assigning and producing matter and meaning and the way in which knowledge is part of this process, rather than being an objective 'discovery' of a pre-existing 'thing'. Thus, legal categorisations of difference – based around sex, race, disability, class, geographical location, age, for example – can be challenged for the way in which legal meaning is assigned to difference, and the normative and concrete repercussions of this. This is not to overlook differences, but to think about *how* differences come to matter. Moreover, recognising these processes of differentiating as boundary making practices, through a variety of technologies and apparatus, enables us to recognise them as agential cuts which *necessarily* create an 'outside' or an other. A key corollary of this is the recognition of *responsibility* for such agential cuts, rather than seeing them as pre-determined boundaries. This will be a key theme running through the book and will be discussed in more detail below when discussing the role of the state and institutions.

Shifting the rendering of the legal subject and agents enables us to see the consequent shifts that then must also take place in shifting our ideas about the role of the state and institutions, about causality and responsibility, and about how relations can be reconfigured. Notions of the state which are bound up in the very rendering of the legal subject begin to unravel once the understanding of agency changes. As will be discussed in turn below, this opens alternative ways of thinking about responses and interventions, processes of change and, as Feely asserts, enables us to "pose new questions and follow creative and experimental trajectories in academic analysis" (Feely, 2016, 877).

Responsibility and responses

A central idea in liberal legal theory revolves around the separation of the state from the private lives of citizens, carefully policed by the public/private divide. In tandem with the ideal of the liberal legal subject as unencumbered, as atomistic and self-actualising, the state is thus portrayed as absent and interfering only in carefully circumscribed circumstances, in turn keeping notions of state responsibility carefully circumscribed. This also shapes our ideas of how, when, and why the state ought to respond. The state might respond, for example, via the criminal law in defining certain actions as criminal, and by punishing those who transgress this. This view of the state as 'hovering over' yet separate, as only responding or interfering in well-defined and bounded circumstances, and as a potential threat to the autonomy and self-mastery of individual subjects, is common in mainstream legal theory. Yet, spatialising our understanding of the state and law challenges this caricature by exposing the role of the state (to be conceived of not as a monolithic entity but as a series of practices and processes) and institutions such as law in the ongoing processes of interaction and reproduction in assemblages. The state and institutions such as law are always, already part of these spatialising processes; they are not simply there as a reaction to them. As will be demonstrated throughout the book, even in the purported absence of the state – for example as portrayed in some critiques of neoliberal policy drivers

– there are active processes which go into the creation of the space of absence, and the shifting of responsibilities that take place as part of this.

An important aspect of these processes of law is the boundary drawing impacts that they often have. It was noted above, for example, that legal categorisation and differentiation between subjects takes place through these processes of assignment. But boundaries are also created around the obligations of the state, through the maintenance and reproduction of the public/private divide, for example. Blomley, Delaney, and Ford draw attention to this, stating that, "[b]oundaries mean. They signify, they differentiate, they unify the insides of the spaces that they make. What they mean refers to constellations of social relational power" (2001, xviii). Boundaries which are being drawn around different spheres become interpenetrating and aid in the mutual reinforcement of each other. For example, the centrality of autonomy and the rendering of the liberal legal subject helps to sustain (and is recursively sustained by) the public/private divide, and by the non-interventionist state and ideals of liberty. What is important to do here, through this spatial and relational analysis of dynamic processes, is to consider the creation and reproduction of norms and knowledges via state institutions and legal processes, and how this is entangled with particular ontologies and representations. We see that the state is *already* responding through these processes, and is engaged in the carving out of boundaries and the creation of knowledge through intra-actions with other agents.

The issue of jurisdiction is a central and perhaps familiar iteration of boundary drawing in law. Often, however, jurisdiction can be viewed uncritically; like other categories or boundaries in liberal legalism, it can be accepted unquestionably as a neutral and pre-political dividing line. Instead, scholars such as Valverde have argued for the need to pay more attention to concepts such as jurisdiction and scale as examples of governance processes and techniques. Valverde suggests that more than simply distinguishing territories, or the where and who of governance, "jurisdiction also differentiates and organizes the 'what' or governance – and, most importantly because of its relative invisibility, the 'how' of governance" (Valverde, 2009, 144). Judicial and legislative statements as to jurisdiction then can be viewed not as the neutral drawing of lines on a map, but as practices of governance, and as the figuring of norms into law. As such, there is a need to focus on these processes, and how they intertwine with other jurisdictional processes, to highlight the broader conceptual architecture being sustained or reconfigured.

Resonating with the ideas of line drawing and mapping, which are entailed in jurisdictional analysis, is the issue of scale. This is another important critical juncture which a spatialised analysis can enable. As Davies puts it, "[r]epresentations – including those implicated in a choice of scales or mapping practices – always select and exclude, while often masking or naturalising the choices involved" (Davies, 2017, 92; also see Hollin et al., 2017). Instead, recognising the issue of scale (i.e. the correct 'scale' of response in law – macro, meso, micro) as an active choice and part of the processes of cementing and reproducing particular norms enables a more critical account to develop. Scale itself can be challenged through this approach – scale, like jurisdiction, is not a neutral or pre-determined 'thing' but something which is created through processes of articulation, and which – as with all boundary drawing practices – necessarily excludes. Scale in this sense becomes a static entity, enabling a false and stratified separation of the state and the citizen. Focusing instead on relational and spatial assemblages, and flattening the various actors within this, demonstrates that scale is not, and cannot be, a separate 'thing', but instead that we have interpenetrating relational dynamics between what have traditionally been seen as scales for response. Barad, for example, discusses scale as an outcome of ongoing processes of production and reproduction (Barad, 2007, 245) and is heavily critical of views which render the global as a large scale, with the local as always being smaller than this, or the macro scale always being bigger than the micro. It is important to avoid reifying this structural view of scales and scale of responses when thinking about transformative legal approaches.

A useful approach for law, based on these spatial accounts, is to think about boundary drawing as an agential cut (Barad, 2007), which opens up new ways to conceptualise responses, the role of the state and institutions, and responsibility. Thus, legal processes of knowledge production – such as legislative processes, or judgments in case law, for example – can thus be seen as active interventions (i.e. agential cuts) which play a role in the broader processes of norm production and reproduction. Again, this poses a crucial challenge to the fiction of the state and its institutions as not intervening – instead, they are actively taking part in the constitution and reiteration of particular assemblages, and linked assemblages. These are not simply processes of external, objective viewing of a given situation, but active embeddedness within the processes of creating.

What this recognition enables for legal theory is careful attention to the issue of responsibility. As noted previously, agential cuts *always* necessarily create an external or outside of the boundary – they are processes of exclusion. As Davies suggests, "Law defines spaces of insides and outsides and in many respects is a large-scale exercise in social line-drawing. Exclusion is widespread and seemingly fundamental to law" (Davies, 2005, 6). This is not to say that this external is 'real', but that it has been created by the prior process or processes. Recognising that agential cuts are active interventions in themselves necessitates appreciation of the responsibility of particular agents in creating this knowledge and these practices of exclusion. As said above, pronouncements as to jurisdiction, scale, or legal response become seen not as external, objective 'readings' of the situation but as agential cuts. As such, there is a degree of control and responsibility over these and the material consequences of them (Barad, 2007, 243; also see Hollin et al., 2017). Such processes feed into the broader creation of particular worlds, and there is a complex path-dependency between such processes which could always have been other. As Barad puts it, "we need to meet the universe halfway, to take responsibility for the role we play in the world's differential becoming" (Barad, 2007, 396). Similarly, Williams recognises that categorising and processes of differentiating in and of themselves are not the problem – they are always necessary to a certain extent through apparatus and legal technologies; however, "the problem is in the failure to assume responsibility for examining how and where we set our boundaries" (Williams, 1991, 102). Recognising the numerous intra-actions and agential cuts which occur in processes of becoming and mattering, of excluding, and the historicity and path-dependency of these, for example, suggests that causality is much more complex than the simple linearity which tends to underpin liberal legalism. Here, through the static idea of state responses, there is a presumed linearity between the intervention by the state and the result or outcome (Allen, 1999, 196). Complicating the picture by the recognition of not just the intra-actions taking place through the apparatus or intervention, but also how these intra-actions will also enable shifts in other relations and contexts, and will have diffuse, multimodal impacts, provides a significant insight for thinking about transformative legal responses.

Moreover, the temporality of liberal legalism is also open to challenge through this recognition. As Valverde points out,

> Liberal legalism is not completely a-temporal: but its temporalization is limited to the highly normative and universalising temporality of the liberal Enlightenment ... which assumes gradual change brought about by economic prosperity and greater education.
>
> (Valverde, 2015, 109)

This linear causality and temporality are intimately connected in the liberal legal imaginary. Rethinking this and the various entangled processes and practices which help to produce and reproduce norms enables us to see how these could be reconfigured and to what potential productive effects. It also importantly enables us to see how particular power relations come to be cemented, through processes of reiteration and reproduction. Here, possibilities for change open up – indeed, change is seen as a constant potentiality as agents are porous and intra-acting. As we saw in the discussion of the legal subject above, changes in the embodied context, and thus their entanglement in particular assemblages, already does impact their subjective experience. Temporally, they can occupy a number of subject positions at the same time, in direct challenge to the linear model of progress and individual development that liberalism portrays. Shifting the spatial and relational dynamics at various different levels and through different processes will have diffuse and tangible impacts in other areas. This allows us to discard the idea that changes in individual experience result from a top-down state response and to think more carefully about where interventions can, and already do, occur.

Conclusion

The implications of these insights, for theory more broadly but specifically for law, are significant and exciting. As Barad has elaborated,

> [I]f causality is reworked, then power needs to be rethought ... Agency needs to be rethought. Ethics needs to be rethought ... Even beyond that,

> it undermines the metaphysics of individualism and calls for a rethinking of the very nature of knowledge and being. It may not be too much of an exaggeration to say that every aspect of how we understand the world, including ourselves, is changed.
>
> (Barad, 2007, 23)

This chapter has introduced the concepts which will be applied and developed through engaging with mental capacity law in the remaining chapters. As will be seen, these offer important tools for wider reconceptualisation of problematic frameworks across law and other disciplines. The discussion in the next chapter will consider the relevance of such insights to the context of disability, and more particularly, to the Social Model of Disability. It is here that the Convention on the Rights of Persons with Disabilities (CRPD) and the invitation to rethink social justice may have the most immediate effect, yet rethinking certain foundational ideas around the legal subject (the *who?* of law) and the role of the state and institutions (the *why*, *how*, *where*, *when*, and *what?* of law) *through* disability will open up space to reflect on the broader implications of these transformative approaches.

References

Allen, A. 2002. 'The Anti-Subjective Hypothesis: Michel Foucault and the Death of the Subject' *The Philosophical Forum Quarterly* 31(2), 113–30.

Allen, J. 1999. 'Spatial Assemblages of Power: From Domination to Empowerment' in D. Massey, J. Allen and P. Sarre (Eds), *Human Geography Today*, 194–218. Cambridge: Polity Press.

Anderson, B., Keanes., M., McFarlane, C. and Swanton, D. 2012. 'On Assemblages and Geography' *Dialogues in Human Geography* 2(2), 171–89.

Barad, K. 2007. *Meeting the Universe Halfway*. Durham, NC: Duke University Press.

Blomley, N., Delaney, D. and Ford, R. 2001. *The Legal Geographies Reader: Law, Power, Space*. Toronto, ON: Wiley.

Blomley, N. 2004. 'Learning from Larry: Pragmatism and the Habits of Legal Space' in I. Braverman, N. Blomley, D. Delaney and A. Kedar (Eds), *The Expanding Spaces of Law: A Timely Legal Geography*, 77–94. Stanford, CA: Stanford Law Books.

Blomley, N. 2005. 'Flowers in the Bathtub: Boundary Crossings at the Public-Private Divide' *Geoforum* 36, 281–96.

Braverman, I., Blomley, N., Delaney, D. and Kedar, A. 2004. *The Expanding Spaces of Law: A Timely Legal Geography*. Stanford, CA: Stanford Law Books.

Conaghan, J. 2013. 'Feminism, Law and Materialism: Reclaiming the "Tainted Realm"' in M. Davies and V. Munro (Eds), *The Ashgate Research Companion to Feminist Legal Theory*, 31–50. Farnham: Ashgate.

Coole, D. and Frost, S. 2010. *New Materialisms: Ontology, Agency, and Politics*. Durham, NC: Duke University Press.

Davies, M. 2005. 'Exclusion and the Identity of Law' *Macquarie Law Journal* 5, 5–30.

Davies, M. 2017. *Law Unlimited*. Oxfordshire: Routledge.

Delaney, D. 2004. 'At Work in the Nomosphere: The Spatiolegal Production of Emotions at Work' in I Braverman, N. Blomley, D. Delaney and A. Kedar (Eds), *The Expanding Spaces of Law: A Timely Legal Geography*, 239–63. Stanford, CA: Stanford Law Books.

Feely, M. 2016. 'Disability Studies After the Ontological Turn: A Return to the Material World and Material Bodies Without a Return to Essentialism' *Disability & Society* 31(7), 863–83.
Ford, R. 2000. 'Laws Territory (A History of Jurisdiction)' in N. Blomley, D. Delaney and R. Ford (Eds), *The Legal Geographies Reader: Law, Power, Space*, 200–17. Toronto, ON: Wiley.
Gill, N., Allsop, J., Burridge, A., Fisher, D., Griffiths, M., Hambly, J., Hoellerer, N., Paszkiewicz, N. and Rotter, R. 2020. 'What's Missing from Legal Geography and Materialist Studies of Law? Absence and the Assembling of Asylum Appeal Hearings in Europe' *Transactions of the Institute of British Geographers*. (online first) https://doi.org/10.1111/tran.12399.
Haraway, D. 1991. 'Situated Knowledges: The Science Question in Feminism and the Privilege of the Partial Perspective' in *Simians, Cyborgs and Women: The Reinvention of Nature*. San Francisco: Free Association Books.
Harding, R. 2017. *Duties to Care: Dementia, Relationality and Law*. Cambridge: Cambridge University Press.
Hogg, R. 2002. 'Laws Other Spaces' *Law/Text/Culture* 6, 29–40.
Hollin, G., Forsyth, I., Giraud, E. and Potts, T. 2017. '(Dis)entangling Barad: Materialisms and Ethics' *Social Studies of Science* 47(6), 918–41.
Kong, C. 2017. *Mental Capacity in Relationship: Decision-Making, Dialogue, and Autonomy* Cambridge: Cambridge University Press.
Leckey, R. 2008. *Contextual Subjects: Family, State and Relational Theory*. Toronto: University of Toronto Press.
Lemke, T. 2015. 'New Materialisms: Foucault and the "Government of Things"' *Theory, Culture & Society* 32(4), 3–25.
Mackenzie, C. and Stoljar, N. 2000. *Relational Autonomy*. Oxford: Oxford University Press.
Massey, D., Allen, J. and Sarre, P. 1999. *Human Geography Today*. Cambridge: Polity Press.
Munro, V. 2007. *Law and Politics at the Perimeter: Re-evaluating Key Debates in Feminist Theory*. Oxford: .
Nedelsky, J. 2006. 'Reconceiving Rights as Relationships' in C. Koggel (Eds), *Moral Issues In Global Perspective*. 2nd Ed., 95–107, Peterborough, ON: Broadview Press.
Philippopolos-Mihalopolos, A. 2018. 'And For Law: Why Space Cannot Be Understood without Law' *Law, Culture and the Humanities*. OnlineFirst, 1–20.
Smith, S. 1999. 'The Cultural Politics of Difference' in D. Massey, J. Allen and P. Sarre (Eds), *Human Geography Today*. 129–50. Cambridge: Polity Press.
Soja, E. 1999. 'Thirdspace: Expanding the Scope of the Geographical Imagination' in D. Massey, J. Allen and P. Sarre (Eds), *Human Geography Today*, 260–78. Cambridge: Polity Press.
Sunley, P. 2008. 'Relational Economic Geography: A Partial Understanding or a New Paradigm' *Economic Geography* 84, 1–26.
Valverde, M. 2009. 'Jurisdiction and Scale: Legal "Technicalities" As Resources For Theory' *Social and Legal Studies* 18(2), 139–57.
Valverde, M. 2015. *Chronotopes of Law: Jurisdiction. Scale and Governance*. Oxon: Routledge.
Walzer, M. 1984. 'Liberalism and the Art of Separation' *Political Theory* 12(3), 315–30.
Whatmore, S. 1999. 'Hybrid Geographies: Rethinking the Human in Human Geography' in D. Massey, J. Allen and P. Sarre (Eds), *Human Geography Today*, 22–39. Cambridge: Polity Press.
Williams, P. 1991. *The Alchemy of Race and Rights*. Cambridge, MA: Harvard University Press.

2 Spatial dynamics and disability

Interrogating the terrain of the Mental Capacity Act 2005

The previous chapter has highlighted the importance of a relational and spatial critical lens for legal analysis. Such an approach allows us to be attentive to the processes and historicity which characterise legal frameworks and practices. Moreover, we can trace the relational dynamics and power relations which are enabled and fostered through such frameworks. We can also more closely track the creation of material and discursive spaces and assemblages, and their entanglement and intra-dependency with other assemblages. A core element of the organising logics in liberal legal frames, as has been suggested in the previous chapter, is the reliance upon binaries. These binaries work to produce conceptual and material boundaries for both critique and legal responses. The approach outlined in the previous chapter calls for us to challenge them and their underpinning assumptions and logics.

Disability provides an important lens through which to undertake a spatial and relational analysis and to utilise the conceptual tools outlined in the previous chapter to challenge the conceptual frameworks that sustain disability as difference in law and society. Disability is a potent concept in society and is often used to organise distinctions between individuals and to buttress the ideal, non-disabled, subject. The Convention on the Rights of Persons with Disabilities (CRPD) offers a vital opportunity to undertake this analysis as it provokes, and necessitates, new thinking around law, disability, and the role of the state. Much of the progressive scholarship in law and social policy to date has been built upon the Social Model of Disability, but as will be advanced in this chapter and throughout the book, there is a need to deepen our understanding of the interaction between law and disability in order to avoid static and linear applications of the Social Model. Current work in critical disability studies and human geography, which foregrounds spatial and relational dynamics of disability, will be engaged with as offering a compelling challenge to the Social Model. Critical disability studies, however, have not always readily or fully engaged with law, often representing law as the positivist, rights-based creature which was contested in the previous chapter. The CRPD thus provides a catalyst to explore convergences between critical disability studies and a spatial and relational legal lens. Bringing it into conversation with law and the conceptual analysis outlined in the previous chapter

DOI: 10.4324/9781351067881-2

has much to offer to critical scholarship in mental capacity law and enables us to reveal more about the role of law and legal processes in the creation and reinscription of the particular concepts and conceptual frameworks which shape disability. It enables a fine-grained and nuanced analysis of the apparatus and technologies of law and challenging the concepts which law claims to represent or discover.

Bringing these disciplines together in this way will offer important insights for other areas which engage with disability, highlighting the role of law within the conceptual frameworks with which they engage. Moreover, it offers a critical challenge to broader legal frameworks, which are often built upon exclusionary non-disabled norms. Such norms shape and create ideas of legal subjectivity which reach beyond disability and work to exclude other groups within society, being implicated in ideas of race and gender for example. In this way, rather than simply thinking about how concepts can be rethought for disability, thus reinforcing problematic distinctions between disabled/non-disabled subjectivity and their effects, the chapter acknowledges the importance of rethinking concepts *through* disability.

After outlining the possibilities offered by engaging disability studies with spatial and relational approaches to law, the chapter will then move on to use this critical lens to begin to trace the development and effects of some of the core binaries through the development of the Mental Capacity Act (MCA) – namely, capacity/incapacity, disability/non-disability, and autonomy/paternalism. The MCA provides a rich case study for this, given that it is built upon a number of interlinked and interdependent binaries, which are reflected more broadly in liberal legalism as well as in policy debates around disability. Outlining the development of the boundaries in this way is an important first step in the analysis of a spatial and relational approach to disability and law as it challenges the idea of a pre-existing disabled/non-disabled legal subject, as well as unsettling taken for granted conceptualisations of the role and reach of the state. Following Keenan, this approach allows us to more usefully explore "how different spaces are produced, how particular subjects come to belong in those spaces and what constitutes the complex relation between space and the subject" (Keenan, 2015, 43). This provides a useful framework for challenging the static and 'given' boundaries of mental capacity law and exposing the effects of the spaces these produce. Such analysis will demonstrate the shaping of the liberal legal subject and a particular vision of the role of the state and institutions as core elements of the Mental Capacity Act. This approach then lays the groundwork for the deeper critical exploration embarked on in later chapters, each of which will engage with the core organising binaries in this context in order to highlight their contingency, their productive effects (both material and discursive), and the techniques through which they are maintained and reproduced in concert with other binaries.

The CRPD: a challenge and an invitation

The CRPD provides an apt opportunity to explore this nexus between critical disability studies, spatial approaches, and new materialist legal theories. Article 1, for example, states that "Persons with disabilities include those who have long-term physical, mental, intellectual or sensory impairments which *in interaction with various barriers* may hinder their full and effective participation in society on an equal basis with others", demonstrating a more Social Model approach to disability (emphasis added). The Convention also places positive obligations on States Parties to give effect to the rights contained within, melding civil and political rights with social and economic rights as it does so. This challenges ideas of the state and more negative approaches to rights (i.e. not to have the state or others interfere with these) which are often seen in other Conventions. It also contains provisions which directly, and potentially fatally, challenge some of the core suppositions of legal frameworks which govern legal responses to disability. A stark example of this is the right contained in Article 12, that persons with disabilities enjoy legal capacity on an equal basis with others in all aspects of life.

As such, the Convention invites us to consider not just a shift in disability rights discourse, but a theory of justice at a broader level. Much of the literature on the CRPD refers to it as signalling a 'paradigm shift' in relation to disability rights, yet – as will be seen in the later discussions in this book – this shift is yet to occur. Notwithstanding the fact that the term 'paradigm shift' is apt to be overused, and is often used unreflectively, Kuhn's notion of the paradigm shift is in many ways instructive here for thinking about the processes through which such shifts occur (Kuhn, 1962). Kuhn contrasted 'normal science' (i.e. everyday, incremental developments in scientific knowledge which tend to occur using the current frame or paradigm) to the less frequent scientific revolutions which shift the broader frame or paradigm being used by scientists. These shifts occur then when 'old' theories or ways of approaching a subject become completely changed or revolutionised, throwing the previous paradigm into doubt and eventual rejection. Such paradigms are most clearly associated with *scientific* methodologies (Newtonian physics being a key example), yet Kuhn speaks to the ways in which epistemological viewpoints can constitute paradigms, such as "the philosophical viewpoint initiated by Descartes" (1962, 121).

In terms of the processes through which a paradigm shift occurs, Kuhn refers to the ways in which the broader conceptual scheme begins to be challenged, and gradually the paradigmatic approach is in crisis as its core foundations are eroded. As will be seen throughout this book, the CRPD has roundly challenged some of the presuppositions that inform our legal frameworks and understandings of disability and the role of the state in shaping and responding to this. Scholarship in disability law and disability studies more broadly has been engaging with what this might mean for our social structures and institutions as we seek to understand and give effect to the Convention. As Kuhn goes on to say, eventually, there comes a point when the conceptual discourse shifts so that the previous paradigm and 'new' paradigm become incommensurate. What is also interesting about Kuhn's influential work on paradigm shifts is that he maintains that the world, or reality, or ontology, cannot be explained independently of the current paradigm through which we work. A shift in the paradigm also changes the world which is being described or engaged with.

As noted above, Kuhn's work focused on scientific revolutions and the shifts in the approaches to and philosophies of science. Yet, his work has had much broader purchase and is useful here for reflecting on how and whether a paradigm shift is occurring in the field of disability justice. There are also interesting resonances between Kuhn's work and that of new materialist theorists discussed in Chapter 1. This interaction between discourse and matter, and the ways that the world itself can be reconfigured through broader shifts in the conceptual terrain, or the apparatus or technologies used to approach matter, is particularly salient. It is not just the conceptual approach taken by scientists or practitioners which changes, but the 'objects' or matter itself. In tandem, these approaches invite us to think about the processes through which a particular paradigm is created and maintained, as well as how it comes to be challenged.

It could be argued then that currently we are on the cusp of the necessary crisis point in the process of the 'paradigm shift', as conceptual debates around issues such as disability, legal capacity, and the role of the state are intensifying following the CRPD. More relational understandings of disability and the dynamic role of actors within this, as well as epistemological challenges to mental capacity law and its core idea of denying legal capacity on the basis of mental capacity, signal a need to move away from the more individualistic liberal legalism we are accustomed to. Yet, as will be seen, this challenge is often taking place at a superficial level, with the conceptual foundations left unscathed and – in the legal and policy context – viewed through a broader liberal legal lens. Critical debates and developments are taking us so far, but then fall back into the (comforting?) binary frames, which will be seen as structuring the boundaries of current debate. The necessary deeper shift to the terrain is certainly not occurring, and it is this broader shift which this book seeks to provoke. The CRPD thus acts as an invitation to more closely scrutinise this background terrain, and why it is so difficult to shift.

Spatial dynamics and disability: beyond the Social Model

The Social Model of Disability – the idea that it is societal barriers, rather than impairments, that cause disability – has been heavily influential in disability activism and scholarship. It has had an enduring influence in disability politics and law, being central to a range of arguments for recognition, rights, and legal change. At the same time, and as with any central theory in a given field, it has not been without criticism. Early critics of the Social Model of Disability expressed the view that the focus on disabling societal barriers overlooked the embodied experience of impairment (Crow, 1996; Shakespeare and Watson, 2002). There was a concern that experiences of pain or discomfort had to be excluded from the Social Model discourse so as not to detract from the core message that it is not impairment that disables individuals, but that it is society that does. Moreover, the binary distinction between disability and impairment was also a target for critique, with the argument that the notion of impairment in itself is already inflected with medicalised discourse and power: as Nirmala Erevelles suggests, this biological focus of impairment always brings into the play the politics of the social (Erevelles, 2011, 19). There was an overarching concern from those whom Tom Shakespeare terms cultural disability theorists that the Social Model was too material, with a particular concern that the British iteration of the Social Model associated with Colin Barnes and Mike Oliver was strongly Marxist (Shakespeare, 2013). More post-modern critiques of the Social Model and approaches to disability thus emerged with scholars drawing on Foucauldian understandings of bio-power and discourse, for example, in order to challenge the materiality of the Social Model and to draw attention to the social construction of both impairment and disability (Tremain, 2005). In many ways, this trajectory reflects that of many forms of social theory in the late 20th century, with materialist approaches falling out of favour in the academy following a post-modern and post-structuralist turn. Yet, even though this dichotomising of material and discursive approaches often misrepresents the insights of the theorists, the debate in the context of mainstream disability studies had unfortunately become somewhat polarised and factional. As Erevelles puts it,

> When even those who espouse radical discourses seem unable to reconceptualise an alternative world without being locked into the political constructions of what constitutes appropriate humanness, then it becomes apparent that the disability movement has a task that goes above and beyond merely extending the boundaries of the discourses that celebrate humanism and instead needs to focus its energy on re-theorising itself.
>
> (Erevelles, 1996, 522)

It has been recognised for some time now by some critical disability scholars that rethinking ontology through new materialisms and post-humanism can disrupt current entrenched ideas of subjectivity as well as moving us beyond a strictly polarised view of materialism and more discursive or constructivist approaches (see Goodley and Ecclestone, 2016; Goodley, Lawthom, and Runswick Cole, 2014). Scholars such as Erevelles were particularly keen to challenge the humanist norm that the Social Model may be seen as reinforcing through the focus on barrier removal. The subject of the Social Model, or the norm to be actualised, was critiqued as reinforcing particular liberal ideals such as autonomy, self-determination, rationality, and independence. Such ideals are seen as problematic in creating and maintaining a disabled 'other', with Fiona Kumari Campbell frequently drawing attention to the ableism which is foundational to such liberal approaches and which has the effect of excluding difference from the very outset (Campbell, 2009). In essence, if the Social Model is simply focused on removing barriers to achieve this (ableist) norm, then such a norm becomes reinforced without question of its foundational presuppositions. The binary is thus reinforced.

As Shakespeare suggested in his earlier work, "perhaps the maintenance of a non-disabled identity … is a more useful problem with which to be concerned; rather than interrogating the other, let us deconstruct the normality-which-is-to-be-assumed" (Shakespeare, 1999, 28). The humanist logics thus structuring the Social Model have gradually become seen by critical disability scholars as an important target for critique. Erevelles has consistently challenged these logics, asking, "[w]hat happens when the very essence of the liberal humanist self is necessarily predicated on the construction of the disabled Other as the embodiment of inalienable difference?" (Erevelles, 2002, 11). These insights also enable us to think more carefully about the Social Model, which despite the debates noted above, has undoubtedly been crucial in disability rights and has influenced radical approaches to disability politics. It is important to think through how rethinking the humanist and liberal subject and the role of the state and institutions through disability might enable us to move beyond Social Model approaches which may reinforce problematic norms, and to respond more carefully to the challenges posed by the CRPD.

Spatial and relational approaches have been engaged with by some working on geography and disability, and this offers a productive way to challenge the static and linear ideas of subjectivity and the role of the state that has proved problematic for those seeking to use the Social Model in radical or progressive ways. Hall and Wilton, writing from a critical geography perspective, have drawn on new materialist theorists such as Barad and Braidotti, and the notion of assemblage, to advance an understanding of "complex and emergent geographies of disability, but also to unsettle broader assumptions about the nature of the 'able-body'"(2016, 727). Unseating the norm of the autonomous, rational, individual legal subject and rethinking subjectivity through and with impairment, interdependence, difference, and relationality enables us to then see the "sheer diversity of embodied experiences that overwhelm any binary opposition between a normative 'able-body' and its disabled other" (Hall and Wilton, 2016, 741). Difference is seen as an emergent and contingent state which is implicated in various webs of material and discursive relations. As such, through a new materialist lens, differential embodied experiences are not erased or ignored – instead the question shifts to how such experiences and embodied forms come to matter.

As Alaimo suggests,

> As the material self cannot be disentangled from networks that are simultaneously economic, political, cultural, scientific, and substantial, what was once the ostensibly bounded human subject finds herself in a swirling landscape of uncertainty where practices and actions that were once not

considered in ethical or political terms suddenly become the very stuff of the crises at hand.

(Alaimo, 2011, 282)

As Bozalek further contends in relation to new materialist and post-human analyses "neither makes the assumptions of enlightenment humanist ethics by regarding the independent rational human actor as the centre of morality, or seeing the human being as the centre of moral thought" (Bozalek, 2016, 80). The understanding of agency is no longer tied to human subjects, and as a result, much of the post-Enlightenment humanistic baggage is discarded.

This shift has particular relevance for mental capacity law which is structured around the ideal of a rational human actor. In this way mental capacity law is driven by Enlightenment humanist ethics, which places the independent, rational human actor as the central figure against which the incapacitous 'other' is placed. Moreover, this is an approach to 'the human' which resonates across liberal legal approaches, whether this be in the context of disability, race, gender, or non-human animals. Disability scholars such as Simo Vehmas have long challenged the focus on humanist ideas of rationality and intelligence that are central to social and legal ordering (1999). As Altermark puts it, "the politics of intellectual disability is the politics of all of us" (2018, 3). Joseph, for example, has exposed the entanglement of categorisation of people as 'types' as part of dehumanising colonial and imperial projects to establish human hierarchies (2015, 1021; also see Simpson, 2007). As such, they urge close scrutiny of "how and why articulations of difference have been inoculated into societies and what historical and contemporary projects they continue to serve" (1037). Discarding this humanist baggage has significant critical potential for challenging this normative ordering and uncovering its effects. The disability context in particular is starkly driven by ideas of disabled/non-disabled, and – as will be discussed in more depth in Chapter 3 – disentangling this binary through spatial and relational approaches can significantly shift conceptual, legal, and policy approaches to mental capacity but also offers important critical insights for other areas of law.

In particular, the focus on intra-actions and embodied experiences as entangled within assemblages of material, discursive, technological, institutional, and socio-economic forces emphasises the processes and temporal, changing nature of our experience. Importantly, this demonstrates experience and identity not as static (a static disabled/able subject) but as changing over time as we move through and between different assemblages. In direct contrast to the more teleological temporality of liberal humanist frames, focusing on progress, the subject here can experience more than one identity, as they are situated in different assemblages at the same contemporaneously. The impact of the various actors and productive forces in these entanglements and intra-actions are also seen not to be linear, but to be diffuse and disparate. This poses a challenge to the Social Model in that the relationship between the disabled subject and the societal barrier becomes much more complex, and the connection between a particular barrier and impairment less concrete and linear. Both medical and social models of disability tend to operate through and along a linear, uni-directional causal paradigm, and further endorse a teleological dynamic of progress, and an assemblage approach provides the critical tools to begin to dismantle such assumptions. Moreover, the focus becomes much broader than disability, as subject positions and identities intersect and shift. As Hall and Wilton suggest, this entails a "decentering of a stable disabled subject in favour of an emphasis on relational becoming" (2016, 727). Allowing this subject to replace the individualistic, atomistic, autonomous subject thus has productive potential. As Schwiek outlined in her discussion of the so-called "ugly laws", which made it illegal in some US states for people with "unsightly" disabilities to appear in public, those seeking to challenge these did so by challenging norms in order to reconfigure them. Terming such activists "spatial dissidents", she suggests that they "insisted not only on exposing themselves to public view but also on occupying and radically reconfiguring public space" (Schwiek, 2009, 6).

Beyond this, the productive, vibrant nature of new materialist approaches enables a more positive, creative, and transformative Social Model approach. There is a sense in which an approach which focuses on removing a particular barrier that disables an impaired subject still individualises the problem, and leaves the broader structural issues including the conceptual framework intact. Whilst it is true that it locates the issue in society rather than individualises it as a medical concern, the locus of action is still this connection between the individual who is impaired and the barrier. Exclusionary practices or frames may still be left to function, so long as the impaired individual is able to function within this. In drawing on ideas of processes and moving away from a uni-directional, linear way of framing disability, it becomes evident that thinking in terms of a relational, interdependent subject is productive within these assemblages and can impact on the broader structures and institutions. The Social Model had attracted criticism for the way in which it simply positioned the disabled body (and the body more generally) as an object waiting to be inscribed by the broader structural processes (a common critique of materialist approaches), "rather than a subject with ontological significance" (Erevelles, 2011, 35), or a "subject as both produced and productive" (46). Instead, engaging with spatial and relational processes sees us not as simply inscribed by practices and processes, but as active (or intra-active) participants. This, importantly, opens up new ways of thinking about responses and responsibility, as was discussed in the previous chapter in relation to spatial legal approaches. As Joseph suggests,

> when we recognise ourselves and each other as deeply imbricated in the confluence of historical oppression, we are left to question any position of anti-, as we are all still functioning within systems and structures of difference, and human hierarchies that make the position of being 'anti' to one particular form of oppression, impossible.
>
> (2015, 1037)

This resonates with Barad's call to recognise that there is no 'outside', and that we are all mutually entangled and imbricated.

It is argued that changing our ontological starting point changes and reshapes the material and conceptual framework of analysis, potentially changing approaches to law and social justice in radical ways rather than leaving them intact or seeing them as natural. As Barad suggests, "embodiment is a matter not of being specifically situated in the world, but rather of being *of the world in dynamic* specificity" (Barad, 2007, 376–7). This echoes Laura Davy's argument for "philosophical inclusive design" which takes universal relationality and interdependence as the central starting point for philosophy, rather than (as often happens) trying to shoehorn disability into existing political and philosophical approaches almost as an afterthought, thus reinforcing the 'otherness' and exceptionality of disability (Davy, 2015). It is important not just to consider the shift in ontology or subjectivity, but to think about how this then impacts and reconfigures the broader theoretical and material terrain.

Rather than simply focusing on how law or policy views a particular subject – as capacitous rather than incapacitous, as non-disabled rather than disabled – this more dynamic approach necessitates a focus on how the processes of differentiation come into being and what their material and discursive effects are. Importantly, this avoids reinscribing the naturalness or pre-givenness of these subject positions (and their opposite). As Power and Bartlett discuss, "The intersecting nature of these three elements (the body, social relations, and place) is fundamental to the relational model of disability … However, place is largely left implicit and muted within this conceptual framework" (2018, 564). As has already been discussed, space is not only material, and we need to be attentive to the backgrounded discursive, organising spaces which contain and maintain boundaries for analysis and action. As will be turned to in the remaining sections, law plays an important role in creating and sustaining discursive and material spaces and their boundaries, although this role has as yet been under-theorised in critical disability literature.

Disability and law in conversation

Whilst there have been important developments in critical disability studies, which will be discussed below, there has been surprisingly little engagement with *law* as a part of the assemblages which have otherwise warranted critical analysis. We see reflected in some of the disability studies debates the idea that law is a positivist phenomenon. So, for example, Oliver and Barnes in their later work advocated essentially for a turn away from law in a paper which argued that legislation and rights were being captured by certain powerful professions and interest groups (Oliver and Barnes, 2006). Whilst this is undoubtedly true and resonates with a longstanding argument against relying upon rights or law to solve issues of social justice, what is missing here is a more critical analysis of how *law itself* could be changed. Moreover, this betrays a particular ideal that law is something which can somehow be escaped in activism, a position which Lobel has critiqued in her argument that the legal and the social are not separate but instead permeate each other (Lobel, 2007). Law is seen in Barnes and Oliver's account as static, a problematic approach which was discussed in the previous chapter. Nik Rose's work, which is much more socio-legally grounded, has at times fallen into this trap of seeing law and/or rights as pre-defined structures. Rose suggests that there are limitations of rights discourse in seeking progressive strategies for social reform (Rose, 1985). Whilst the critique is undoubtedly historically accurate and warranted in light of liberal rights frameworks, missing from this account is the recognition that law and rights discourses can shift and are contingent. This turn away from law, as Munro suggests, still allows these power relations and norms to persist, albeit unchecked (Munro, 2007, 68). Similarly, Tom Shakespeare's influential *Disability Rights and Wrongs Revisited* seems to caution against relying upon law or rights to solve all disability problems, yet still seems to endorse legal means throughout the second part of the book (Shakespeare, 2013). The critical realist approach which Shakespeare takes is interesting here in that it seems to accept the concepts which have troubled and divided disability studies scholars, as well as the given-ness of the structures within which these concepts work, including the legal and political structures. Again, a static, ordered, and positivist approach to law is taken without recognition of the ways in which law itself is a dynamic, ongoing process with shifting boundaries. There is a need to interrogate how law and legal processes occupy an important role within disability: they help to define and solidify difference; they help to create, cement, or dismantle roles and relations; and they define the boundaries of responsibility and appropriate response.

This is not necessarily a criticism of these scholars as it is an approach echoed across many fields, including in some legal analysis. As Philippopolous-Mihalopolous suggests, "law presents itself as immaterial, abstract, universal, non-geographical. This is of course one of law's greatest tricks" (2014, 410). There is real scope here for productive engagements between critical disability studies and socio-legal theorists in order to more carefully expose the intra-actions between legal processes and the problematic concepts which critical disability studies has grappled with and to challenge their given-ness. This is not a new concern. In 1998, Nik Rose and Mariana Valverde urged for a similar focus on the interaction between processes of law and problematisation. Whilst this is a long quotation, it needs to be shared in its totality to fully capture the essence of the point.

> Law, as a unified phenomenon governed by certain general principles is a fiction ... While it might seem obvious to begin by asking "what does law govern?", from the perspective of government we would not start from law at all. Instead, we would start from problems or problematizations. A problematization, here, is a way in which experience is offered to thought in the form of a problem requiring attention ... As an example, it is now commonplace to ask how 'the law' regulates 'sexuality'. But we would

> prefer to ask how does a particular problem – say that of homosexual relations or prostitution – come to emerge as a target for government, and what role is played by legal institutions, functionaries and calculations in this?
>
> (Rose and Valverde, 1998, 545–6)

This sees legal 'problems' not as pre-existing issues which the state, via legal institutions and government, must respond to, but as created and emerging through a number of societal and institutional processes. Disability offers a rich example for interrogation here, shifting from looking at how law responds to disability, towards thinking about how particular problems (such as decision making by people with impairments) emerge as a target for government. With this need to focus on the processes (and their genealogy) through which 'problems' emerge, the rest of this chapter will outline the development of the Mental Capacity Act, through the Law Commission processes, and the boundaries that this created for discourse in this field. This will have a particular focus on the problematisation and framing of the legislation as being (1) limited to those with a 'mental disorder' and (2) about autonomy rather than paternalism. This is not to suggest that these are or were the only drivers of the legislation, yet this approach to the development of the Act demonstrates that these are stark organising binaries of the legislative framework. Moreover, the processes underpinning the creation of legal binaries such as capacitous/incapacitous and disabled/non-disabled offer important insights for critical disability studies and work which seeks to challenge these categorisations. Being attentive to these processes enables us to see how approaches to legal subjectivity are created and maintained and how this is closely linked to the broader boundaries of the state. As will be seen in later chapters, these binaries also play a key role in the development and sustainment of other binaries in the conceptual framework in the context of mental capacity law and liberal legalism more broadly.

Development of the Mental Capacity Act: foundational binaries

The Mental Capacity Act 2005 was enacted after a long and tumultuous period of consultation, drafting, and debate. A number of factors triggered the need for law reform in this area, including cases such as *T v T* [1988] Farn 52 and *Re F* (Mental Patient: Sterilisation) [1990] 2 AC which exposed the problematic lack of legal authority for medical interventions in the lives of those deemed unable to consent. Additionally, the Law Commission 1995 Report on *Mental Incapacity* (Law Commission, 1995) outlined various reasons for the need for reform. The Law Commission pointed to the way in which the law governing decision making for adults deemed to be incompetent was "unsystematic and full of glaring gaps" (Law Commission, 1995, 1.1) and had "failed to keep up with developments in our understanding of the rights and needs of those with mental disability" (1.1). Furthermore, there was perceived to be a lack of an effective framework for resolving disputes about the care of people without capacity or for legitimating or regulating the substitute decision making that regularly took place in practice (Law Commission, 1995, 1.5). The social context was also deemed to be an important factor in pushing for legal reform, with the Law Commission pointing to deinstitutionalisation, the ageing population, medical advances, and a rights-focused law and policy agenda as being key social and political drivers for change in this area (Law Commission, 1995, 2.31).

The resulting Mental Capacity Act 2005 sets up a clear, and perhaps deceptively simple, framework for decision making, with a central distinction drawn between capacity and incapacity, based on the existence of an impairment or disturbance in the functioning of the mind or brain, drawn in s2 and 3. Should a patient be deemed to have mental capacity, then their decision cannot be interfered with – they are ultimately seen as exercising their autonomy. Should a patient be deemed to lack mental capacity in relation to a particular decision, then any decision made has to be made in their best interests, in accordance with s4. The binary divide then is crucial in guiding the legal trajectory and available responses.

Much of the literature in this area also tend to under-theorise or under-appreciate the political underpinnings of the legislation and policy in this area. As will be seen, mental capacity law does not exist in a vacuum. The Act itself is premised upon particular ideals of subjectivity and the role of professionals and other institutions. It sets up a framework of legal and spatial relations, drawing boundaries around and within these relations as it does so. These boundaries are inflected with an interwoven network of binaries which help to shape and form the logics of the legislation as well as broader legal frameworks, including autonomy/paternalism, capacity/incapacity, empower/protect, public/private. Delving into the spatial boundaries that are drawn in the jurisprudence enables us to see how the workings of the Act and its logics play an active role in shaping and buttressing ideas of (disabled) legal subjectivity and the role of the state in creating and maintaining this.

Disabled/non-disabled

In many ways, the legislation consolidated and codified the existing law, which had developed through a number of cases. The case of *Re C* (Adult: Refusal of Medical Treatment) [1994] 1 All ER 819 is often highlighted as a key illustration of the origins of the 'test' for assessing mental capacity. The now infamous case involved a man who was diagnosed with paranoid schizophrenia who was detained under the Mental Health Act 1983. His doctors were recommending the amputation of his gangrenous foot, but C was refusing this for a number of reasons which the medical professionals argued were delusionary. It was held by Thorpe J that the presence of schizophrenia did not prevent C from having the capacity to make this particular decision about his medical treatment and so allowed the refusal. The case is interesting for a number of reasons, including the way in which the test of capacity was formulated, and the way in which the interaction between disability and incapacity was considered.

Whilst it appears that the test for capacity in the MCA, stemming as it did from *Re C*, is a legal construct, its origins belie a more than subtle medical influence. The medical expert in the case, Dr Nigel Eastman, was invited to give his assessment of the capacity of C. His assessment drew on three factors which he saw as relevant to assessing capacity in relation to health care decisions, namely retaining information, believing information, and weighing up that information. Keywood highlights how Thorpe J then "borrowed" these criteria to form the legal threshold of mental capacity, suggesting that

> this judicial annexation of a clinical assessment measure is highly problematic for it conceals the fact that clinical determinations of patients' decision-making abilities are given a normative force that they were never intended to have. Moreover, the manner of this judicial appropriation has meant that a range of nonclinical issues that impact on people's decision-making abilities have been obscured from critical examination by the courts.
>
> (Keywood, 2003, 605)

Indeed, there is a heavy emphasis on clinical diagnosis in the MCA. Whilst we see from *Re C* and the legislation that a mental disorder alone is not sufficient for a finding of incapacity, it is a *necessary* element. The applicability of the legislation intrinsically depends on there being a disorder or disturbance in the functioning of the mind or brain which *causes* the inability to use, weigh, retain, or communicate the information relevant to the decision (see *PC & Anor. v City of York Council* [2013] EWCA Civ 478).

This diagnostic or status element to the legislation was not uncontroversial in the consultation and debates leading to the Act. In their consultation paper 'A New Jurisdiction', the Law Commission stated that

> From the responses received to our consultation paper it appears that more distress is caused by over-extensive use of protective powers than by any stigma found to attach to the term 'mental disorder'. It also seems that the requirement [inclusion of a diagnostic element] goes at least some way towards providing *a safeguard against improper interference in the lives of those whose perceived failure to manage is attributable merely to a lack of inclination or eccentricity*.
>
> (Law Commission, 1992, 3.13; emphasis added)

In their 1995 report *Mental Incapacity*, the Law Commission signalled that the balance fell in favour of including a diagnostic element so as to ensure that "the test is stringent enough *not* to catch large numbers of people who make unusual or unwise decisions" (Law Commission, 1995, 3.8). Recognition was given to the criticisms propounded at the time by Carson, who argued that both a test for capacity and a diagnostic element to this were misconceived (Carson, 1993).

The Commission reported Carson's view as being a rejection of a "medical model" of the assessment of mental capacity (Law Commission, 1995, 2.15) yet gave a number of reasons to reject this "mainstreaming approach", as they termed it, including that

- It puts a heavy burden on the test of incapacity.
- Another respondent could not agree that there could be mental incapacity without mental disorder.
- The Law Society Mental Health Sub-Committee and General Council of the Bar had included some test of mental disorder in addition to the test of functional competence.
- A further respondent had suggested that "where incapacity is used to justify imposing restrictions on freedom of movement, Art 5 of the European Convention on Human Rights would require the establishment of a true mental disorder before a competent authority on the basis of expertise" (2.16).

It is interesting here that the idea of 'capacity' is tacitly accepted as an objective and measurable 'thing' through this discussion by the Law Commission, with seemingly no prior consideration of *why* we utilise the concept or question it in the first place. We can also see a professional wrangling around the meaning of capacity going on, with a clear agreement from the Commission with the Law Society Sub-Committee and the Bar Council. Similarly, the Article 5 issue raised seems to place acceptance upon medicalised approaches to capacity and disorder and is, in a sense, the tail that wags the dog of necessitating mental disorder, notwithstanding the specific purpose and context of Art 5. The medicalised focus of the legislation will be further explored in Chapter 3, yet it is interesting to note here that there is a consolidation of the dominance of the medical profession in the legislation through the perceived necessity of the diagnostic element. Mental capacity becomes (or continues to be) seen as a medical concern, firmly within the realms of medical expertise. This retention of a diagnostic element can be seen as reinforcing and repeating what had previously occurred unchecked in medical practices: the legislation simply provides a solid legal basis for such actions, and the opportunity to more critically engage with or challenge the foundations and justifications for such actions was thus sidelined. This may be due to the roots of the legislation being situated in medical cases such as *Re F* as discussed above. Yet, as will be seen, the reach of the Act goes far beyond the medical realm. Despite claims that the legislation is empowering, or about enabling autonomy – claims which will be further interrogated in later chapters – we see here a sense in which it was actually more of the same, with the broader institutional frames and structures enabling professional dominance left intact.

As we have seen then, the distinction drawn between those with and those without a mental disorder in the capacity/incapacity distinction was central to the Law Commission consultation and recommendations when crafting the legislation, swayed by a concern not to intervene unduly in otherwise simply "eccentric" decisions. We can see this strict boundary being policed in subsequent Court of Protection case law, most recently in the high-profile case of *Kings College v C* [2015] EWCOP 59. The case involved a woman wanting to refuse lifesaving renal dialysis following an attempted suicide. A great deal of the judgment in this case is given over to an in-depth discussion of her ability to understand, use, and weigh the information relevant to this decision, it ultimately being found that she was able to do so and thus 'passed' the functional test for capacity. However, there is an interesting discussion following this about the causal link between this ability and an impairment of, or disturbance in, the functioning of the mind or brain,

> had I been satisfied that C was unable to use and weigh information in the manner contended for by the Trust, I believe I would have had difficulty in deciding that this inability was, on the balance of probabilities, because of an impairment of, or a disturbance in the functioning of, the mind or brain. Whilst it is accepted by all parties that C has an impairment of, or a disturbance in the functioning of, the mind or brain, the evidence as to the precise nature of that impairment or disturbance was far from conclusive. Further, and more importantly, with regard to the question of causation, and in particular whether what was being seen might be the operation of a personality disorder or simply the thought processes of a strong willed, stubborn individual with unpalatable and highly egocentric views the evidence was likewise somewhat equivocal. However, as I say, I need say no more about this in light of my conclusions as set out above.
>
> (para 93)

Macdonald J did not have to engage in the space of the incapacitous subject. However, as will be discussed further in Chapter 3, this static distinction between disabled and non-disabled becomes increasingly unsustainable when we engage with the more recent critical disability literature. It will become clear that this legal distinction is one which is produced, rather than discovered.

Autonomy/paternalism

It is also pertinent to reflect on the broader context in which the consultation and legislative process were taking place in order to think about the material and discursive drivers and context which played a role in creating the distinctions between subjects and the role of the state. The ascendency of medical law and bioethics as disciplines helped to bring debates about patient autonomy, paternalism, and rights to the fore. Traces of this are evident through much of the Law Commission's work on mental capacity. Their early consultation documents, for example, emphasise the importance of balancing "choice" and "protection" (Law Commission, 1992; Law Commission, 1993a), and the 1995 report similarly emphasises this need to balance "autonomy" and "protection" (Law Commission, 1995). In all instances, these terms are presented as in need of being balanced, implying their separateness and tension. At the same time, however, what is meant by these terms is not explained. The MCA Code of Practice states that "the Act also aims to balance an individual's right to make decisions for themselves with their right to be protected from harm if they lack capacity to make decisions to protect themselves" (paras 1.4 and 2.4). This attention to the importance of autonomy and nervousness about perceived paternalism and interference in the lives of individuals is also prominent in the above discussion about the diagnostic threshold. The importance of constraining any powers to interfere in decisions to those who have a particular mental disorder, and not encroaching on merely eccentric or unwise decisions, is paramount in the debates surrounding the legislation.

These binaries play an important role in shaping the legal framework surrounding mental capacity, and their representation and uncontroversial deployment throughout the Act's development reflects broader legal and political debates at the time. They have a productive role, however, in both creating the legal subject and in drawing boundaries around the role of the state. The view perpetuated through this framing is that the legal subject is self-determining and autonomous – rational and capable of justifying or explaining decisions. Such a subject is highly reflective of the liberal legal subject we encountered in Chapter 1. The incapacitous subject, on the other hand, falls outside of the liberal norm and becomes a state of exception: other. Yet, this exception must be carefully circumscribed so as to uphold the shape and logics of the liberal state. The state is thus presented through the development of the legislation as largely absent, enabling this necessary self-determination, and thus only interfering when the individual falls into this separate, carefully constructed realm.

What begins to surface from the previous section is the way in which this disabled/non-disabled binary feeding into the distinction drawn between capacity/incapacity becomes justified through and maps onto the autonomy/paternalism binary. It was felt overall by the Commission that inclusion of the diagnostic threshold would provide clarity and prevent "net widening". What becomes apparent here is this creation of a necessary connection between recognising incapacity and a "paternalistic intervention". This leads to a perceived need to keep the category of incapacity small, to reduce intervention. What this does not explain is *why* purportedly "paternalistic interventions" are the only responses conceivable here. It is starkly evident that this binary understanding is constraining, and is recursively constrained by, the conceptualisation of potential responses.

Such presuppositions involved in this framework become evident in many Court of Protection judgments, including this statement by Eldergill J,

> Society is made up of individuals, and each individual wills certain ends for themselves and their loved ones, and not others, and has distinctive feelings, personal goals, traits, habits and experiences. Because this is so, most individuals wish to determine and develop their own interests and

> course in life, and their happiness often depends on this. The existence of a private sphere of action, free from public coercion or restraint, is indispensable to that independence which everyone needs to develop their individuality, even where their individuality is diminished, but not extinguished, by illness. It is for this reason that people place such weight on their liberty and right to choose.
>
> (*Westminster City Council v Manuela Sykes* [2014] EWHC B9 (COP), per Eldergill J, para 20)

This distinction drawn between the public sphere of interference and the private sphere of non-interference has been challenged by many feminist legal theorists and is undoubtedly problematic when particular practices become normalised or viewed as an aspect of 'nature' or individual responsibility when relegated to this private realm. As will be seen in later chapters, by shifting the focus to entanglements and connections in assemblages, and drawing attention to the temporal aspects of decisions as ongoing, produced through a number of connections and intra-actions over time, this private realm of individual self-determination becomes difficult to sustain. This zone of non-interference ignores the ongoing, embedded relations between individuals with each other, with the state, with institutions and with cultural, economic, technological, and discursive forces – relations which shift and change over time as new connections are made. What is important here is that even those spaces which the state and its institutions claim to be absent from are actively produced by norms which shape this absence.

The conceptual reach of the binaries – adult safeguarding

It has been seen that the focus on autonomy, as opposed to paternalism or protection, and the binary divide between capacity and incapacity, linked to disability (discussed further in Chapter 3) has played a central role in shaping the legal frameworks and responses of institutions and professionals in this area. It is important to also look at the developments in adult social care law and policy alongside this to note the way in which legal and professional responses were being shaped in the context of social care, and to think about how this is entangled with the legal and ethical discourses around autonomy, paternalism, and capacity. We see the binary frames which emerged through the development of the MCA, stemming themselves from broader legal and policy commitments at the time, beginning to reach into linked areas of policy, assisting in the cementing of the conceptual boundaries. Whilst the Mental Capacity Act 2005 is heavily rooted in the medical jurisprudence and concerns around consent and battery in tort, it is important to recognise and consider its practical impact in shaping adult social care, as it touches upon decisions about contact, residence, and access to services in the community. The initial Law Commission work on mental incapacity envisaged focus and reform of public law issues around jurisdiction and obligations in relation to those who were termed "vulnerable adults" (Law Commission, 1993b). This was seen as important given the diffuse and unclear nature of local authority duties and obligations in this context, as well as the "outdated" nature of any existing powers, such as under the National Assistance Acts 1947 and 1951, given more modern approaches to rights and autonomy. What is interesting about the work of the Law Commission here is the way in which they envisaged setting up a jurisdiction alongside the mental capacity legislation, which encompassed a group of adults who were deemed vulnerable and at risk (Law Commission, 1993b). In their early work in this area, they stated that,

> Mental incapacity should also be distinguished from the concept of vulnerability, which is increasingly used to characterise groups of people who may need either protection from harm or help in obtaining the services to which they are entitled. Some vulnerable people are also mentally incapacitated, but many are not. Nevertheless, some of the legal mechanisms available at present can be used, not only for people who are incapacitated but also for wider categories of mentally disordered or vulnerable people, and we shall inevitably have to consider these in the course of this review.
>
> (Law Commission, 1989, 2)

The core focus of the consultation on the public law issues, and the resulting 1995 report, was on issues of abuse and safeguarding, with the framing of the problem being posed as being about

> how the balance between protection from harm and respect for individual rights … should be struck and maintained.
>
> (Law Commission, 1995, 9.1)

Despite the extensive consultation, however, the government in their Green Paper *Who Decides* (Lord Chancellor's Office, 1997) stated that law reform here was unnecessary and instead favoured developing clearer processes and powers in relation to social care through policy mechanisms. Whilst wholesale reform was abandoned, the social care legislation and policy trajectories intersect in fundamental ways with the workings and interpretation of the Mental Capacity Act 2005.

No Secrets, which was (prior to the Care Act 2014) the key policy framework underpinning adult safeguarding, interestingly drew on the Law Commission's work to shape the realm of the "vulnerable adult" and core values in this area. In particular, the way in which the term "vulnerable adult" had been framed in the consultation paper and 1995 Law Commission report was used to underpin the policy. *No Secrets* defined a vulnerable adult as,

> A person aged 18 or over who is or who may be in need of community care services by reason of a mental or other disability, age or illness; and who is or who may be unable to protect himself or herself against significant harm or exploitation.
>
> (Department of Health, 2000, 2.3)

Here the idea of vulnerability is seen as broader than incapacity yet is still intimately and necessarily linked with ideas of illness or disability. *No Secrets* also reproduced the centrality of capacity as guiding responses in this area, stating that,

> The vulnerable adult's capacity is the key to action since if someone has "capacity" and declines assistance this limits the help that he or she may be given. It will not however limit the action that may be required to protect others who are at risk of harm. In order to make sound decisions, the vulnerable adult's emotional, physical, intellectual and mental capacity in relation to self determination and consent and any intimidation, misuse of authority or undue influence will have to be assessed.
>
> (Department of Health, 2000, 6.21)

This interaction between the adult social care policy and the mental capacity legislation helped to structure the foundations for conceptual development going forward. It set the categories, obligations and scope of responses and built them upon a framework of capacity/incapacity and vulnerability/invulnerability, a framework that was also heavily suffused with notions of disability and protection. In many ways, these realms of incapacity and vulnerability became seen as exceptions to the norm of capacitous and autonomous choice: different, other, and warranting special responses. This has the effect of buttressing notions of the ideal subject and shaping the 'other'.

These concepts and values can be traced through the developments following *No Secrets,* which further shaped the contours of the adult social policy agenda. Whilst *No Secrets* was concerned with safeguarding and protection of the vulnerable, issues of access to services and the values underpinning these developed through a different agenda. The White Paper *Valuing People* (Department of Health, 2001), for example, aimed to set up the policy agenda for services for people with learning disabilities. Choice featured as a central focus of this document, alongside control and independence. Such concepts became the central drivers and focus for initiatives following *Valuing People,* being echoed in *Independence, Wellbeing and Choice* (Department of Health, 2005), *Our Health, Our Care. Our Say* (Department of Health, 2006), and *Valuing People Now* (Department of Health, 2009). These ideas of choice and independence that are central to much of this agenda resonate with the focus on patient autonomy and self-determination, which was increasingly framing debates in medical law and ethics, and which featured so heavily as a framing device in the legislative process leading to the Mental Capacity Act 2005. As a number of commentators have identified, the trajectories of access to services on one hand, and safeguarding and protection on the other, have developed separately, with very little engagement with one another (Fyson and Kitson, 2007; Sherwood-Johnson, 2016; MacKay, 2017). This separation of underpinning values echoes in many ways the development of mental capacity law and enables the demarcation of binary distinctions around identity and corollary obligations or responses. Again, incapacity or vulnerability are distinguished at both a conceptual and policy level from capacity, invulnerability, and independence. This is then entangled with questions about how and whether the state should intervene – whether this is paternalistic, and whether interventions in the lives of those outside of the autonomous realm should be aimed at empowerment or protection. Just as the balance to be struck between autonomy and paternalism has framed much of medical law and the development of the Mental Capacity Act 2005, the balance between empowerment and protection, or independence or protection, has framed much of the debate and policy agenda in relation to adult social care.

Fyson, for example, has highlighted that,

> Much of the difficulty lies in the fact that social care policies and adult safeguarding policies, despite both existing for the intended benefit of the same groups of people, have each developed within a completely separate paradigm.
>
> (Fyson, 2009, 6)

This has helped to shape the frameworks for approaching and defining problems in this context for social workers, lawyers, judges, and academics. However, the way in which these concepts and their dualistic, binary nature are deployed often belies their complexity. In the same way that we have seen the concept of autonomy in medical law and mental capacity law being subject to criticism in relation to its almost parochial individual and narrow deployment, the concepts that resonate with it in the social policy literature – choice, control, independence, and empowerment – are facing similar charges. As we have seen, these are set up against (negative) ideas of intervention and protection, echoing concerns of paternalism. Yet, as Sherwood-Johnson argues in the social care context, it is important to consider such binaries through a 'construction' rather than 'discovery' model in order to draw awareness to conflicts over meaning, contingencies in application of policy concepts, and the consequences of their deployment in terms of creating meaning (Sherwood-Johnson, 2016).

Conclusion

This chapter has outlined the importance of a relational and spatial critical lens for law in tandem with critical disability studies, in order to illuminate the processes through which well-recognised problematic conceptual boundaries in relation to disability come to be developed. The conceptual approach has been seen to challenge and build on Social Model approaches and provide the critical tools for detailed legal analysis and progressive reform.

The discussion so far has introduced the early roots of some of these key organising binaries in mental capacity law, which will be further interrogated in the subsequent chapters. It has also begun to reflect on the ways that such binaries have rendered particular ideas about the legal subject and the role of the state. Such an approach to the MCA is particularly important now given the opportunities posed by the CRPD; yet, as will be seen, these opportunities have not yet been taken, as the current conceptual boundaries are being accepted and employed by many scholars, policy makers, and legal professionals in order to give effect to the Convention. This will be seen in the next chapter, which turns to consider the distinction between capacity and incapacity and the problematic ways in which this is drawn, as well as the productive effects of this binary in terms of shaping the ideal of the legal subject. Bringing critical disability studies and spatial approaches to law into conversation in this way offers new conceptual tools to deepen the critique of the current legal framework and to respond more dynamically to the challenges posed by the CRPD. Whilst the focus here has been on the domestic context, this approach will have resonance for scholars in other jurisdictions seeking to implement the CRPD or to challenge legal frameworks based on capacity or competence. Moreover, given the entanglement of ideas of capacity and rationality with the ideal of the liberal legal subject, which has historically worked to exclude and oppress other groups in society, the critical lens and excavation of the development of binaries opens up the critical space to challenge conceptual starting points, with repercussions for law and other disciplines engaged with social justice.

The next chapter will more closely analyse the capacity/incapacity binary using the conceptual tools offered by spatial and relational approaches to law and disability, to reveal the ways in which this binary is maintained and its material and discursive effects, but also to challenge and dismantle the logics that sustain it.

References

Alaimo, S. 2011. 'New Materialisms, Old Humanisms, or, Following the Submersible' *Nordic Journal of Feminist and Gender Research* 19(4), 280–4.

Altermark, N. 2018. *Citizenship Inclusion and Intellectual Disability: Biopolitics Post-Institutionalisation*. London: Routledge.

Barad, K. 2007. *Meeting the Universe Halfway*. Durham, NC: Duke University Press.

Bozalek, V. 2016. 'The Political Ethics of Care and Feminist Posthuman Ethics: Contributions to Social Work' in R. Hugman and J. Carter (Eds), *Rethinking Values and Ethics in Social Work*. London: Palgrave Macmillan. 80–96.

Campbell, F. K. 2009. *Contours of Ableism: The Production of Disability and Abledness*. Basingstoke: Palgrave Macmillan.

Carson, D. 1993. 'Disabling Progress: The Law Commission's Proposals on Mentally Incapacitated Adults' Decision Making' *Journal of Social Welfare and Family Law* 15(5), 304.

Crow, L. 1996. 'Including All Our Lives: Renewing the Social Model of Disability' in C. Barnes and G. Mercer (Eds), *Exploring the Divide: Illness and Disability*. Leeds: The Disability Press. 55–72.

Davy, L. 2015. 'Philosophical Inclusive Design: Intellectual Disability and the Limits of Individual Autonomy in Moral and Political Theory' *Hypatia* 30(1), 132–48.

Department of Health 2000. *No Secrets: Guidance on Developing and Implementing Multi-Agency Policies and Procedures to Protect Vulnerable Adults From Abuse*. London: Department of Health.

Department of Health 2001. *Valuing People: A New Strategy for Learning Disability for the 21st Century. A White Paper*. London: Department of Health.

Department of Health 2005. *Independence, Well-Being and Choice: Our Vision for the Future of Social Care in England*. London: DoH.

Department of Health 2006. *Our Health, Our Care, Our Say: A New Direction for Community Services*. London: DoH.

Department of Health 2009. *Valuing People Now*. London: DoH.

Ecclestone, K. and Goodley, D. 2016. 'Political and Educational Springboard or Straightjacket? Theorizing Post/Humanist Subjects in an Age of Vulnerability' *Discourse: Studies in the Cultural Politics of Education* 37(2), 175–88.

Erevelles, N. 1996. 'Disability and the Dialectics of Difference' *Disability & Society* 11(4), 519–38.

Erevelles, N. 2002. 'Cognitive Disability, Race and the Politics of Citizenship' *Disability, Culture and Education* 1(1), 5–25.

Erevelles, N. 2011. *Disability and Difference in Global Contexts: Enabling a Transformative Body Politic*. New York: Palgrave Macmillan.

Fyson, R. 2009. 'Independence and Learning Disabilities: Why We Must Also Recognize Vulnerability' *Journal of Adult Protection* 11(3), 18–25.

Fyson, R. and Kitson, D. 2007. 'Independence or Protection: Does It Have to Be a Choice? Reflections on the Abuse of People with Learning Disabilities in Cornwall' *Critical Social Policy* 27(3), 426–36.

Goodley, D., Lawthom, R. and Runswick Cole, K. 2014. 'Posthuman Disability Studies' *Subjectivity* 7(4), 342–61.

Hall, E. and Wilton, R. 2016. 'Towards a Relational Geography of Disability' *Progress in Human Geography* 41(6), 727–44.

Joseph, A. 2015. 'The Necessity of an Attention to Eurocentrism and Colonial Technologies: An Addition to Critical Mental Health Literature' *Disability & Society* 30(7), 1021–41.

Keenan, S. 2015. *Subversive Property: Law and the Production of Spaces of Belonging*. Oxfordshire: Routledge.

Keywood, K. 2003. 'Rethinking the Anorexic Body: How English Law and Psychiatry "Think"' *International Journal of Law and Psychiatry* 26, 599–616.

Kuhn, T. 1962. *The Structure of Scientific Revolutions*. Chicago: University of Chicago Press.

Law Commission 1989. *Mental Incapacity*. London: HMSO.

Law Commission 1992. *Mentally Incapacitated Adults and Decision Making: A New Jurisdiction*. London: HMSO.

Law Commission 1993a. *Mentally Incapacitated Adults and Decision Making: Medical Treatment and Research*. London, HMSO.

Law Commission 1993b. *Mentally Incapacitated and Other Vulnerable Adults*. London, HMSO.

Law Commission 1995. *Mental Incapacity*. London: HMSO.

Lobel, O. 2007. 'The Paradox of Extralegal Activism: Critical Legal Consciousness and Transformative Politics' *Harvard Law Review* 120(4), 937–88.

Lord Chancellor's Office 1997. *Who Decides? Making Decisions on Behalf of Mentally Incapacitated Adults: A Consultation Paper*. London: TSO.

Mackay, K. 2017. 'Choosing to Live with Harm? A Presentation of Two Case Studies to Explore the Perspective of Those Who Experienced Adult Safeguarding Interventions' *Ethics and Social Welfare* 11(1), 33.

Munro, V. 2007. *Law and Politics at the Perimeter: Re-evaluating Key Debates in Feminist Theory*. Oxford: Hart.

Oliver, M. and Barnes, C. 2006. 'Disability Politics and Disability Movement in Britain: Where Did It All Go Wrong?' *Magazine of Greater Manchester Coalition of Disabled People* 1–13.

Philippopoulos-Mihalopoulos, Andreas 2014 'Critical Autopoiesis and the Materiality of Law' *International Journal of the Semiotics of Law* 27, 389–418.

Power, A. and Bartlett, R. 2018. '"I Shouldn't Be Living There Because I am a Sponger": Negotiating Everyday Geographies by People With Learning Disabilities' *Disability & Society* 33(4), 562–78.

Rose, N. 1985. 'Unreasonable Rights, Mental Illness and the Limits of the Law' *Journal of Law and Society* 12(2), 199–218.

Rose, N. and Valverde, M. 1998. 'Governed by Law?' *Social and Legal Studies* 7(4), 541–51.

Schwiek, S. 2009. *The Ugly Laws: Disability in Public*. New York: New York University Press.

Shakespeare, T. 1999. 'What is a Disabled Person?' in M. Jones and L. Basser Marks (Eds), *Disability, Divers-Ability and Legal Change*. The Hague: Matinus Nijhoff. 25–34.

Shakespeare, T. 2013. *Disability Rights and Wrongs Revisited*. London: Routledge.

Shakespeare, T. and Watson, N. 2002. 'The Social Model of Disability: An Outdated Ideology?' *Research in Social Science and Disability* 2, 9–28.

Sherwood-Johnson, F. 2016. 'Discovery or Construction? Theorising the Roots of Adult Protection Policy and Practice' *Social Work Education* 35(2), 121.

Simpson, M. 2007. 'From Savage to Citizen: Education, Colonialism and Idiocy' *British Journal of Sociology of Education* 5, 561–74.

Tremain, S. (Ed) 2005. *Foucault and the Governance of Disability*. Michigan: University of Michigan Press.

Vehmas, S. 1999. 'Discriminative Assumptions of Utilitarian Bioethics Regarding Individuals with Intellectual Disabilities' *Disability and Society* 14, 37–62.

3 Capacity/incapacity

A dynamic disability critique

The previous chapters have provided the conceptual tools to interrogate the binaries which frame the Mental Capacity Act (MCA) and which build the conceptual spaces within which issues around mental capacity circulate and come to be viewed. Chapter 2 in particular highlighted the dominant framing of autonomy/paternalism as well as disabled/non-disabled. Whilst the discussion so far has touched briefly on the capacity/incapacity divide, it has not gone into any real depth on its role. The discussion here will focus on the processes through which the binary divide between capacity/incapacity is created and sustained, and what the material effects of this are. Later chapters will explore more fully these material effects, but we will begin to see here the emergence of the space of 'freedom' (and consequent evading of responsibility) that is central to the construction of 'capacity'. It will be seen that this capacity/incapacity distinction is perhaps the primary method by which law in this context sorts individuals into different legal spaces and situates them within the broader framework of binaries (i.e. autonomy/paternalism, empowerment/protection).

The chapter will consider the way this binary is understood and deployed by the judiciary, and some of the real struggles they have in containing it. Going beyond current critical literatures on mental capacity law, the conceptual tools outlined previously will be seen to enable a more thorough interrogation of the very foundations of this binary divide, drawing on critical disability studies in tandem with a spatial and relational approach. In doing so, the chapter brings to the fore the urgency of bringing critical attention to the workings of the capacity/incapacity binary, and that the existence (and persistence) of this binary need not be presumed as objective or necessary. As Martin and Dennis suggest, such oppositions are "so deeply dyed in the post-Enlightenment Western intellectual wool as to be nearly invisible much of the time" (Jenkins, 2010, 86). Similarly, the contingency of this binary divide, like those with which it is entangled, will begin to surface.

The legitimacy and objectivity of the divide will be challenged through considering the ways in which the rational, atomistic ideal of legal subjectivity can be decentered. Bringing attention to the assemblage, and the apparatus through which differentiations are drawn, challenges the ideas of temporality,

DOI: 10.4324/9781351067881-3

causality, responsibility, and agency that currently inhere within the mental capacity framework. Instead, the idea of assessing or measuring capacity will be seen as an apparatus which works to both create knowledge and obscure broader concerns. The productive effects of this capacity/incapacity divide will then be considered, highlighting the material and discursive consequences of this method of legal ordering, both in terms of shaping the ideal legal subject and in the crafting of the boundaries and role of the state. The idea of assessing or measuring capacity will be seen as an apparatus which works to both create knowledge and obscure broader concerns. These reflections will bring to the fore what is invisibilised in these current representations of autonomy, capacity, and empowerment. As Davies suggests, "borders and domains are actively produced" (Davies, 2017, 83) and the lines drawn are not fixed, but shape norms and perceptions at a given moment. What is evident through this analysis is that the binary concepts that frame the boundaries of debate are not natural or neutral – they can be deployed in ways which preclude certain responses and obscure other relevant factors. Importantly, once we begin to unravel the capacity/incapacity binary, and to reveal the broader structures it is bound up in (here and in later chapters), the wider legal landscape and boundaries within it similarly begin to unravel. These insights have resonance beyond the immediate context of mental capacity law for broader social justice movements which are similarly constrained by a normative ideal legal subject which is rooted in exclusion. Moreover, as will be seen here and in later chapters, the discussion opens up a more critical stance towards the role of the state and institutions as part of assemblages, feeding into wider debates in philosophy, political theory, and geography as to responsibilities and responses.

Finally, the chapter will return to Article 12 of the Convention on the Rights of Persons with Disabilities (CRPD) in order to expose one of the core challenges currently facing the concept of mental capacity. Some of the dominant debates on this, and ways of potentially ensuring compliance with the CRPD, will be presented. These debates however will be critiqued in terms of the ways in which they reinforce the problematic broader logics of the mental capacity framework. It will be argued here, as throughout the book, that the broader spatio-temporal frame offered by the CRPD needs to be considered more fully as a challenge to the logics of our current framework.

The stark divide

This section will introduce the general framework of the Mental Capacity Act and present the boundaries that are drawn by it then cemented, justified, and reinforced through case law. Essentially, the legislation draws the parameters of legitimate legal intervention in relation to adults deemed to lack mental capacity. Thus, the distinction between mental capacity and incapacity is crucial. In essence, if an adult is deemed to have mental capacity to make a particular decision, then that decision cannot be interfered with – it is seen as a manifestation of the individual's choice and self-determination, and as such, worthy of respect as an autonomous decision. Conversely, if an individual is deemed to lack mental capacity in relation to the particular decision, then it is deemed to not be an autonomous decision worthy of such respect, and a substitute decision can be made by another in their best interests.

The Act governs a wide range of decisions, from the minutiae of day-to-day decisions such as what to eat, what to wear, and what to do, to medical treatment decisions, residence decisions, decisions as to contact with particular individuals, marriage, and capacity to consent to sex. One of the key principles guiding the Act is the presumption of mental capacity (MCA, s.1) which means that everyone is assumed to have mental capacity to make a decision, unless it can be shown that they lack capacity. Section 2 outlines the diagnostic element of mental capacity, and that

> a person lacks capacity in relation to a matter if at the material time he is unable to make a decision for himself in relation to the matter because of an impairment of, or a disturbance in the functioning of, the mind or brain.

Section 3 of the Act goes on to define what is meant by "unable to make a decision" and, if a finding of incapacity is made, the Act further lays out that decisions must be made for that individual in their "best interests" (s4).

Critiquing capacity/incapacity

The MCA framework and dividing line between capacity and incapacity has not escaped criticism, and such criticism is becoming increasingly ramped up in light of the CRPD. Yet, at the most surface level, there has been concern about the workings of the legislation. The House of Lords Select Committee, in their post-legislative scrutiny of the statute, stated among their headline findings that "the empowering ethos of the Act has not been widely implemented" (House of Lords Select Committee, 2014, para 2) but moreover that,

> The presumption of capacity, in particular, is widely misunderstood by those involved in care. It is sometimes used to support non-intervention or poor care, leaving vulnerable adults exposed to risk of harm. In some cases this is because professionals struggle to understand how to apply the principle in practice. In other cases, the evidence suggests the principle has been deliberately misappropriated to avoid taking responsibility for a vulnerable adult.
>
> (para 3)

This point is particularly instructive here, as it recognises the way in which the binary set up in the statute between capacity and incapacity has significant consequences for the legal and policy trajectories that can then follow. However, underpinning the Select Committee's analysis and recommendations is a tacit positivity towards the values and concepts underpinning the legislative framework, with recommendations focused on improving their application in practice. Training and increased awareness were seen as important, yet the validity of the underpinning framework seemingly remained incontrovertible. Ruck Keene also argues that the concept of mental capacity is inescapably "in the eye of the beholder", and that greater attention ought to be given as a result of this to processes of assessment and potential biases and subject positions of those undertaking the assessing (Ruck Keene, 2017). This is a persuasive analysis, yet it ascribes to the idea that mental capacity assessments as envisaged by the Act are unproblematic, and that the problem lies in their application – the legitimacy of the background framework is left unscathed. Kong has also criticised the legislation from a more relational standpoint, highlighting, among other things, the power imbalances and devalued subject positions that occur through the legislation (Kong, 2017). However, again, the solution to these problems is to undertake these assessments 'better' – to acknowledge the power imbalance whilst making the assessment, or to engage more fully with the situatedness and experiences of the individual being assessed. The boundaries and their legitimacy are implicitly reaffirmed.

Much deeper criticism of this binary or oppositional framework is spurred by the CRPD and, in particular, Article 12 and debates about universal legal capacity. At present, much of the literature on the CRPD, particularly in the mental capacity and medical law field, has focused on this Article – the right to legal capacity on an equal basis with others (universal legal capacity). It states that:

1 States Parties reaffirm that persons with disabilities have the right to recognition everywhere as persons before the law.
2 States Parties shall recognize that persons with disabilities enjoy legal capacity on an equal basis with others in all aspects of life.
3 States Parties shall take appropriate measures to provide access by persons with disabilities to the support they may require in exercising their legal capacity.

This particular Article has provoked a number of commentators to suggest that the MCA is fundamentally incompatible with the Convention, given that it draws a distinction between those with and without disabilities, and that it enables best interests decision making (essentially substituted decision making, rather than supported decision making as required in Art 12(3) on the basis of this). The UN Committee on the CRPD, in General Comment Number 1 on Article 12, took a decidedly 'hard line' approach to this issue, stating that there be no substitute decision making practices and that

> The Committee reaffirms that a person's status as a person with a disability or the existence of an impairment (including a physical or sensory impairment) must never be grounds for denying legal capacity or any of

> the rights provided for in article 12. All practices that in purpose or effect violate article 12 must be abolished in order to ensure that full legal capacity is restored to persons with disabilities on an equal basis with others.
>
> (UN Committee on the Rights of Persons with Disabilities, 2014, para 9)

There has been a great deal of debate about the legitimacy and correctness of the Committee's approach here as well as what it means for domestic legislation. Supported decision making, under Art 12(3), is seen as the alternative framework which ought to form the basis of law and policy, however some scholars and professionals are concerned that supported decision making is not always possible, and that it might overlook the realities of decision making and cognitive impairments, and the perceived need, at times, to intervene in an individual's decisions (Freeman et al., 2015). It is seen by some professionals and academics as ideological but potentially dangerous, ignoring the need for safeguarding or life-saving interventions (Ward, 2011; Kohn and Blumenthal, 2013; Dawson, 2015; Applebaum, 2016). As will be seen, however, there is a sense in which this thinking is situated within current legal and conceptual boundaries, which, in turn, enables them to be reinforced. As Sheppard has discussed however, this sort of backlash often occurs in such moments and can be seen through assertions of the normative superiority of the present framework (Sheppard, 2006).

The purpose of this discussion here is not to get mired in these debates, but to propose that we are not confined by current conceptual boundaries when thinking about the challenges raised. As Weller says, "a danger for those who wish to promote a radical interpretation of the CRPD is that the entrenched position of capacity in modern legal systems may encourage an impoverished interpretation of Article 12" (Weller, 2015, 512). This statement then invites a more thorough exploration of the capacity/incapacity binary: the justifications for it, the contingencies within it, and the productive effects of it. The critique offered through this will be seen to have wider relevance beyond the immediate capacity/incapacity divide in the domestic legal framework, as the underlying logics and effects reverberate across other jurisdictions, and are deeply intertwined with the 'othering' of other oppressed groups. Moreover, it offers critical insights for scholars working on ideas of space, relationality, and disability, demonstrating the subtle ways in which the law here works to shape disability and obscure broader spatial relations.

An objective category?

One of the consequences which flows from critiquing the concept of capacity and incapacity through this dynamic spatial and relational lens is an appreciation of the fact that it is not an objective and neutral concept – the binary construction here is historically framed and contingent, and – of course – could be otherwise. This provides a more complex understanding of the ways in which such concepts *do* take on the cloak of neutrality and do come to be accepted as given. They can draw attention to the historical and political structures which help to frame a particular issue and the socio-historical processes of meaning making.

Interestingly, the Committee on the CRPD, in their General Comment on Article 12, provided some useful insights into the concept of mental capacity, which demonstrates a similar line of thinking. Here, the Committee articulated that,

> The concept of mental capacity is highly controversial in and of itself. Mental capacity is not, as is commonly presented, an objective, scientific and naturally occurring phenomenon. Mental capacity is contingent on social and political contexts, as are the disciplines, professions and practices which play a dominant role in assessing mental capacity.
>
> (para 14)

This echoes the work of a number of STS scholars including Stefan, who suggests that a finding of incompetence is part of a dynamic process between the individual and a professional – a process that is "a matter of both interpersonal dynamics and social and political structuring of roles and communciation" (Stefan, 1993, 778). Such insights resonate with the growing interest in non-representational approaches, such as that of Haraway and Barad, who emphasise the processes involved in assigning and producing matter and meaning, and the way in which situated knowledge is part of this process, rather than being about an objective 'discovery' of a pre-existing 'thing'. This is part of a challenge to the way in which "representationalism would have us focus on what seems to be evidentially given, hiding the very practices that produce the illusion of givenness" (Barad, 2007, 359) and that representations always "select and exclude, while often masking or naturalising the choices involved" (Davies, 2017, 92). Challenging the 'given-ness' of particular categories enables us to see the different processes which feed into these and the various power relations at stake in creating them. Importantly, this is not to suggest that differences do not exist and are wholly constructed. Instead, it draws attention to the processes through which these differences become interpreted and come to matter, highlighting alternative trajectories and elements that are marginalised or overlooked as well as prompting us to question *why* such alternative trajectories were discounted.

As critical disability scholars have pointed out, the liberal, rational, and autonomous subject is problematic given the ableist foundations which underpin and sustain it. This is not a neutral account of subjectivity or the ideal subject – it is, from the outset, exclusionary of disability. A more spatial understanding of the social politics of knowledge production and "disabling spaces" (Glenn Smith, 1999, 50) invites us to recognise

> [s]pace as a produced and ideological arena that is a blurring of the built, the social, the cultural and the mental. Space, as it is understood here, is thus considered to be socially produced through specific socio-economic modes of production and related societal and cultural values, reproduced through dominant social and cultural 'myths' and 'realities' and lived, accepted and contested through language and behaviour, thoughts, action and even ... silence.
>
> (Glenn Smith, 1999, 50)

This enables us to be attentive to how such space is performed, as well as to the "social spatialisation of difference and the pragmatic effacement, denial or recalibration of difference" (Delaney, 2010, 18). As we have seen, the capacitous liberal legal subject is built upon the Enlightenment and humanist ideals of rationality and logic, of self-actualisation and progress and is in stark contrast to the relational ontology increasingly argued for in critical approaches. The 'other' to this subject – the incapacitous, disabled, 'less-than', actively produces a hierarchical ranking in subjectivity, what Feely terms "devalued subject creation" (Feely, 2016). Moreover, as Erevelles argues, these essentialising assumptions "[locate] persons with cognitive/severe disability outside the margins of 'active' citizenship" (Erevelles, 2011, 148). Importantly, each side of the capacity/incapacity binary is important for reinforcing the broader liberal legal logics here. A finding of incapacity reinforces the ideal of the capacitous and autonomous subject which this particular individual is deemed to fall short of. Indeed, it is interesting that often in cases in which judges go on to find that an individual lacks capacity that they will make the strongest pronouncements of capacity and autonomy as of central importance to law. This identification of the 'other' is necessary to liberal individualism in order to reify and reinforce the humanist self.

As Carson maintained at the time the mental capacity legislation was being drafted,

> Life is not so simple as mental disorder or no mental disorder, capacity or incapacity, though it is regularly portrayed by the law as being such. The Law Commission's interim proposals, if implemented, would continue this dichotomous legal view of the world and avoid meeting the challenge or incorporating and rationalising legal developments such as misrepresentation, consent and undue influence into a more general law about when decisions made by *anyone* are validly made.
>
> (Carson, 1993, 314)

The mental capacity framework overlooks similarities between people and our shared interdependence and situatedness in networks, then, in an attempt to make clear categories for legal responses. Importantly, this critique does not seek to suggest, or necessitate the conclusion, that differences in decision making ability should be overlooked. It could be surmised that given that we are all entangled within these processes and relations, then the law ought to either treat us all as 'lacking capacity' or, conversely, avoid judging capacity and instead respect all decisions. However, quite aside from then reinforcing the broader conceptual framework that is being dismantled in this book, this would be to overlook the deeper and more nuanced consequences which flow from recognising the ubiquity of relationality. One of the important points to consider here is then how differences come to be legally relevant or meaningful – how "matter comes to matter" (Barad, 2003).

It is in this regard – in recognising differential embodiment, and how it comes to 'matter' – that insights from critical disability studies can significantly enhance and build on these spatial and relational approaches. There have been productive engagements between the Social Model and vulnerability theorists. Herring has begun to explore this nexus, suggesting that

> the concept of universal vulnerability … provides a powerful tool for disability advocates. The arguments here, that it is the provision or absence of social supports that can render some vulnerabilities as more visible or potent, echo and indeed support the social model critique of vulnerability.
> (Herring, 2016, 36)

Yet, the vulnerability literature and some of the Social Model literature can tend to take a linear and static approach to the norms and roles of agents involved in particular social practices. The Social Model might focus on a linear connection between a barrier and its disabling effects, and provide an individualised response to its removal. Similarly, with vulnerability theory, there is a tendency to conceptualise this as requiring a response from the state to provide resilience in situations of particular vulnerability, but again this can individualise the issue and at the same time maintain the broader structural and institutional framework. This can often, however, leave the broader logics underpinning a norm in place. In this vein, Mitchell and Snyder have suggested that a commonly made argument in disability studies and in activism is that "the mark of social success is the capacity for disabled people to live as non-disabled people live" (Mitchell and Snyder, 2018, 193). This is often the case in discussions of relational autonomy and mental capacity law or autonomy in law more broadly. There is thus a "dangerous paradox" (Holloway et al., 2019, 5) in reclaiming agency or autonomy within or through liberal ideals of the subject, given that such a subject is also implicated in and intertwined with broader structural manifestations of its exclusionary tendencies – exclusions which are woven into the very fabric of the logics. As such, as well as critiquing and challenging the category of 'incapacity', there is also a need to interrogate and dismantle the other side of the binary – that of the capacitous norm. The relational and spatial dynamics central to new materialist approaches take these processes and intra-actions all the way down – taking into account historical contingencies and connections, and the multiple agents and material and discursive forces involved in particular phenomena. Yet, as the next sections and chapters show, it is precisely such an approach which is often foreclosed by the centrality of the capacity/incapacity binary. Looking through the lens of the assemblage and foregrounding spatial and relational dynamics allows us to disrupt the ideas of causality, temporality, responsibility, and agency that shape the mental capacity framework through the capacity/incapacity binary.

Causality

One of the key questions then is how, in practice, this seemingly simple process of assessing whether somebody is "unable to make a decision" actually occurs. What is the connection that is required between an impairment and incapacity? This was fleshed out in the case of *PC & Anor v City of York Council* [2013] EWCA Civ 478, in which the idea of the "causal nexus" between the impairment or disturbance in the functioning of the mind or brain *and* the inability to understand, use or weigh information, or communicate a decision, was highlighted.

PC was a complex case involving the question of capacity to consent to contact. PC had married NC during the course of a 13-year prison sentence which NC was serving for a number of serious sexual assaults. PC however did not believe that he was guilty of these offences. There was an expectation that upon NC's release, PC and NC would cohabit, and there was a concern for PC's safety. In particular, it was felt that due to her learning disabilities, she was unable to fully examine the issue of his guilt, and thus that her capacity to make this decision was felt to be impaired. At first instance, Hedley J had found that PC lacked capacity in relation to this decision, stating that,

> She is undoubtedly within section 2(1) requirements of impairment. Applying the section 3(1) test I am not satisfied that she is able to understand the potential risk that NC presents to her and that she is unable to weigh the information underpinning the potential risk so as to determine whether or not such a risk either exists or should be run ... I am satisfied too that that significantly relates to the impairment in section 2(1), though I do accept that there is an element in it of an instinctive impatience simply to bring about the desired result whatever, which, if it stood alone, would simply be an unwise decision. Accordingly, I find that in relation to the decision as to whether to resume cohabitation with NC, PC lacks capacity so to decide and thus the jurisdiction of the Court of Protection is engaged in respect of that particular issue.
>
> (para 21)

However, this was then appealed to the Court of Appeal by PC and NC, with the core focus being on the "person-specific" rather than "act-specific" approach to capacity which was applied by Hedley J in the Court of Protection – that the perceived unsuitability of NC had driven the finding on incapacity, rather than the assessment of PC's actual decision making abilities. However it was also argued that the finding of incapacity to make the decision to cohabit based on being "referable" to or "significantly relating" to her learning disability fell short of finding that the inability was "because of" her disability as required by MCA s 2(1).

Macfarlane LJ thus stated that,

> There may be many women who are seen to be in relationships with men regarded by professionals as predatory sexual offenders. The Court of Protection does not have jurisdiction to act to "protect" these women if they do not lack the mental capacity to decide whether or not to be, or continue to be, in such a relationship. The individual's decision may be said to be "against the better judgment" of the woman concerned, but the point is that, unless they lack mental capacity to make that judgment, it is against their better judgment. It is a judgment that they are entitled to make. The statute respects their autonomy so to decide and the Court of Protection has no jurisdiction to intervene.
>
> (para 53)

It was held here that the causative nexus between the incapacity and the diagnostic element was not sufficiently made out. Lewison LJ concurred, suggesting that,

> I well understand that all the responsible professionals take the view that it would be extremely unwise for PC to cohabit with her husband. But adult autonomy is such that people are free to make unwise decisions, provided that they have the capacity to decide. Like McFarlane LJ I do not consider that there was a solid evidential foundation on which the judge's decision can rest. We must leave PC free to make her own decision, and hope that everything turns out well in the end.
>
> (para 64)

This judgment illustrates the carefully constructed boundaries of the legal framework – capacity/incapacity, autonomy/paternalism, impaired/non-impaired. Thinking about these judicial statements as agential cuts, the binary divide that is emphasised and shored up in this case creates the space within which responses can occur, and who can be brought within this framework. This framework is carefully intertwined with a diagnostic and medicalised element. Essentially, if there is no cognitive impairment present, then there is no lack of capacity. Likewise, even if there is an impairment present, the individual will be deemed to have capacity if it cannot be shown that it is that impairment which is causing the inability to understand, use, weigh, or communicate information. The result of this assessment of mental capacity is crucial; if an individual is deemed to have capacity, then their decision will be respected and they will be deemed to be autonomous. On the other hand, if they are deemed to lack mental capacity, then a decision can be made in their best interests.

This is reflected heavily in the dicta of MacFarlane LJ and Lewison LJ in *PC and NC* above in their careful policing of the causal nexus, and references to freedom to make unwise decisions as the basis of autonomy. Such judgments have an important structuring role in carefully delineating the boundaries of the legislation, and the mutually reinforcing binaries that shape them and create the 'other', the 'outside'. What is presupposed within this framework is an idea of freedom or liberty as non-interference, which enables autonomy and self-determination to flourish unimpeded. It is evident then that a very stark legal boundary is created by this distinction between capacity and incapacity, and much hinges upon it. There is an almost visible movement of the individual from a (fictitious) capacitous, autonomous space into the realm of incapacity based upon the capacity assessment. Again, as we saw in the earlier chapters, this separate realm has had to be carefully crafted and justified through the Law Commission documents and through subsequent case law.

The linearity of causality which inheres in this framework is stark here. The complex nature of entangled interactions, presupposed in new materialist and more dynamic relational approaches emphasising the assemblage, disrupts the idea of causality that underpins the mental capacity legislation, and has been reinforced in the Social Model and relational autonomy approaches encountered in the earlier chapters. It was reiterated in the case of *PC & Anor v City of York Council* [2013] EWCA Civ 478 that the "causal nexus" between the cognitive impairment and the inability to satisfy the capacity assessment must be shown. That is, that it must be shown that the inability to use, weigh, or communicate is because of the cognitive impairment. This is a particularly linear way of understanding causality and is problematised when we recognise the ongoing and shifting relations and contexts which impact upon and shape decision making abilities. From a critical disability perspective, this individualises and internalises the disability – seeing the relationship between an impairment and an inability to use, weigh, understand, and communicate as internal to the individual. This ignores the contingency of disabling or incapacitating effects flowing from a cognitive impairment, and the myriad ways in which these could be different. Instead, we end up with a linear idea of the link between an impairment and inability to pass a functional test for capacity, as well as a static notion of disability, rather than seeing the varying ways in which the impairment effects are created and mediated by a number of other forces.

Hall and Wilton, writing from a critical geography perspective, have drawn on the new materialist theorists such as Barad and Braidotti, and the notion of assemblage, to advance an understanding of "complex and emergent geographies of disability, but also to unsettle broader assumptions about the nature of the 'able-body'" (Hall and Wilton, 2016, 741). Unseating the norm of the autonomous, rational, individual legal subject and rethinking subjectivity through and with impairment, interdependence, difference, and relationality enables us to then see the "sheer diversity of embodied experiences that overwhelm any binary opposition between a normative 'able-body' and its disabled other" (Hall and Wilton, 2016, 741). This is particularly salient in the mental capacity context, where we see a real focus on rationality and individual decision making abilities. Rather than perpetuating this, challenging the norm of the autonomous, 'capacitous' subject enables us to more fully interrogate the broader structures which are entangled within this and which maintain its preeminence. The focus on the spatial and relational context here entails a more shifting and fluid notion of subjectivity and the ways in which individuals can simultaneously occupy different subject positions, challenging the linearity and static nature which we see in some Social Model accounts. Shakespeare and Watson discuss how this emerging, embodied focus on ontology and rejection of the autonomous, rationalistic and disconnected (disembodied?) subject breaks down the presupposed qualitative difference between disabled and non-disabled people (Shakespeare and Watson, 2002, 26): we are all impacted upon by societal processes and structures. I would add that this entails recognition of the fact that we are all also impact*ing* upon such processes – we are not passive objects simply being inscribed by these. Further, as Shildrick points out, this is not just about "revaluing multiple variant forms" but about "a celebratory positioning of difference and transcorporeality as the very difference of life" (Shildrick, 2015, 28). However, as Shakespeare and Watson go on to suggest, not all of us are oppressed on the basis of our embodied subjectivity – only some experience these processes in this way (2002, 28). This calls then not just for a de-centring on the able-bodied, able-minded autonomous liberal legal subject, but at the same time, a focus on how particular processes work at different levels, and with different histories, to create differential embodied experience, as part of an assemblage. Currently the capacity/incapacity binary obscures this, as the process of knowing and understanding, and agency, is seen as a disconnected and abstract concept, separated from material forces.

Temporality

The requirement of the causal connection between the impairment and inability to make a decision is also tied to a requirement for the assessment to be made in relation to a particular decision – not to global decision making abilities or in relation to future decisions. Thus, temporally, the legislation requires the assessor to focus on the present and the current abilities of the individual. It is perhaps understandable that the legislation was written this way given the medical roots of the legislation – remember that one of the key driving forces for the legislation was the need for a legal basis upon which doctors could obtain the required consent for medical treatment or interventions, and this consent in the medical context is often contemporaneous.

Yet this static framing can lead in practice to a malleability in ways of framing or describing the decision-specificity in order for the judges to contain the more complex temporality of decision making in reality. This is evident in a case involving "fluctuating capacity", which is seen as a particular difficulty for the legislation when somebody is assessed as having capacity at one time but then can lose it periodically. *RB Greenwich v CDM* [2018] EWCOP

15 involved a dispute as to a woman's capacity in relation to residence, personal affairs, and the management of her diabetes. The difficulty for the medical expert in this case however was that capacity was seen to be fluctuating – it seemed to vary according to her control of her diabetes. Cohen J surmised the position that poor diabetic control led to unwise decision making and inability to engage with professionals, stating that "when making appropriate decisions she has capacity but when making manifestly inappropriate decisions she lacks capacity" (para 52). Yet, the difficulty here is that this in practice may lead to a finding that she lacks capacity in a particular situation *because* the decision seems unwise, which goes against the grain of the principle in the legislation that a person is not to be treated as lacking capacity merely because it is an unwise decision. Moreover, it individualises the decision, suggesting that the inability arises as a result of her inappropriate decision making, rather than recognising the ways that such abilities will always hinge upon a number of other actors and resources being made available.

The case returned to the Court of Protection in light of fresh expert evidence. Here, Newton J tried to deal with the difficult temporality of such cases by essentially sorting decisions into macro and micro decisions. In framing diabetic management and control as global macro decisions (comprising a number of smaller, micro decisions), he was able to declare that she lacked capacity in relation to such decisions, thus side-stepping the problematic pragmatic issue of having to continually assess and re-assess capacity.

This static demarcation of a decision as 'macro', and the consequent ability to make a declaration of incapacity here to enable decisions to be made, provides a convenient way to avoid troubling the boundaries of the mental capacity framework. In doing so, however, it reinforces the abstract, binary idea of decision making as individualised and constant, rather than recognising that abilities will and do ebb and flow in a multitude of directions as the context shifts. The pragmatic necessity of a flawed framework thus takes precedence in this judgment over recognising and challenging its problematic assumptions.

Another case in which we see judicial creativity in the face of this temporal messiness, in order to reaffirm and maintain the framework, is *United Lincolnshire Hospital Trust v CD* [2019] EWCOP 24. This case involved a woman with schizophrenia who was 35 weeks pregnant and had been detained under the Mental Health Act 1983. The issue arose as to the management of her labour, as clinicians were concerned that she may come to lack capacity during labour (although she was deemed at the current moment as having capacity to make such decisions). The question arose as to whether and how the Mental Capacity Act would and could apply here – could declarations be made about anticipated incapacity in the future, and did the Court of Protection have jurisdiction to do so in relation to somebody who at present has capacity? Francis J summarised the problem here as,

> The practical position, however, is that if (as those treating CD consider very likely) CD subsequently loses capacity to make decisions about her

> delivery, this is likely to be in an urgent situation where a renewed application would cause unacceptable delay with potentially catastrophic consequences as discussed above. In my judgement it would be dangerous and plainly wrong to do nothing. This court cannot and will not take what is regarded by all as an unacceptable risk. If, as has been summarised above, a medical emergency were to arise and if it were to be determined that CD has again lost capacity to make decisions about herself, the treating clinicians would find themselves in the invidious position of possibly carrying out invasive surgery and administering anaesthetic or other drugs without lawful authority.
>
> (para 13)

It was held, then, that the court could make an anticipatory declaration of lawfulness should the obstetric team need to intervene, contingent upon CD losing capacity. Francis J went on to say that he was doing this on the basis that

> For so long as CD retains capacity to make decisions about her obstetric care and the delivery of a baby, she will of course be allowed to do so, even if those decisions are considered to be unwise. If, however, her mental health deteriorates and she loses capacity I consider that it would be in the best interests to try for a normal vaginal delivery if possible and this is consistent with either CD's expressed wish or best interests. The care plan drawn up by the applicant records the expectation that CD will comply with what is proposed but also includes fall back options, including for appropriate minimal restraint, should this not be the case. Restraint would potentially be used to transfer her to the maternity suite, insert a cannula (although only if medically required) or provide general anaesthetic in order to proceed to a caesarean section. A caesarean section would be very much a last resort.
>
> (para 16)

Again, here the court is having to work creatively to contain the difficult temporality of such cases without disturbing the boundaries around the framework. Yet, despite the fact that the power afforded to the medical professionals here is said to be wholly contingent upon CD coming to lack capacity, the spectre of the legislation is brought forward and will arguably impact upon the power relations prior to labour. Statements above such as that "the care plan drawn up by the applicant records the expectation that CD will comply with what is proposed" trouble the idea that this is simply about placing the Mental Capacity Act 'on ice' in case it is needed, but instead is about stretching the relational (power) dynamics to a prior moment, and bringing its presence (albeit spectral) into the pre-labour space.

Another case illustrating the difficulties with time-specific applications of capacity assessments and the judicial attempts to neutralise and side-step the temporal messiness here is *Cheshire West and Chester Council v PWK* [2019]

EWCOP 57. The case involved a 24-year-old man who had had a difficult childhood, growing up in care following neglect as a young child. Declarations of incapacity were sought in relation to issues such as care and support needs, contact with others, social media use, financial and property affairs, and use or possession of a car under the Motability Scheme. The difficulty summed up by Hedley J was,

> When PWK was relaxed and in a good place he might well be regarded as having capacity. However, when he became anxious his position could be very different. Moreover, there were many things that could trigger anxiety and quite often his carers would be confronted with irrational behaviour that could be difficult to manage.
>
> (para 9)

To navigate this difficulty and the fluctuating capacity issue that has again emerged, Hedley J adopted a "longitudinal" approach. It is similar to the macro/micro distinction from CDM in that it sees certain decisions, such as management of financial affairs, as ongoing over time, rather than well-defined, individual decisions. The benefit of this, according to Hedley J, is that it provides clarity and recognises the ongoing nature of a decision. It was thus stated that

> In PWK's case all the relevant decision-making with which I am concerned lies in the field of repeat rather than isolated decisions. Dr Rippon's view, which was not really the subject of challenge, was that where a longitudinal perspective was adopted then PWK lacked capacity in all relevant areas.
>
> (para 21)

It is evident that the pragmatic concern for maintaining the workability and structure of the legislative framework is prioritised through re-defining the boundaries of a decision. The fact, that was well-recognised, that PWK could make decisions when not anxious, seemed to become submerged in this case. The shifting context and relational dynamics which could produce or mitigate against this anxiety, and changes over time, was overlooked. Indeed, the declaration of a lack of capacity as part of these "longitudinal" decisions seems to mitigate against attempts to reconfigure these broader relational dynamics and context of decisions to ameliorate this anxiety, or, to use the language of Article 12, to support the exercise of legal capacity.

What is also troubling in this case is that the court readily recognised that the issue of the use of the car is what is driving much of PWK's anxiety and provoking the difficulties in other areas of decision making. Essentially, as PWK has a visual impairment, he cannot drive the car himself. At the same time, the private care provider is unwilling to provide or require care workers to drive it for him. This is recognised as the source of much of PWK's anxiety, "matters relating to this wholly dominated PWK's written observations" (para 28). As such, the approach taken in the judgment is to separately declare a lack of capacity in relation to the car. However, the artificial separation of all of these decisions, at the same time as recognising that the car is causing PWK acute anxiety and impacting his wider decision making abilities, is problematic here. It ignores the reality that these decisions are closely intertwined and relate to his ability to assert his agency in his life. Extending the reach of the mental capacity framework to deny his agency as to the car, and in turn shifting and configuring particular relational dynamics between PWK and care providers and other professionals, may serve to further entrench this anxiety. Whilst it is recognised that there may be occasions when certain decisions might be able to be made by PWK, despite the longitudinal assessment of incapacity, this ignores the way that the legislation will be actively shaping the relations at this time too, with an absent presence undoubtedly shaping decision making trajectories. Again, this seems to be the cost to be borne at the expense of maintaining the structural integrity of the legislation, which seemingly is incapable of containing or addressing these various contingencies at the same time. As the opening quote to the chapter alludes, the world is precisely what is lost through these purportedly objective assessments. In a recursive and iterative process, the conceptualisation of these norms becomes naturalised and further entrenched. To exceed them, or allow other concerns in, becomes impossible, lest the whole structure falls down.

These cases, demonstrating the struggles to contain the messy temporality and causality within the binaries of the legislation, become more problematic when viewed in light of what these capacity/incapacity determinations do, in terms of their broader effects as boundary drawing practices.

Depoliticising through agential cuts

The measurement or assessment of capacity in practice can be viewed through the Baradian idea of 'apparatus', or Latourian 'technology'. In this sense, we have to be attentive to the productive effects which occur through the active process of measuring, as well as the problematic sense of objectivity which can stem from seemingly neutral and scientific processes such as assessing capacity. As Barad has pointed out, whilst there may appear to be an objectivity in terms of utilising the same apparatus and gaining the same results, we have to also recognise that the apparatus itself is an active agent within the act of measuring, and will necessarily exclude or foreclose alternative modes of thinking or assessment. In the mental capacity context then, the capacity assessment can be viewed through this lens as in itself an active apparatus or technology. Whilst this is one which may seem objective in terms of the repeated results which occur through its application or at the very least, we might be able to glean some logic to its application in case law (see e.g. Coggon, 2016; Skowron, 2019); yet this is also one which actively produces a particular outcome which forecloses other insights. Here, the narrow vision provided of capacity as autonomy produces and reproduces the liberal legal subject, and the spatial context of this subject within a broader web of binaries.

One area which demonstrates this starkly is in relation to capacity to consent to sexual relations. A number of cases demonstrate the struggles that the judiciary has in outlining the relevant test for such capacity, with debates ranging around whether this test should be act-specific or person-specific. Linked to these was a concern not to encroach on sexual autonomy, given that a declaration that somebody lacked capacity to consent to sex would inevitably mean that they would have to be prevented from having sex. As a result, in an authoritative Court of Appeal judgment, Sir Leveson outlined that the test must be act-specific, "a general evaluation which is not tied down to a particular partner, time and place" (*IM v LM and Others* [2014] EWCA Civ 37, para 76). This, however, sits uneasily with the necessarily relational character of sexual decision making – at an obvious level, sexual acts are interpersonal and so are always tightly interconnected with others. The interpersonal dynamics involved, as well as broader structural factors such as education, spaces in which to engage in sexual activity, and moral judgements about such activities, will mean that capacity to consent is always contingent. A later case, *Derbyshire CC v AC* [2014] EWCOP 38, demonstrates the continuing dissatisfaction with the approach taken in *IM v LM*. Here, Cobb J discussed the statement of a Dr Milne, who reported that the woman in the case, AC, "said that even if she did not want sex she would have to go along with it as she wants to be 'lovey dovey'" (para 33). Cobb J expressed his unease with this and the way that the test for capacity to consent to sex as currently framed in *IM v LM* does not include this within its scope (para 36). It is evident in these cases that the all-or-nothing framework here, with everything hinging upon capacity/incapacity, constrains the ability to recognise or speak to broader issues. There is a tangible – and ongoing – judicial struggle to contain something which is so inescapably relational within an Act that is premised upon an individualistic methodology.

We also see this malleability starkly in the line of *TZ* cases which involved assessments of capacity to consent to sex (*A Local Authority v TZ* [2013] EWHC 2322 (COP); *A Local Authority v TZ (No.2)* [2014] EWHC 973 (COP)) – after declaring that TZ had capacity to consent to sexual relations, there was a concern that TZ, in exercising this in particular instances (at some unspecified point in the future), may lack capacity. To avoid the pragmatic pitfall that a best interests decision cannot be made with regard to sexual consent (MCA s27), the question in *TZ (2)* was posed as,

> whether TZ has the capacity to make a decision whether or not an individual with whom he may wish to have sexual relations is safe.
>
> (para 18)

According to Baker J, this focused on the "specific factual context" (para 17); however, it is contended that this is no less abstract or artificial than a general declaration of either capacity or incapacity in relation to sex. It ignores the contingency of this upon a number of different other contextual connections over time and in different spaces. We see again the spectre of a static and linear notion of causality which overlooks the role of broader actors and institutions in impacting the future trajectory. Moreover, the future orientation presumes a static legal subject, and ignores the various shifts in interpersonal and institutional relations which will impact on this. Interestingly, it was also raised that if TZ lacked capacity in relation to this first point, then it also had to be asked whether he has the capacity to "make a decision as to the support that he requires when having contact with an individual with whom he may wish to have sexual relations" (para 18). Again, the boundaries of the capacity concept are shaped in order to shoehorn in and neutralise what are otherwise broader, ongoing processes involving a multiplicity of other actors and agents. This is then justified and naturalised by a cloak of objectivity in the terms of the Act, such as 'capacity' and 'best interests'.

It is important, however, to bear in mind the pragmatic questions facing the judiciary. Given the framing of the legislation and the lack of ability to make a 'best interests' decision in relation to sexual relations (s27), it is perhaps then understandable that given this all-or-nothing approach, the judges are somewhat constrained by pragmatic concerns and a low threshold may be seen as the optimal way to protect sexual rights. Indeed, this is clear in Baker J's assertions in *A Local Authority v TZ* that a low threshold for capacity here is "more consistent with respect for autonomy in matters of private life" (para 23). However, this serves to highlight the struggle central to the binary here, and the way in which it constrains and is constrained by itself. It is limited by a sense of inevitability that recognising these additional factors *necessarily* means that the response needs to be, or will be, paternalistic and that autonomy is buttressed by non-interference. This then leaves these additional aspects unsaid, neutralised, depoliticised, and outside of the scope of concern – although this does not extinguish their very tangible, ongoing impacts.

These cases demonstrate then the real constraints that capacity/incapacity binary has in practice for the judiciary, and the ways that the reassertion of the binary maintains a static and linear, decontextualised and abstract idea both of the individual and the role of the state. The state appears as a distinct and separate actor, only getting involved in tightly circumscribed situations in order to avoid sweeping paternalism, and with only a particular type of individualised response being possible within the state's scope and remit. In this sense, the capacity/incapacity binary is dependent upon this rendering of the state, and as will be further elucidated in later chapters, once the binary begins to unravel, the linked, mutually constraining binaries around the role of the state similarly emerge for critique.

Rethinking agency through the assemblage: dynamics of capacity/incapacity

Through looking at the workings and underpinnings of the capacity/incapacity binary, relational and spatial analysis can provide the tools to expose the broader, co-dependent logics that the binary is entangled with and begin to dismantle them. In the context of the capacity/incapacity binary, we can challenge the dominant framing through consideration of the assemblage, through insights from critical disability studies, through exposing the static and abstract framing of the MCA, and through considering capacity assessment as an apparatus rather than an objective measurement. These ongoing, dynamic processes, impacted by different intra-actions, which then shift and shape experience, destabilise static, ordered understandings of the (legal) subject, and dividing lines between public/private, self/other, nature/culture, mind/body. Our physicality and historicity within the world, interdependence and material interconnectedness become the starting point for theoretical approaches. Unlike the disembodied subject that resides in liberal theory, we instead see the body (and the mind) as embodied, embedded, enacted, and extended (Davies, 2017, 88).

This requires a move from atomism towards agential intra-actions; the individual is no longer the methodologically prior concern. The focus becomes on relational dynamics over time – how various agents intra-act in the active production of differential relations and workings of power (Barad, 2007, 65). An important element of this is seeing the body not as simply inscribed upon, but as an active agent within these processes. As Whatmore puts it, agency becomes seen as a relational achievement "spun between social actors rather than a manifestation of a unitary intent" (1999, 26). Unlike the individualistic rendering of autonomy, these processes are always, already entangled with others and with other forces (material, discursive, cultural, technological, etc.) as well as emerging "through social practice within time/space-specific regimes of power" (Holloway et al., 2019). It could be suggested that such an approach may result in an abdication of responsibility on behalf of agents, given that we are all then seen as interdependent and part of much broader processes. If we are not then autonomous in the sense suggested by liberal theories, then how can we be held accountable or responsible for our actions? How can we say we have made a decision? Moreover, extending this to institutional or state responsibilities, how can we trace this when we are just as much a part of these processes? However, such conclusions do not necessarily follow. As will be discussed further in the later chapters, recognising that we are all entangled within such processes and relations of becoming and that a number of human and non-human agents are imbricated does not lead to a conclusion that the abilities to effect change or exert power in such assemblages or entanglements are equally distributed or located. A core element of the analysis developed in this book is on the power relations which are central to particular relations, their reproduction, and maintenance.

The legislation, with its rationalist foundations and focus on understanding and comprehending, places an overt focus on internal abilities of the mind – evidenced further by the focus on cognitive impairments. As Shildrick suggests, "the knowing subject is disembodied, detached from raw material" (1997, 14). When it is recognised that we are all similarly shaped by, and actively shaping, our context and relations and that these can be differentially experienced as embodied beings that inhabit and move between different contexts, then the role of experience and embeddedness within particular assemblages of the material and discursive becomes central to creating agency. Agency does not spring internally or *in spite of* our material, cultural, relational, emotional, structural, corporeal, institutional, technological, economic entanglements but through and *because of* them.

As has been discussed above, these insights call for going beyond a static and linear Social Model of Disability in order to more carefully trace the different disabling effects of particular spatial contexts. It is here that calls for *transformative* rather than merely *inclusive* approaches are particularly salient, given the danger of simply reinforcing disabling norms and practices (Erevelles, 2011). Part of this broader tracing of problematic norms is to shift the focus away from the idea of a static and representable subject, such as we see in the capacity/incapacity binary and individualised focus, and instead to be more attentive to context (not just the immediate interpersonal or spatial context, but to the various assemblages which this is intertwined with, and the different intersecting scales which have shaped this). This contextually driven and relationally embedded approach to agency thus requires not just challenging the idea of 'incapacity', but also the other side of the binary – the norm of the 'capacitous' individual and all that that is bound up in.

As such, rethinking agency in this way calls for a rethinking of responses and responsibility – recognising the always, already nature of 'responses' which have shaped and are shaping experience. Rather than building responses based on a pre-conceived categorisation (which is already inflected with societal norms and processes) in order to facilitate bringing the individual up to a normative standard (rational, non-disabled, for example), the purpose, location, and temporality must also shift. This avoids the problematic bind that progressive literatures in this context currently find themselves in, where, whilst there is an appetite to critique assessment processes, there is also a tendency to endorse the broader justification for the mental capacity concept and everything that then flows from it (Kong, 2017; Ruck Keene, 2017). This seeming objectivity and necessity of the framework sidelines any broader questioning of its foundational justifications, or *why* certain groups are (and have historically been) excluded from the autonomous norm, and why such a norm exists and persists in the face of purportedly progressive critique.

Article 12 CRPD

As noted at the beginning of this chapter, Article 12 of the CRPD has provided an important conceptual challenge to the very basis of the MCA and the capacity/incapacity binary. The core idea of legal capacity on an equal basis with others, and obligations on States Parties to provide support to exercise legal capacity, is an exciting prospect for those interested in critiquing mental capacity and disability studies more broadly. There is here the potential to avoid the capacity/incapacity binary that structures domestic law and legal frameworks across a number of jurisdictions, and the problematic effects of this, as well as to open up new ways of thinking about the role of the state and institutions as part of "support to exercise legal capacity".

The broader logics which guided decision making in relation to individuals seen as cognitively impaired prior to the legislation thus have been left intact through the legislation, despite the positive claims to the contrary. The capacity/incapacity binary however acts in many ways to detract from this historical legacy, through presenting itself as simply an application of an objective or neutral test. These insights resonate with broader disability literature which traces the historic treatment of disabled people occurring through exclusion from communities, and the different bases upon which this has occurred (Ben Moshe et al., 2014). What is interesting here is the point that it is still the same groups which are excluded, despite the shifting political justifications for this. Even in the age of liberalism and the purported neutrality of capacity assessments which is core to the justifications for the MCA (seen in Chapter 2), the same groups are captured, normatively shaped and excluded through its logics.

However, current debates on the implementation of the CRPD have tended to focus primarily on Article 12 as the lynchpin for progress, creating the assumption that once supported decision making is in place then the equality required in the Convention will follow. As will be seen, this is not necessarily the case, and to argue this misunderstands both the CRPD and the pervasiveness of capacity/incapacity and the broader binaries with which it is entangled and which are mutually sustaining. In relation to supported decision making, which is seen as a revolutionary aspect of the Convention, we need to be cognisant of the difficulties discussed earlier regarding seeing a decision as a single moment in time, or a one-off event. We need to ensure that we see it as an ongoing process and a practice which is not solely located in the individual and question, for example, *why* decision making ability is being called into question, *who* is doing this and based on *what* knowledge, *when* this is occurring, and the various factors that have fed into this process so far. Art 12(3) specifically refers to States Parties providing access to "support they may require in exercising their legal capacity", which is a much broader framing that simply supported decision making. It implies an ongoing process or practice of exercising legal capacity, and does not refer to this being based upon assessments of 'capacity' at any point to trigger this. The idea of *exercising* legal capacity here is more akin to the active idea of agency which we see in new materialist thought. There is undoubtedly a temporal aspect to Art 12(3), which requires further reflection so that we do not fall back into seeing it through the problematic lens of the existing legislation. The discussion in the following chapters, engaging with the wider binaries that capacity/incapacity is entangled with and ideas as to the role of the state and responses, will be useful for those seeking to utilise the CRPD in progressive ways and to understand how this agency can be more fully enabled outside of the spatio-temporal limits of the concept of capacity.

A further difficulty with framing Art 12 as an issue of "supported decision making" rather than "support to exercise legal capacity" is that the focus then becomes on isolated decisions. This can then transpose the difficulties that have been discussed above regarding the way in which this still sees the individual as the locus of concern – somebody who is falling below particular standards at a particular time and who needs to be supported to reach these. Moreover, narrowing the scope of Art 12 to simply being about supported decision making, and thus focusing on *who* supports and *how* may perpetuate static identities of supporter and supported. Formalising the idea of support and distilling it into an exchange that takes place at a particular moment (perhaps in response to a concern about decision making ability) similarly overlooks the support or care that is ubiquitous and necessary for all individuals. Exceptionalising support as a one-off transaction can thus similarly reinforce, rather than dismantle, the ableist norms of autonomy, rationality, and self-determination, situating this as the yardstick to which those in need of support must reach through this formalised (yet still exceptional) process. This retains an idea that these (externally verifiable) abilities are individually produced in an unencumbered realm, and once these deficiencies are discovered by professionals, then support can be provided. It overlooks the ongoing processes underpinning this and the role of others in these assemblages. As will be explored in more depth in the next chapter, it perpetuates the idea that the locus of concern, and site of response, is the individual who is seen as 'other' and deficient. Perhaps due to its historical roots in tort law and medical law, the MCA currently perpetuates this given that its core focus is 'informed consent'. Often it is assumed that providing more information or providing a particular type of information will do enough to redress any power imbalances in this doctor–patient relationship and enable an autonomous decision. As Harrington suggests, this is problematic as such tests "attempt to compress the interactive process which is the therapeutic relationship into an isolated moment altering the legitimate balance of power between doctor and patient" (Harrington, 1996, 355), which then diverts criticism away from broader structural issues of power and dominance. There is a similar danger here that in focusing on supported decision making, we inadvertently reinforce the idea that an individual, at a particular moment in time, is deficient and that we can support them to reach the required level of understanding to achieve autonomy. The response then similarly becomes individualised, allowing the background processes to endure. Importantly, this can then feed into broader policy aims which become built upon this problematic idea of support as exception, or something to be provided in singular instances. Such an approach then reinforces the idea of support as antithetical to the autonomous norm. Similarly, it ignores the various modes of support or care which we all rely on yet are not recognised as 'formal' support – the support which hinges upon a particular liberal subject and is thus invisibilised as a background condition to enable such a subject to function. Aside from this diverting attention from the broader structural issues, this also leaves them intact – reifying and perpetuating exclusionary norms.

Disability neutrality has been suggested as a way to potentially advance the CRPD and Art 12. Indeed, the reiteration of "on an equal basis with others" throughout the Convention underpins such an argument. Such an approach might mean, for example, taking out the diagnostic element of the mental capacity assessment. Yet this may problematically overlook the ways that the current legal framework has been built upon and shaped by ideas of legal subjectivity and agency as ability, rationality, and autonomy (and its other). In this way, the assumptions around disability would still haunt and drive the legislation, but would do so in a less overt way (see Steele, 2017, for a discussion of this in relation to a disability neutral doctrine of necessity approach). The potential for law to obscure these underpinning logics is evident in the very creation of the Mental Capacity Act. The broader logics which guided decision making in relation to individuals seen as cognitively impaired prior to the legislation were essentially left intact through the legislation, despite the positive claims to the contrary around respecting autonomy, empowering individuals, and having a legislative test for capacity. The capacity/incapacity binary however acts in many ways to detract from this historical legacy, by presenting itself as simply an application of an objective or neutral test. These insights resonate with broader disability literature which traces the historic treatment of disabled people occurring through exclusion from communities, and the different bases upon which this has occurred (Ben Moshe et al., 2014). What is interesting here is the point that it is still the same groups which are excluded, despite the shifting political justifications for this. Even in the age of liberalism and the purported neutrality of capacity assessments which is core to the justifications for the MCA (seen in Chapter 2), the same groups are captured, normatively shaped, and excluded through its logics. As such, there is a need to tread carefully with arguments for disability neutrality and for an appreciation of the various logics built into the legal framework, which are mutually entangled with the capacity/incapacity binary. Moreover, such a move should concern other social justice movements if legal reform purporting to be disability neutral occurs – what 'norm' is being advocated for as the yardstick for the response as part of such a move, and what other exclusionary ideals are internally structured within this? As seen in previous chapters, ideas of ability/disability and rationality are intertwined with the exclusion and oppression of other groups within society.

Thus, there is a need to carefully engage with Art 12 and the CRPD as a whole and rethink ideas of responsibility, response, and causality through this. At present, our preoccupation with drawing boundaries in engaging with the CRPD is hindering the opportunity for transformative legal and policy approaches and is overlooking the broader webs that particular binaries are entangled with.

Conclusion

It is becoming apparent that changing our ontological starting point changes and reshapes the material and conceptual framework of analysis, potentially changing approaches to law and social justice in radical ways rather than leaving them intact or seeing them as natural. It is important not just to consider the shift in ontology or subjectivity, but to think about how this then impacts and reconfigures the broader theoretical and material terrain and the norms that are deeply implicated in current conceptualisations of capacity, such as what we mean by responses, interventions, and causality. It is important to question what happens – what are the consequences for the rest of the structure – when these "unspeakable subjects" (Lacey, 1998) become central. At present, the desire to do this is constrained by the sense in which recognising relationality and interdependence would *necessarily entail* responding in 'paternalistic' ways. Thinking in terms of shifting these frames,

> a change in scale involves (by definition) a change in frame of reference, and also in the modes of authority, the definition of a legal subject, the sources of normativity, the affective ties between norms and subjects and so forth. Certain elements are made visible, while others recede. Everything, in other words, is up for re-analysis and the scholarly imagination must be attentive to new types of objects not seen, or perhaps sometimes seen and marginalised, at the level of state law.
>
> (Davies, 2017, 106)

We have seen then that through a more spatial and relational lens, a number of broader factors that are currently hidden by the capacity/incapacity framework come to the forefront of analysis and begin to dismantle the given-ness and purported neutrality of the current approach. Yet, it is also important to build upon this and to consider the productive effects of this binary divide. As Delaney has argued, it is important not just to focus on fragments, such as how the binary is deployed in particular cases, but to look at the wider connections and processes which stem from the binary and its deployment (Delaney, 2010, 13). As has been seen, current debates about implementing Art 12, for example, are often constrained by these binaries, and tend to endorse the current spatio-temporality, which inheres in the legal framework without question. If the debate is framed as simply hinging upon capacity/incapacity, then "transformative legal norms will in effect be mapped onto an unchallenged institutional status quo – a recipe for non-enforcement and even further entrenchment of non-inclusive systemic norms and practices" (Sheppard, 2006, 267). Considering the spatial as the mutual constitutivity of the material and the discursive enables us to consider "not simply analysis of spatial imaginaries *as such* but their productive, constitutive effects on *other aspects of social being* such as identity, personhood and power" (Delaney, 2010, 15). It is thus important to consider in more depth the mutually constraining, but also mutually reinforcing, binaries to which capacity/incapacity is connected. The next chapter moves to further trouble and dismantle these problematic binaries in the context of the static subject positions pre-determined in ideas of carer and disabled person in mental capacity law, as well as in policy more broadly. It will be seen that the depoliticising and individualising effects of both the capacity/incapacity and care/disability binaries enable the role and responsibilities of the state and institutions to be obscured.

References

Appelbaum, P. 2016. 'Protecting the Rights of Persons With Disabilities: An International Convention and Its Problems' *Law & Psychiatry* 67, 366–8.

Barad, K. 2003. 'Posthumanist Performativity: Toward an Understanding of How Matter Comes to Matter' *Signs* 28(3), 801–31.

Barad, K. 2007. *Meeting the Universe Halfway*. Durham, NC: Duke University Press.

Ben-Moshe, L, Chapman, C. and Carey, A. 2014. *Disability Incarcerated – Imprisonment and Disability in the United States and Canada*. New York: Palgrave Macmillan.

Carson, D. 1993. 'Disabling Progress: The Law Commission's Proposals on Mentally Incapacitated Adults' Decision Making' *Journal of Social Welfare and Family Law* 15(5), 304–20.

Coggon, J. 2016. 'Mental Capacity Law, Autonomy, and Best Interests: An Argument for Conceptual and Practical Clarity in the Court of Protection' *Medical Law Review* 24(3), 396–414.

Dawson, J. 2015. 'A Realistic Approach to Assessing Mental Health Laws' Compliance with the UNCRPD' *International Journal of Law and Psychiatry* 40, 70–9.

Davies, M. 2017. *Law Unlimited*. Oxfordshire: Routledge.

Delaney, D. 2010. *Nomospheric Investigations: The Spatial, The Legal and The Pragmatics of World Making*. Oxfordshire: Routledge.

Erevelles, N. 2011. *Disability and Difference in Global Contexts: Enabling a Transformative Body Politic*. New York: Palgrave Macmillan.

Feely, M. 2016. 'Disability Studies after the Ontological Turn: A Return to the Material World and Material Bodies without a Return to Essentialism' *Disability & Society* 31(7), 863–83.

Freeman, M., Kolappa, K., de Almeida, J. M., Kleinman, A., Makhashvili, N., Phakathi, S., Saraceno, B. and Thornicroft, G. 2015. 'Reversing Hard Won Victories in the Name of Human Rights: A Critique of the General Comment on Article 12 of the UN Convention on the Rights of Persons with Disabilities' *Lancet Psychiatry* 2, 844–50.

Glenn Smith, R. 1999. 'Reflections on a Journey: Geographical Perspectives on Disability' in M. Jones and L. Basser Marks (Eds), *Disability, Divers-Ability and Legal Change*. The Hague: Matinus Nijhoff. 49–64.

Hall, E. and Wilton, R. 2016. 'Towards a Relational Geography of Disability' *Progress in Human Geography* 41(6), 727–44.

Harrington, J. 1996. 'Privileging the Medical Norm: Liberalism, Self-Determination and Refusal of Treatment' *Legal Studies* 16(3), 348–67.

Herring, J. 2016. *Vulnerable Adults and the Law*. Oxford: Oxford University Press.

Holloway, S., Holt, L., and Mills, S. 2019. 'Questions of Agency: Capacity, Subjectivity, Spatiality and Temporality' *Progress in Human Geography* 43(3), 458–77.

House of Lords Select Committee on the Mental Capacity Act 2005 2014. *Report of Session 2013–14, Mental Capacity Act 2005 Post Legislative Scrutiny*, London: TSO.

Jenkins, R. 2010. 'Beyond Social Structure' in P. Martin and A. Dennis (Eds), *Human Agents and Social Structures*. Manchester: Manchester University Press. 152–65.

Kohn, N. and Blumenthal, J. 2013. 'A Critical Assessment of Supported Decision-Making for Persons Aging with Intellectual Disabilities' *Disability & Health Journal* 7(1), S40–S43.

Kong, C. 2017. *Mental Capacity in Relationship: Decision-Making, Dialogue, and Autonomy*. Cambridge: Cambridge University Press.

Lacey, N. 1998. *Unspeakable Subjects: Feminist Essays in Legal and Social Theory*. Oxford: Hart.

Mitchell, D. and Snyder, S. 2018. 'Low Level Agency: Disability, Oppression and Alternative Genres of the Human' in K. Ellis, R. Garland-Thomson, M. Kent and R. Robertson (Eds) *Manifestos for the Future of Critical Disability Studies*. London: Routledge. 189–99.

Ruck Keene, A. 2017. 'Is Mental Capacity in the Eye of the Beholder?' *Advances in Mental Health and Intellectual Disabilities* 11(2), 30–9.

Shakespeare, T. and Watson, N. 2002. 'The Social Model of Disability: An Outdated Ideology?' *Research in Social Science and Disability* 2, 9–28.

Sheppard, C. 2006. 'Constitutional Equality and Shifting Conceptions of the Role of the State: Obstacles and Possibilities' *Supreme Court Law Review* 33, 251–68.

Shildrick, M. 1997. *Leaky Bodies and Boundaries: Feminism, Post-modernism and (Bio)ethics*. London: Routledge.

Shildrick, M. 2015. '"Why Should Our Bodies End at the Skin?": Embodiment, Boundaries, and Somatechnics' *Hypatia* 30(1), 13–39.

Skowron, P. 2019. 'The Relationship between Autonomy and Adult Mental Capacity in the Law of England and Wales' *Medical Law Review* 27(1), 32–58.

Steele, L. 2017. 'Temporality, Disability and Institutional Violence: Revisiting in re F' *Griffith Law Review* 26(3), 378–400.

Stefan, S. 1993. 'Silencing the Different Voice: Competence, Feminist Theory and Law' *University of Miami Law Review* 47, 763–815.

UN Committee on the Rights of Persons with Disabilities 2014. General Comment Number 1: Article 12: Equal Recognition Before the Law. UN Doc CRPD/C/GC/1.

Ward, A. 2011. 'Adults with Incapacity: Freedom and Liberty, Rights and Status: Part 1' *Scots Law Times*, 5, 21–5.

Weller, P. 2015. 'Reconsidering Legal Capacity: Radical Critiques, Governmentality and Dividing Practice' *Griffith Law Review* 23(3), 495–518.

Whatmore, S. 1999. 'Hybrid Geographies: Rethinking the Human in Human Geography' in D. Massey, J. Allen and P. Sarre (Eds), *Human Geography Today*. Cambridge: Polity Press. 22–39.

4 Care/disability

Challenging the divide through relationality

The previous chapters have developed a critical frame which draws on spatial and relational theories in order to challenge the binary frameworks that underpin and draw the conceptual boundaries of mental capacity law. This relationality resonates with insights from care ethics, relational autonomy, and vulnerability theory, yet moves beyond these to provide a broader and more pervasive understanding of relationality, disentangled from the liberal web of logics which constrains the analysis. The focus on space and spatial dynamics has opened up ways to engage with the historicity and processes of creation and reiteration of taken-for-granted norms in the legal landscape. Critical disability theory has similarly been drawn on to disrupt the ableist logics of the broader framework, as well as to highlight some of the failings of the Social Model imaginary. This has been engaged to challenge the central capacity/incapacity binary that guides the legal framework and to highlight the effects of this in practice. This chapter will further engage with the legal subjectivity that inheres in the mental capacity framework, highlighting the problematic static and separate subject positions of carer/disabled person, which are created and opposed through the statute and jurisprudence. In doing so, it will demonstrate the importance of a spatial approach in both advancing critical approaches to care, moving beyond a dyadic approach and instead focusing on landscapes of care. As Daly and Lewis suggest, "[c]are lies at the interstices of the most interesting dichotomies at the heart of social provision" (Daly and Lewis, 2000, 282).

To some, this may seem a strange approach in a book which is engaging with disability; historically, care and disability theories have been viewed antagonistically by both theorists and activists. The concept of 'care' has been viewed as essentialising and entrenching the powerlessness of disabled people, viewing them as in need of care and as 'less than'. On the other hand, there has been a concern from care theorists that the focus on disability rights overlooks the experiences and burdens placed upon carers, with little social or political acknowledgement of the importance of care. This has been a longstanding point of contention which, unfortunately, has often resulted in missed opportunities to harness the critical insights emerging from both camps – insights which often converge in productive and disruptive ways. Drawing these

DOI: 10.4324/9781351067881-4

together through engaging with the spatial and relational dynamics of care enables us to sharpen these insights for law and policy, offering new perspectives and critical alliances for progressive social justice movements concerned with care and disability more broadly.

Care and disability in conflict?

Care ethics literature has been fruitful in providing a critical avenue to challenge liberal ideas of autonomy, rationality, and individualism over the last 40 years. The ethics of care literature has long called for a focus on interdependence and relationality rather than fetishised ideals of independence and self-determination, which were seen as dogging ethical discourses of autonomy. At the centre of the ethics of care is the privileging of networks of human interdependence, a challenging of the public/private divide, and a focus on the values arising from refocusing on interdependence. The work of Carol Gilligan, *In a Different Voice* (Gilligan, 1982), provided the impetus for the development of the ethics of care. Initially, so-called 'first generation' care ethicists focused primarily on the distinctions between feminine and masculine morality, and furthermore on distinguishing care ethics from theories of justice. Nel Noddings, for example, in *Caring* (Noddings, 1984), focused on the idea that care should replace justice as the central concept of morality. Justice was perceived as a product of a masculine system, which was exacerbated by the public/private divide in relation to rights which was seen to propagate the relegation of women's interests to the private sphere. As Spring discusses, the feminist critique of rights regards the traditional liberal understanding of rights as overly individualistic, as obfuscating the real political issues, and as isolating people from one another (2011, 69). Instead, care ethics foregrounded the importance of *relationality* and *interdependence* as opposed to the *independence* and *individualism* which was seen as at the heart of justice and rights concerns.

However, the care/justice dichotomy has gradually been eroded through later developments in care theory. As care ethics has moved on, there has been a renewed focus on care as a political theory which is free of ties to gender. Clement notes that "the most recent theoretical discussions of care include the assertion that care is not a superior form of morality and that there are dangers in excluding justice considerations in deliberations about care" (Clement, 1996, 112). An early attempt at positing a relationship between care and justice was undertaken by Joan Tronto in her 1993 work *Moral Boundaries* (Tronto, 1993). Here, Tronto suggested that it is important to contend with the ways in which "even conventional liberal thought will be transformed if we take care seriously" (xi) and introduced the values of attentiveness, responsiveness, responsibility, and competence to inform care policy (127). She distinguished her approach from those preceding her by insisting that "we cannot understand an ethic of care until we place such an ethic in its full moral and political context" (125). Central to this more political ethic of care then was thinking not just about the importance of relationality and interdependence at an interpersonal level (i.e. between carer and cared-for) but thinking about the ways in which political institutions and frameworks such as liberalism are (in) attentive to and respond to this. Reconceptualising the distinctions between public and private as part of this thus allows more targeted scrutiny at a policy level of obstacles to caring practices. Rather than relegating issues arising in the 'domestic sphere' to the realms of private individuals, and outside of the scope of the state, reconceptualising this private/public divide presents such issues as a matter of societal and political importance.

There are clear conceptual affinities between care ethics and the Social Model of Disability, which was discussed in Chapter 2, as both engage with experience in a relational way in contrast to the individualistic, social vacuum which has been the caricature of traditional approaches, and both draw attention to the societal role in shaping experience. At the same time, there has been considerable debate between both camps as to the dangers of emphasising the needs and rights of one group in society over others. In essence, the distinction between the theories was seen as one of a point of emphasis; where care ethics was seen as emphasising the needs of carers, the disabled people's movement buoyed by the Social Model of Disability was concerned with the needs of 'care-recipients'. The engagement with care at a policy level, particularly in the British social policy context, has been around highlighting the often-hidden role that carers play in society as well as the ways in which their interests are overlooked. Moreover, this lack of recognition has been translated into a lack of support for carers (financial and institutional), which is particularly problematic in contexts in which carers face challenging circumstances. Feminist care theorists often aligned these arguments with more familiar debates about the gendered nature of care and the burdens placed on women to undertake caring responsibilities and social reproduction, and the relegation of these concerns in policy to the "private" or domestic domain. One example of this can be seen in the context of community care policies in the 1980s where the primary policy driver was deinstitutionalisation. As Fine and Glendinning discuss,

> feminist scholars argued that as the burden of caring in the home falls on women, community care policies needed to be understood as regressive and patriarchal, effectively transferring responsibility from the state to the family and, within the family, to women.
>
> (Fine and Glendinning, 2005, 603)

Underlying this then was a concern about privatising – or further embedding care relations – in the private sphere and abnegating state and societal responsibility. There was a fear that deinstitutionalisation would thus place further burdens upon (primarily) women to undertake care with little support or recognition.

It is not difficult to see how this stance may jar with the Independent Living Movement and the Social Model perspective underpinning it. One of the core principles of the Independent Living Movement is the need to move disabled people out of institutions and to remove the barriers to their full inclusion and participation in communities. Essentially, it is about enabling meaningful independence, choice, and control over everyday life and decisions. As such, deinstitutionalisation – in theory, if not in practice – ought to be seen as an important goal for the Independent Living Movement. As such, the resistance to the deinstitutionalisation policies among some feminist care theorists was heavily criticised by disability activists. At one level, the debate was seen to reinforce the idea of disability as a burden and the vision of disabled people as dependent upon care. As Watson et al. discuss, the concept of 'care' came to be viewed by many in the disabled people's movement as a "byword for dependency" (Watson et al., 2004, 335) and instead, there was a preference for the idea of 'personal assistance' to connote empowerment and liberation. Moreover, through this lens care is seen as a problematic exercise of power over the disabled person, and as potentially stifling, overbearing, and a barrier to inclusion. There was also perceived to be an overlooking of the potential for abuse in care relationships by care theorists who tended to portray care as a benign activity. Instead, the need for independence, choice, and control was advocated for by the disabled peoples' movement, as opposed to the recognition of dependence and interdependence which ran at the heart of the ethics of care. As Jenny Morris starkly argued, "The only way to empower people is to throw off the ideology of caring which is a form of oppression and an expression of prejudice" (Morris, 1997, 54).

Thus, it is evident that there has been a critical rejection of care theory in the disability rights literature. In contrast to the care ethics focus on revaluing dependence and relationality, the disability rights literature focused instead on empowerment through policies enabling independence, choice, and control. As will be discussed through this chapter however, this dichotomous view of care and disability approaches is apt to be overstated, and there are good reasons to productively engage with convergences in their conceptual underpinnings. Indeed, it is perhaps the policy and political context which has necessitated the distinct and seemingly antithetical focus of the care and disability movements, rather than the theoretical underpinnings themselves. However, both care ethics and Social Model approaches are not without their problems. Critiques of the Social Model were discussed in depth in Chapter 2, and similar critiques exist of care ethics literature. For example, Chris Beasley discusses the ways that, whilst

> care ethicists can be credited … with offering a critique of the rational atomistic self/citizen associated with neo-liberalism in their emphasis on an embodied altruistic politics … in important ways the asymmetry at the heart of the political vision of care ethics tends to leave in place the active independent subject/citizen of neo-liberalism, who is distinguished from dependent others.
>
> (Beasley, 2017, 240)

Moreover, Beasley goes on to suggest that care ethics can responsibilise the carer, and rather than providing an alternative to neoliberal individualism, can inadvertently support its structure (Beasley, 2017). These critiques are similar to those of the Social Model in that, despite problematising the subject (carer, disabled), the approach often leaves the broader context and norms untouched. There is thus a need for "a more expansive conception of embodied interconnection than care commands" (Beasley, 2017, 241).

The spatial and relational approach which has been developed through the book so far offers a way to avoid reinforcing and reinscribing the problematic norms that care and Social Model approaches have tried to distance themselves from. Spatial dynamics enable a focus on processes of division, boundary drawing, and categorisation and to see the material effects of these. Moreover they offer ways to disrupt causality and ideas of responsibility, moving away from static and linear ideas, which often foreclose a focus on broader agents and relations. Spatialising care in the way that feminist geographers have called for enables a focus on the wider context and the power relations – the networks or assemblages which care is both situated in and part of. Milligan and Wiles talk about this in terms of "landscapes of care" (2010, 738) and refer to the "complex social, embodied and organizational spatialities that emerge from and through relationships of care" (738). Bowlby (2012) looks at this through the terms "carescape" and "caringscape". "Caringscapes", according to Bowlby, focus on the particular caring relationship, whereas "carescapes" situate this within a broader resource and services context, looking at how the "carescape" shapes the "caringscape" terrain (Bowlby, 2012, 2112). Alongside spatial and relational approaches to disability, considering care through this lens not only enables a deeper, critical exploration of the processes and dynamics at play in the construction of care, but also offers a way forward for care and disability theorists to escape the antagonisms and build critical alliances for progress.

Shaping the divide through the Mental Capacity Act (MCA)

This section will look at some of the ways that the carer/disabled dichotomy plays out in practice in mental capacity law before moving to more closely interrogate what a spatial and relational dynamic, attentive to the carescape or landscapes of care, allows us to do beyond critiquing the separateness and categorisation of carer/disabled. There has been recognition in the mental capacity literature of the separateness created in the best interests framework of the Mental Capacity Act 2005 (Herring, 2007). The focus of the best interests assessment is solely on the individual deemed to lack mental capacity. Section 4 sets out the factors to be considered as part of the best interests assessment once somebody has been deemed to lack mental capacity, including whether it is likely that capacity will be regained and whether steps have been taken to permit and encourage participation (s4(3) and 4(4)). As I have discussed in previous work (Clough, 2014), the best interests criteria work to sideline the interests of carers as part of this assessment, and to ignore the context of the care relationship. The framing of the MCA and section 4 in particular continues the problematic logics of separation, and similarly positions the carer or family members as instrumental – there as part of the assessment process to enable a clearer picture of the wishes, feelings, beliefs, and values of the individual deemed to lack capacity. This framing is echoed by the Convention on the Rights of Persons with Disabilities (CRPD), which seems to also envisage the carer as there to enable the rights of the disabled person. Whilst the CRPD does refer to family members or carers of persons with disability (see e.g. Preamble, Art 16, Art 23(4), and 28(1)), when it does so, they are essentially placed as the means by which the rights of the person with disability can be achieved – there is no support given to facilitating the carers interests as an end in itself, nor focusing on the caring relationship as a whole. The Preamble, for example, states that

> the family is the natural and fundamental group unit of society and is entitled to protection by society and the State, and that persons with disabilities and their family members should receive the necessary protection and assistance *to enable families to contribute towards the full and equal enjoyment of the rights of persons with disabilities*.

Whilst on the face of it this statement appears to lend support to a relational ideal of recognising the interests of all of those within a caring relationship, a closer reading reveals that the underpinning logics underpinning support provided to families is to enable them to contribute to the enjoyment of rights of persons with disabilities – see the emphasis added, for example. The family member is positioned as primarily instrumental. As Kayess and French (2008) discuss, in drafting the Convention, the Ad Hoc Committee had keenly argued about whether the interests of family members ought to be included. This was answered in the negative,

> on the basis that in most societies family needs and rights tend to be privileged above those of persons with disabilities and, notwithstanding the enormous importance and contribution of families to the realisation of rights and dignity of person with disability, it is sometimes family members who are principally responsible for, or collude in, human rights violations against them.
>
> (Kayess and French, 2008, 25)

Whilst this may not completely overlook the role of family members as carers, and does not foreclose considering them in a distinct treaty, it does perpetuate the idea of separate interests and static identities and subjectivity. We see here distinct echoes of the liberal spatio-temporality being repeated, without challenging the underpinning logics of this: without challenging these boundaries then the CRPD (or attempts to implement it) may problematically reproduce them.

Returning to the domestic legislation, there seems to be little, if any, recognition on the face of the MCA framework of the ways in which such interests are intertwined with those of those legally positioned as carer. Instead, the idea of non-interference, of separateness and separability, and of individual interests is the dominant frame. Legal principles regarding informed consent to medical interventions, for example, view family or other external involvement with suspicion (*Re T* (adult: refusal of medical treatment) [1992] 4 All ER 649). Ho perceives "a general concern that family involvement will muddle the patient's decision-making process, such that a focused, individual decision is more valid and well-considered than a tainted one that involves the voices and considerations of others" (Ho, 2008, 129). As Bridgeman contends,

> [t]he work of caring for dependents and emotional interdependency with our children, spouses, partners and families must remain concealed lest we appear not to be independent souls suited for the public world. Consequently, the nature of dependency, the responsibilities of those who care for dependents and responsibilities of others, or the state, for those in need of care remains relatively unexamined.
>
> (Bridgeman, 2007, 308)

The simplistic framing of section 4 betrays then this liberal legal logic as underpinning the legislation. The interests of the carer – contemporaneous or conflicting – or of the effect of the decision on the carer or the overall caring relationship are not relevant considerations. Yet, there may be concerns that taking into account the interests of wider parties such as carers and/or family members might detract from the interests of the individual deemed to lack capacity, who, in many ways, will be in a less powerful position. Such an approach though artificially suggests that these interests and relations are separate and easily separable. This liberal imaginary seems to thus map onto (and perhaps be inspired by) the logics of the carer/disabled person dichotomy, which we traced in the above section and which has historically dogged debates around rights and activism in this area.

This is not to say that when *applying* the legal framework in practice, there is not scope to interpret the provisions as enabling consideration of more relational interests, including those of the carer. One case which predated the MCA, and which has attracted significant critical attention, is that of *Re Y* (Mental Patient: Bone Marrow Donation) [1997] 2 WLR 556. This case involved a 35-year-old mentally and physically disabled woman who was incapable of understanding others' needs but could express her own basic needs. Her older sister had the pre-leukaemic bone marrow disorder myelodysplastic syndrome. She needed a bone marrow transplant, preferably from a sibling, to significantly prolong her life. The court referred to evidence that Y benefited from her sister's visits and that it helped her maintain a link with the outside world. It was further submitted that if the application was unsuccessful then there was evidence that this would have an adverse effect on her mother's health so that her relationship and contact with Y would be affected. Therefore it was of benefit to Y to act as donor. The court also relied on the argument that disadvantages were very small and involved no real long-term risks. As such, it was to Y's emotional, psychological, and social benefit to grant the declaration that she should be a bone marrow donor for her sister. The court emphasised that

> the root question remains the same, namely, whether the procedures here envisaged will benefit the defendant and accordingly, benefits which may flow to the plaintiff are relevant only in so far as they have a positive effect on the best interests of the defendant.
>
> (Connel J)

Putting aside ethical debates as to the correctness of the court's approach here, this approach to best interests can become problematic for a number of reasons. As I have argued elsewhere,

> instead of explicitly recognising the plurality of interests at stake, issues such as the interests of the sister in receiving the bone marrow, and gratitude from the mother and sister were viewed as aspects of the best interests of Y. This consequently prevents the real reasons behind a decision from being openly reflected, which in turn denies an open basis for challenging the decision or more openly and transparently grappling with the undoubtedly complex issues at stake, such as relationality and obligations.
>
> (Clough, 2014, 135)

In the case of *NK v VW* (2010) Unreported (case no. 11744555), the Court of Protection was faced with the issue of whether the son could bring welfare proceedings in relation to his mother, who had dementia. He wanted her to be moved to a closer care home to facilitate more frequent contact with fewer restrictions than were imposed at the time. An important part of the rules regarding bringing proceedings is the need to consider the benefit to the person to whom the proposed order relates (s50 MCA, and Rule 50 of the Court of Protection Rules 2007). In refusing this application, Macur J placed substantial weight on the importance of viewing benefit from the perspective of VW, rather than her son, and further on the evidence of Dr A, who is "unable to conceive that any living conditions, no matter how physically superior to those in the present home occupied by VW will benefit her emotional/welfare needs". Macur J is clear that

> The sad fact of the matter is that NK lives at a considerable geographical distance from VW. His journeys to exercise contact with VW are difficult and costly. They are uncertain in that dependent upon VW's moods, she may not be in a fit state to receive him. Those difficulties, unfortunately, are his, and I am not required to have regard to the benefits that would flow from the proposed order or directions to anyone other than VW.
>
> (para 13)

Again, the legislation frames benefit as pertaining to the individual lacking capacity. The 'exceptionality' of cases which do engage with interdependence reflects the way that the legal framework sets it up as in contrast to the 'independent' norm. There thus seems little scope for recognition of the *relationship*, as opposed to recognising A's interests and B's interests. As Nedelsky puts it, "when the dominant metaphors turn our attention away from relationships, we cannot give either the relationships or the legal concepts that mask them the critical scrutiny they require" (Nedelsky, 1990, 178). Finally, and perhaps most importantly, even when the interests of others may become a factor in cases, there is danger that such interests and the actions of individuals within what is legally recognised as a caring relationship become viewed in an individualised manner. By this, it is meant that the broader relations which feed into and shape this particular caring relationship become hidden by the individualistic methodology of the case law, driven by the MCA.

As such, whilst there has been recognition and critical engagement with the way that mental capacity law separates the carer and cared-for within the current framework, and tends to reinforce liberal individualistic ideals in doing so, there is a need to deepen this analysis. How and why does the legal framework work in this way, and what are the material effects of doing so? What broader processes and logics are these processes of categorisation, individuation, and boundedness part of? As will be discussed in the next section, the more contextually driven, relational and spatial lens provides the critical tools to consider in more depth both how the care/disability dichotomy plays out in case law in the MCA and the particular ideals that this reveals, but also how the dichotomy itself can be more carefully challenged, with the insights emerging being harnessed to enable a critical perspective which takes forward the shared concerns of both disability and care theories.

Resisting the divide

Interdependence

One of the central arguments that has played out between care ethicists and disability theorists has been around issues of interdependence and independence. There is a legitimate concern that a care theory which emphasises the burdens of care can present the disabled person as the source of this burden (Herring, 2014, 5). Such a framing of relations and subject positions is problematic and misses the point of a relational analysis. At the same time, the language of independence, choice, and control which permeates much of the disability rights debates can be criticised as simply reversing the concerns of the disabled people's movement and reflecting it back onto carers – as entrenching the individualistic dichotomy that was the target of criticism. As Bernardini puts it,

> although the word in question has a profound political meaning in the perspective of persons with disabilities, it being connected with emancipatory ideals, and despite its content being remarkably different from the common one, it still runs the risk to remain associated to the logic of self-mastery and isolation which characterises the liberal and neo-liberal discourses.
>
> (Bernardini, 2018, 117)

However, as noted above, there is also a sense in which the disability rights position in the Independent Living Movement similarly challenges the individualistic rendering of independence. In the National Centre for Independent Living definition of independence, we see the emphasis on meaningful choice rather than endorsing a narrow view of independence as self-determination and actualisation.

> Independent living for disabled people means being able to live in the way you choose, with people you choose. It means having choices about who helps you and the ways they help. It is not necessarily about doing things for yourself, it is about having control over your day to day life.
>
> (NCIL leaflet, quoted in Hasler, 2003)

Yet, in the policy articulations of the core principles of the Independent Living Movement, such as independence, choice, and control, there is a sense in which this more relational definition has not been actualised, and instead independence has become a byword for self-actualisation and responsibilisation. Carers can become seen simply as sources of assistance based on demand, carrying consumerist connotations which are particularly prevalent in neoliberal discourse. As Hughes et al. contend, this is a "wrong-headed strategy" (Hughes et al., 2005). It "does not adequately observe the role of interpersonal relations between parties involved in the caring nexus" (Watson et al., 2004, 335). Similarly, as Herring suggests, such an approach reinforces the idea of separation rather than interdependence and relationship (Herring, 2014). Instead, calls have been made for a bridging of such approaches, based on mutual recognition, need, and embodiment. A similar point has been argued by Williams, maintaining that a political ethics of care is required in order to reconsider interdependence as the basis of human interaction; at different times, in different places, and in different ways we all need to be cared for (Williams, 2001, 487).

However, criticism has been levelled here that the idea of interdependence and reciprocity advocated by the ethics of care does not fully reflect the experiences of those needing care. As Shakespeare points out, "[t]here is a major difference in degree between interdependence of non-disabled people, and the forced dependence of some people with impairments" (Shakespeare, 2013, 147). This is quite right and illustrates the reality that whilst all those within society are in the main interdependent, those with long-term impairments or disability are often *more* dependent, or at least may have dependencies of a different nature. However, this is not an insurmountable criticism of care theory. In fact, relational theories are in a better position than less contextual theories to appreciate this. Whilst it is true that those in need of care may be more dependent than others within a particular caring relationship, at a given time, this should not take away from the fact that carers rely on those that they care for too. As will be discussed further in the next section, positions in the care relationship are not set in stone and the ability of new materialism, underpinned by care ethics, to recognise and more importantly to respond to this is notable.

The spatial and relational lens propounded in earlier chapters allows for further depth in the analysis of interdependence and the positioning of people as carer or cared-for. Care ethicists and relational autonomists have often called for recognition of the contextual realities and interdependencies facing *all* individuals as a starting point, and the ways in which choice and agency is always mediated by this. Agents are seen as inevitably and ubiquitously interconnected, becoming *through* relations. In this sense, the relational and spatial dynamics of the new materialist lens build on these insights from care ethics, placing emphasis not just on interpersonal relations but situating these within a broader political, social, historical, cultural, and material positioning. Importantly, this interdependence is always historical, contingent, and specifically situated within a particular assemblage or web of broader connections. We can begin to trace the ways in which these identities and subject positions have been created and to highlight the processes through which this has occurred. Rather than simply taking the care relationship and dependency within this as the point of analysis, such a frame invites us to consider the historical relations through which this particular relationship has been formed – the carescape which has shaped the caringscape. The interdependence at the heart of this, as noted above, is not simply at the interpersonal relational level, but takes account of the temporality of this relation, and ways it could be otherwise. The relations with broader institutional actors, as well as the material and discursive frameworks within which such a relationship is situated, also become particularly pertinent through this analysis.

The case of *WMA* [2013] EWCOP 2580 in the Court of Protection provides an interesting illustration of some of the *legal* processes which take place in framing the care relationship and responding to them. The case involved a 25-year-old man with atypical autism and a pervasive development disorder. He had lived at home with his mother, however there was a history of local authority and police involvement due to concerns about WMA's care at home. Previously, for example, the family had been moved out of their home into new accommodation due to concerns about the lack of hygiene in the home. Delos, who provided care to WMA, were also concerned that both WMA and his mother, MA, did not engage with their services and found the mother to be obstructive. It seems that WMA did not want the level of support that Delos was offering (12 hours a week) and wanted this to be reduced. However, the local authority wanted to move WMA into a supported living arrangement to facilitate his independence. Ultimately, it was decided that WMA lacked capacity and that it was in his best interests to move to supported living. The judgment describes the situation thus,

> He [WMA] leads an isolated and insular life with MA, who has also sight and mobility problems of her own. The local authority ... has reluctantly come to the conclusion that he needs to be moved into supported living accommodation, despite the difficulty of the initial move, because in the long term this will help WMA and MA to develop a more healthy relationship. It is argued that there is currently an unhealthy degree of interdependence. The local authority alleges too that MA is unable to care for WMA properly, she is likely to be harming his development and it is against his best interests to remain with her.
>
> (para 6)

The mention of interdependence here is interesting, and it is unusual for judgments to specifically highlight a relationship in these terms. Yet, we get a real sense that this interdependence is something to be avoided, and is perceived as unhealthy. We see this further at other points in the judgment, for example, "MA in the meantime regards WMA as her eyes and is dependent on him and there is no evidence that she would co-operate with help offered to her either" (para 28).

Interdependence, or dependency here, is seen as in contrast to the independence and empowerment of WMA. The professionals and the judge in this case were in agreement that WMA's abilities were limited not by his impairment, but by his mother. The evidence of the care manager neatly encapsulates this attitude: "She felt that WMA needed to be moved, to be 'encouraged to push the boundaries' in B [the care home]. He would be 'empowered', she thought" (para 88). MA – WMA's mother – is viewed as a barrier to such independence. Yet, recognition of interdependence through relational and spatial theory calls for a more nuanced focus upon the genesis of this perceived barrier. The relationship between WMA and MA must be situated – spatially and relationally – within broader dynamics of the carescape, as well as historically located. Later sections will highlight these elements as well as further developing the claim that such concerns are important for both critical disability studies and care theorists.

The judgment allows us to see the formation of the ideal legal subject that underpins the divide between disabled or incapacitous and the normative 'other' to which they are measured against through the following exchange regarding WMA's wishes and 'potential',

> He could not decide where he wanted to live but he liked to choose food for his lunch and, whilst he could not cook, he helped her (MA) by regulating the gas knobs on the stove. He could not, however, determine when food was ready and cooked. She had tried to teach him things but he would go into "meltdown". WMA struggles with understanding instructions and would shout and swear and punch doors in frustration.

> She agreed this probably meant he cannot make decisions for himself and she accepted the diagnosis of autistic spectrum disorder. "He does not like change", she said later. He could not decide whether to move home, for example. But, "He can be more intelligent than I am", she insisted, yet people expect too much of him. Delos tried to plan two to three days ahead and he liked to plan just one day at a time. He did not like new routines, though seemed to me to be a defeatist approach.
>
> (para 48)

At a conceptual level we see that WMA's abilities and his wishes here (although it is not clear as to the accuracy of them) are seen as in need of fixing. Differences in embodiment and in ways of being, for example not making concrete plans for days in the near future, or making food in particular ways, is seen as in need of remedy, regardless of whether the individual would like to, or indeed can, perform this type of subjectivity. The dismissal of this by the judge as "a defeatist approach" is telling as to the broader normative framework within which mental capacity law occupies and plays a part, one which sees a particular able-bodied and minded norm as the yardstick.

This is reflected in some of the statements in WMA regarding his wishes. We see, for example,

> WMA unequivocally told me he wanted to be "permanently" with his mother. The work done by Delos, he said, was too much and he thought three hours of support four days a week was just not acceptable. He wanted one hour two days a week. Delos did not leave the home when he asked them to go. They would not listen to him. He wanted proper appointments and did not want extra people turning up on visits. As to spending his time, he liked to watch DVDs and watch the TV. He likes to take his dog, Joe, for a walk in the park. He does not like mixing with people. "That's my choice", he said. But, of course, he really has not experienced a life that is other than isolated hitherto.
>
> (para 45)

> I have no doubt as to the strength of WMA's wishes and feelings but what became clear to me was how much he dislikes change and fears the unusual, that which he has not experienced. What came over too was the degree of interdependence with his mother ... It is clear that he has simply not weighed up the advantages and disadvantages of moving or, indeed, what will happen when his mother becomes unwell and he did not contemplate properly the risks to himself, nor understand his lack of life skills.
>
> (para 47)

We see here a problematic disavowal of the strength of WMA's wishes, which is seemingly driven by a suspicion of his interdependence on his mother as well as the hierarchical nature of the weight given to the views of particular actors here.

WMA's wishes become mediated through those of other, more powerful, actors such as Delos and the local authority, as well as being seen as driven by his mother.

At another level, we also see the constrained focus which the MCA necessitates through its framework of capacity assessment and best interests response here. The narrow lens which the Act must utilise becomes individualised and sets MA up as a separate and separable entity – albeit here one who is a barrier to WMA's individual development. The focus of the capacity assessment, and the best interests assessment in terms of the response available to the court, similarly entails an individualised response.

> The position of MA has been a somewhat unusual one … I regard, for my part, MA as a vulnerable person and, whilst I have no direct evidence that she, too, lacks capacity, I am concerned at the way in which she keeps her home. She is obviously dependent to a degree upon WMA for care of herself and I am concerned too by her reluctance to engage with social services and any organisation seeking to assist.
>
> (para 18)

Again, the mental capacity legislation seems to struggle with this, given the dominant framing of the individual lacking capacity, with the carer seen as simply a factor in certain assessments. The fact that concerns as to MA's "vulnerability" is mentioned by the judge here is noteworthy – yet the lack of ability of the judge to further engage with this reflection speaks volumes about the constraints in the legal framework and what it leaves 'outside'.

In many ways, this case offers a tangible sense of the care/disability dichotomy discussed in the previous section at play in the framing of the legislation and the ways that this then plays out in judgments. The "moralising sting" in care (Beasley, 2017) also becomes apparent here, as MA is seen to fall below the standard of the responsible citizen that Beasley suggests care ethics approaches may inadvertently uphold: "establishing altruism towards the vulnerable as an ethical starting point typically involves the promotion of care as a desirable moral quality or disposition held by 'responsible' individual citizens" (240). Interdependence is seen as in contrast to the ideals of independence and empowerment. Some of the processes through which the dichotomous approach plays out in practice are evident in the above discussion of the WMA case, yet further attention to processes helps to elucidate more fully how these insights are beneficial to those seeking a critical theory taking us beyond care/disability.

Shifting subjectivity

Looking at care through the lens of spatial and relational dynamics demonstrates the importance of care as a process rather than an identity. This is particularly evident in the work on care ethics which stems from geographers, who view care "not as a separate kind of relation, but as endemic to (potentially) all social relations that matter" (Lawson, 2007, 3). In this sense, care is not something which occurs between a 'carer' and cared-for – it is much broader than this; it is "a way of relating to others" (McEwan and Goodman, 2010, 103), echoing the idea of the carescape within which the caringscape (the particular relationship) is entangled. This approach resonates with a focus on shifting subjectivity and the lack of static identity in the new materialist literature. We see that particular subject positions are shaped by a number of processes, and moreover that such positionings can be occupied simultaneously. This avoids the linear trajectory which is often associated with liberal discourse around care, in which there is seen to be a progressive need for care, or point at which an individual becomes a carer. Instead, we begin to be able to unravel how, rather than static identities of carer or disabled person, interdependence and the flows of care (importantly, not emanating from or solely from a particular individual agent) become centralised.

In this vein, care ethics does not valorise 'carers'; rather, it draws attention to the care processes which we are all reliant on in different spaces and temporalities. As such, identities of care-giver and care-receiver are avoided through the recognition of the shifting subjectivity, which is dependent on context. As Williams has argued, and as has occurred in the care/disability debates discussed previously, policies often 'freeze' identities, and reinforce the discourse of dependence versus independence, thus forcing individuals to align with a particular group to access particular services (Williams, 2012). As Molyneaux et al. suggest, the term 'carer' itself is a "mark of bureaucracy, turning what is a normal human experience into an unnecessarily complex phenomenon" (Molyneaux et al., 2011, 422). This, in turn, acts as an important governance technique for the shaping of a particular static subject, thus enabling the development of a particular normative subject through such policy and legal process. We saw this in particular in WMA above, where the static subjectivity of WMA as care recipient and MA as carer became central to the legal response, despite the judgment straining in parts under the recognition (and ultimate disavowal) of interdependence.

Being attentive to the various care processes which occur, and the multilateral rather than unilateral ways in which these occur, avoids this problematic framing and draws attention to the intersecting interests of different parties to relationships. Moreover, as Ward has discussed, there is increasing recognition of the growing number of carers who are themselves disabled (Ward, 2011). Through exposing this, Ward suggests that we can see care as an activity "that binds us all … to undermine the binaries of disabled and non-disabled, carer and cared for, dependent and independent" (Ward, 2011, 172).

This lack of static identity which emerges through this lens clearly poses a challenge to the reliance on such identities in liberal legal approaches, and in mental capacity law more particularly. Thinking back to WMA again, and the statement that "MA in the meantime regards WMA as her eyes and is dependent on him" (para 28) starkly exposes the difficulty in reality of situating individuals in legal identities as either carer or cared-for. As Braidotti has argued, "identities are [largely] … imaginary tales, which project a reassuring but nonetheless illusory sense of unity over the disjointed, fragmented, and often incoherent range of internal and external fractures that compose them" (Braidotti, 2011, 78). This echoes scholarship from geographers of disability and critical disability studies, seen in previous chapters. Hall and Wilton, for example, develop a relational model of disability which focuses on "decentering a stable disabled subject in favour of an emphasis on relational becoming" (Hall and Wilton, 2016, 275). Moreover, their relational approach is explicitly grounded in a spatial lens, echoing Imrie and Edwards notion of the "recursive relationship between identity and space" (Imrie and Edwards, 2007, 626). In the context of disability, this entails recognising "social environments not as pre-determinedly exclusionary and oppressive … but rather as contexts within which people engage and perform their embodiment and in so doing re/produce and transform both themselves and their surroundings" (Hall and Wilton, 2016, 273). As with more spatial approaches to care, we see a real challenge to the idea of a static subject or identity, such as has informed the care/disability debate in theory and in political activism. Instead, *all* bodies become viewed as "emergent, unfinished and relational" (Hall and Wilton, 2016, 282) as part of an "affirmative conception of dependency" (283). As Simpson puts it, the focus is on *how* "subjects come to be differentiated and distributed through such relationality and becoming … [D]ifference that is not pre-given but rather emerges from a contextual set of forces and aggregations that take place in, between, across and through bodies" (Simpson, 2017, 8). The mental capacity framework is thus one such mechanism that acts to reproduce such difference, as part of the carescape, both in terms of separating and cementing identities of carer and cared-for, but also in terms of setting up the normative able individual which those lacking capacity are situated as 'other' to. This relational and spatial approach, building on convergences of critical disability studies and geographies of care, emphasises,

> displacing the sovereign subject, not simply to point out the ways in which we are all dependent or interdependent. Rather we do so in order to conceptualise that which not only displaces the language of dependence/interdependence but also demonstrates active assemblages of "becoming-in-the-world-with-others" as a way out of the self and the telos of autonomy.
>
> (Price and Shildrick, 2002, 72)

The normative liberal legal subject (independent, empowered) we thus encountered as the progressive aim of the intervention in WMA becomes displaced through this spatial and relational analysis. Such an approach also equips us with the tools to more carefully analyse the particular temporality and spatiality of this legal framework and the broader logics it is entangled with.

Temporal and spatial dynamics

The discussion of the shifting nature of the subject above draws particular attention to the ways in which 'identities', such as legal categorisations of carer and disabled person, are formed through a number of processes which occur over time and through specific spatial configurations. There is no static identity of carer or disabled person. A person can simultaneously be disabled and not disabled depending upon the spatial setting; likewise, a carer can simultaneously be caring for somebody as well as being cared for themselves. This spatial context is formed through a range of processes, including but not limited to the interpersonal relations between those traditionally viewed as forming a care relationship. The various agents within these processes (both historically and currently) affect this spatial context in different ways. Moreover, these processes are linked to broader structural, political, and material contexts – both being affected by them and affecting them. Here, a topological understanding of care is instructive: "thinking topologically … demonstrates that caring actions and practices ripple out into the world beyond the immediate caring relationship or the immediate moment" (Hanrahan and Smith, 2020, 230). It is important to recognise that this is not solely a topological account but also topographical – being attentive not just to the various different flows and agents but also to the power relations within these and how these are formed. Similarly, Simpson suggests that a spatial understanding of active and continual weavings, as part of subjectivity, is important,

> within these weavings our inhabitation of space is taken not just to relate to our situation vis-à-vis various social formations and the symbolic structures but also the quite literal material-situatedness of bodies within spaces which are themselves variously scaled, agentive objects and things.
>
> (Simpson, 2017, 4)

Here, we get a sense of the multidirectional, multiscalar nature of care and care relationships, or, to use Bowlby's term, of carescapes (Bowlby, 2012). As Hanrahan offers, "Care's relationality hinges on the fact that multiple components are brought into relation and connection" (Hanrahan, 2020, 245). Moving away from the unilateral or dyadic model of care which seems to inhabit much of the theoretical and policy debates in the care/disability dichotomy, we instead begin to situate both care and disability spatially and relationally. This avoids essentialising care and disability as both identity or practice, at the same time as drawing attention to otherwise obscured factors in the current critical lens.

Moreover, it begins to reveal the problematic spatial assumptions underpinning much of the deinstitutionalisation debates, which provided the convenient backdrop to many of the more vociferous disagreements between care theorists and disability scholars. The static presumption of particular spaces – the institution, the community, the home – as being sites for particular types of care relation becomes less tenable when we see care as a practice involving a number of actors and institutional relations. As will be seen further in later chapters, the walls of the home are permeable and the relations within the domestic sphere are intensely mediated by 'external' actors. Similarly, the institution is not a static site of closure (despite being experienced as such by residents) but similarly shaped both materially and discursively by 'public' interventions. Care and family relations do not cease at the walls of the institution, just as institutional processes can and do permeate what are otherwise viewed as community or domestic spaces.

As well as considering the spatial construction of particular contexts, the call to consider processes also necessitates an understanding of the historical connections and dynamics which lead to a particular situation, as well as how such temporalities may be disrupted in order to produce new configurations or experiences. There are a number of ways in which temporality is important in the context of care/disability debates. One of the key insights emerging when attention is drawn to interdependence and relationality, as we have seen, is the way that subjects can be both carer and cared-for in a relationship at the same time. Yet, some argue against such a proposition, suggesting that it overlooks the extent of disability in some circumstances, and ignores the extent of caring labour that is undertaken. It could potentially (and contradictorily) be viewed as *overlooking* the lived experience of care or disability, for example, despite claiming to be a lens which is contextually grounded and focused on embodied experience. Yet such a critique ignores the disruptive temporality that this relational account offers, as well as overlooking the various other actors and forces shaping the context. For example, in terms of those who are seen as disabled providing care themselves, the notion of reciprocity is often provided. Such reciprocity, however, does not need to be immediate, direct, or quantitively equal (Bowlby, 2012). This is not a claim that the same 'acts' are offered at the same time, such as in an exchange. Reciprocal care can be enabled through a variety of different means, through different actors and at various temporal junctures. Care then becomes a process over time, rather than a simple exchange between two individuals. As Guest and Corrigan suggest,

> Caring is not a static experience, it is relational, affective, spatial and temporal. Our participants' accounts of care illustrate that policy decisions are felt through the home and shape relationships and identities and this is a vital consideration for understanding experience and providing support.
>
> (Guest and Corrigan, 2018, 77)

Similarly, in relation to the claim that such a critical lens overlooks the reality of disability or care, again recognising both spatial and temporal aspects of processes points to seeing the experience of disability, or of care-giving, as contingent and as always potentially different. Spatial reconfigurations (past, present, and future) can alter the experience of a particular context. Moreover, care as a process takes a variety of forms, and ableist understandings of what care is perpetuate the idea that individuals with impairments are not capable of providing care. The linearity and unilateral nature of care which has pervaded the care/disability debates is thus challenged through this approach.

Another sense in which temporality is important in dismantling the care/disability debate is through the way it disrupts linear, progressive accounts of empowerment or autonomy. Often, even in more critical relational autonomy debates, there is a sense in which autonomy is seen as something which develops over time, albeit through relational support. We see this reflected further in WMA, for example, where the concern is to enable WMA's autonomy and empowerment through moving him into a supported living arrangement. Moreover, we see the urgency in this reflected in the idea that it needs to occur before his mother passes away in the future.

> People like WMA can cope with a parent's death but that is when they have other sources of support and WMA does not.
>
> (para 29)

> So what would happen, asked Mr. O'Brien, when she died? She became confused and spoke of seeing a lawyer and making a will but that was not the point … She conceded that upon her demise WMA would have to live in the social services accommodation. Was it not better for him to learn new skills now? She did not agree and that seemed to me to be entirely unrealistic.
>
> (para 58)

There is a clear normative idea here of development occurring in a linear temporality, through the reference to changing his life and longer-term implications. Moreover, the certainty of his mother dying prior to WMA reflects a normative ideal of a life course and of an ideal subject (becoming independent prior to a parent's passing) which is not reflective of real life. What this normative ideal perpetuates then, in a similar way to some forms of relational autonomy, is a linear trajectory through life, with autonomy being accrued or attained through support. This ignores the shifting nature of the subject and experience and its entanglement with the spatial context, as well as non-sequential modes of becoming. As discussed above, a number of positions can be occupied simultaneously and the relative 'autonomy' experienced within such contexts is highly dependent on a number of broader factors going beyond individual knowledge. These contexts are constantly being shaped and reshaped through a number of processes, challenging the linear and teleological idea of progress which has informed and underpinned liberalism, and which is central to some best interests assessments such as *WMA*.

Responsibility in the assemblage

A crucial point which is often overlooked in the dichotomising care versus disability debates is that the relationality being advocated, and the recognition of the ubiquitous nature of care and interdependency, goes beyond the dyadic portrayal of relationships and extends to much broader, intermingled webs of relations – between individuals but also placing these within wider relations with others, with institutions, and the state. Tronto, in her argument for the need for a political ethic of care concerned with going beyond the domestic sphere, draws attention to the "interweaving, complex web of care" (Tronto, 1993, 103). This goes some way to avoiding the tendencies in some of the early care theory, and which seems to have carried through in some critiques of ethics of care, to "romanticize care as a sentiment or dispositional trait, and reveals the breadth of caring activities as globally intertwined with virtually all aspects of life" (Klaver et al., 2014, 759). As well as exposing the universality of interdependence and our relations with broader social institutions and structures, this approach to care helps to envisage the intermingled relations between individuals in a caring relationship and how these are equally shaped by (and come to shape) relations with different services and institutions. Focusing simply on the dyad – on seeing care as simply a relation between two individuals – misses out the complexity of these wider relations and the tangible impact they have on the interpersonal care process.

There have previously been attempts to bring the literature on care and disability together in order to avoid the problematic dichotomising and to bring attention to socio-political factors. The work of the philosopher Eva Kittay has been recognised as reconciling some of the concerns which have pervaded the debates around care ethics and disability rights. Whilst much of Kittay's work advances the debate, there is a sense in which it is haunted by both a static approach to carer and care-receiver identities and by a fixation on the dyad. One of the cornerstones of Kittay's argument is the idea of derivative dependency, which she claims occurs in care-givers through turning their time, attention, and efforts to caring for another (Kittay, 2001, 565). As well as reinforcing the idea of carer and care-receiver as fixed positions, this notion is also problematic in overlooking the pre-existing dependencies that the person occupying the carer position already has upon societal institutions, *and* problematically locates those being in need of care at a given time as the source or conduit of the dependency. This is exacerbated further by Kittay's idea of 'nested obligations' which, building on the idea of derivate dependency, creates an argument for the provision of resources to enable the carer to care for the person receiving care. This positioning of care-giver and receiver becomes hierarchical and uni-directional, with the person in need of care seemingly disconnected from the societal and institutional network which Kittay argues ought to be responding to the derivative dependency of the care-giver. As Back has argued, this hierarchical positioning within this concept of "nested dependencies" also overlooks the civic or political membership of the disabled person, problematically hinging it upon their carer or family member (Back, 2015) and, in turn, dislocating the individual from the carescape. Moreover, such an approach seems to suggest that the care relationship itself is pre-political and that, outwith this relationship, the care-giver may function free of dependence. This leaves in place a linear idea of care, divorced from the broader relationality shaping relations, resonating with Beasley's critique of care approaches as problematically leaving in place, and buttressing, the neoliberal structures that it claims to challenge.

As such, focusing on the interweaving webs of care that *all* individuals are embedded within and avoiding the dyadic focus which locks individuals into particular subject positions provides a means through which to avoid the problematic inferences which stem from Kittay's framing. The insights from a relational and spatial account here pose a central challenge to the logics of the care/disability dichotomy in theoretical and policy debates. The spatial discussions in care theory and disability theory similarly have important convergences which allow a more nuanced understanding of what is at stake in these debates, the complexities of which are often ignored or left outside of the liberal legal and policy framework. Insights as to shifting subjectivity and the lack of a static identity here are particularly key, highlighting the spatial and temporal aspects which tend to be overlooked through current debate. Importantly, these insights point to consideration of a broader range of actors as part of the context, which opens up the space to consider the importance of responses and responsibility. As will be seen here and in later chapters, the interaction between the legal subject and the role of the state as part of liberal theory is particularly important for the drawing of binaries and the broader legal logics which underpin these. Rethinking the subject entails rethinking responsibility and the role of the state, and it is through this that the more productive and generative insights from the relational and spatial account come to the fore.

One particularly important insight which flows from the recognition of interweaving webs or networks of care processes relates to responsibility. Responsibility is an aspect which Morris has previously discussed as troublesome from a disability perspective, arguing that 'care' in policy becomes synonymous with "taking responsibility for someone" rather than "caring about" them (Morris, 1997, 54). This, Morris suggests, results in potentially oppressive care arrangements as carers become the dominant or controlling party. However, the carescape provides a more complex approach to responsibility which avoids this framing. As Barnes, Brannelly, and Ward suggest, central to a more political ethic of care is the question of *responsibility* (2015). This centrality of responsibility is important as it draws attention to the various different agents and actors involved in what has otherwise been framed as a dyadic care relationship, and in focusing on their role in particular processes, complicates the concept of responsibility and the tendency to ascribe this to individuals. It brings to the fore the broader societal and institutional processes involved in shaping the care relationship and the options available to those situated within it. Moreover, and perhaps more importantly, as well as drawing attention to these factors, Lawson notes that "it also moves us beyond critique and towards the construction of new forms of relationships, institutions, and action that enhance mutuality and well-being" (Lawson, 2007, 1).

This point is particularly salient for considering the social, legal, and political responses to care and the various forms that these may take. Rather than individualising the responses based upon a static identity of carer or disabled person, there can be a greater focus on changes at a number of different levels and in different policy processes. One area where this lens is key is in relation to the potential for abuse in caring relationships. As noted previously, there has been vociferous criticism of care ethics from disability rights activists and from broader theoretical scholarship, suggesting that it valorises care at all costs, and can support what would otherwise be viewed as oppressive or abusive relationships. Cooper, for example, discusses how the ethics of care idealises care through romanticising it (Cooper, 2007). Disability scholars similarly have argued that in viewing care as an always positive practice, the elements of control and abuse may be overlooked. Kittay's work, some of which has been previously discussed above, has also been critiqued on the basis that it has a tendency to romanticise or idealise care relationships, yet this has been on the basis that it ignores the abuse that care-*givers* can experience at the hands of those they are caring for (Clifford Simplican, 2015). Clifford Simplican recognises that in Kittay's account of caring for her daughter Sesha, the "vulnerability" of her daughter is essentially frozen as an identity, with the carer seen as more powerful and, by extension, less vulnerable. As Clifford Simplican goes on to argue,

> An unintentional consequence, however, is that Kittay's emphasis on permanent vulnerability forecloses the possibility that dependents can be both vulnerable and aggressive. This foreclosure silences experiences of violence and leaves us unequipped to respond to abuse.
>
> (Clifford Simplican, 2015, 219)

Building on the idea of identities and subjectivity as fluid and shifting, rather than frozen, as well as recognising the wider webs of relations shaping the processes of care, enables a more careful understanding of abuse and responses to it. This lens opens up the space to recognise and respond to the particularities of a given relationship and to consider the various processes which have shaped the relationship in such a way. For example, it may be that certain policies which shift responsibility (and accountability) from the state to the individual might exacerbate powerlessness or a lack of support to those in care relationships. Whilst the axes of power are always present, and power imbalances are almost certain to pervade most care relations (viewed both interpersonally and as broader networks), a more relational approach informed by a political ethic of care helps to attend to the particularities of how these power relations are formed, sedimented, and perpetuated and how they are experienced in relationship. This also enables responses which are attentive to such particularities and which do not necessarily need to be targeted at the individual level. Moreover, abusive, exploitative or harmful 'care' is the very antithesis of the practices which care ethics seeks to engender, given that it cannot, by definition, be attentive, responsive, or competent. Care ethics analysis pinpoints and actively recognises precisely these problems with what are otherwise viewed, through the current lens, as 'caring' relationships.

This is an important lens through which to consider the *WMA* case. We see a very real concern in the judgment as to the quality of 'care' that WMA is receiving from his mother. A few instances include,

> There has been long term neglect and damage to local authority provided accommodation. So poor was the state of repair of the previous property at P that WMA and MA were allocated that new property in October 2012 at E.
>
> (para 14)

> She [MA] complained about the criticisms as to the state of the home regarding its cleanliness, though it seems to me it is very clear that mother has failed to keep the home in an appropriate state of cleanliness from CG's reporting … They live in poverty and that was the problem, she said. That may be true; but it seemed to me from the photographs I saw of the first home and what I have heard of home since that mother is content at times, simply because she is unable to deal with cleanliness properly, to live in a filthy state.
>
> (para 51)

This paints a very bleak picture of the lives of both WMA and MA. Yet, what the spatial and relational account allows, beyond focusing simply on care, is consideration of the way this relationship – this caringscape – has been structured through different relational dynamics in the carescape. Thinking more broadly about responsibility and responses, we can begin to trace the genesis of the care relationship, paying attention to relations with broader institutional actors. There is certainly a sense of these actors in the above paragraphs – through the housing relocation, and through Delos. Yet, we see a portrayal of the relationship between WMA and MA mediated through this lens: such institutional actors are in a position of greater power than both WMA and MA here and their evidence appears as epistemologically stronger throughout the judgment. Again, we see attention to the material and spatial environment through the paragraphs here, and the way that it is seen to transform the quality of the care relationship into a poor and unsuitable one. A change in the spatial environment through a move to different accommodation is seen as providing the means by which better care could be facilitated, yet what is missing here is an understanding of how if the broader relations – with institutions, for example – remain the same then such change is not likely to occur. A very static ideal of space is evident in this judgment, without the necessary attention being given to broader responses (or *active* lack of response) from other actors and the ways in which these play a role in the spatial constitution of a particular context.

Similarly, we get a real sense through this judgment, and these paragraphs in particular, of the multiple actors involved in a care relationship despite the framing of it as dyadic. Such acknowledgement poses an interesting challenge to the common portrayal of the 'home' as a private site with minimal intrusion from the state. At the same time however, the *responsibilities* of these wider actors and their historical positioning and power relations are missing, particularly when it comes to thinking about legal responses to the situation. Responsibility is placed squarely on the shoulders of MA,

> There are a number of matters that arise out of MA's evidence that caused me the greatest of concern. First, the fault is always somebody else's. She criticises her GP, the social workers, the help or lack of help she has had with money, failure to repair the property, the housing department and Delos. Everyone, according to her, is in the wrong and she in the right, whereas the truth is, it appears to me from the evidence I subsequently heard, that she turns help away and does not engage with professionals.
>
> (para 64)

This is a particularly stark example of the way that, as somebody rendered as capacitous and autonomous herself, MA can be portrayed as holding the responsibility here and failing to act responsibly. She can be brought into the broader machinery of the state and social welfare and within a normalisation and responsibilisation agenda. There is no recognition here of the role of broader services and institutional actors here – how they have engaged with WMA and MA, whether they have taken responsibility for their role, as well as what policy and material frameworks they are working within. Moreover, the legal response is individualised, with WMA being moved to supported living. Regardless of the legal or ethical correctness of this response, it demonstrates the real inability of the mental capacity framework to fully appreciate the relationality at the heart of such situations. Whilst there is some recognition of the broader context, this is heavily constrained by the individualistic methodology. We have seen judicial recognition of the interdependency prevalent in the relationship, the lack of static cared/cared-for identity here, and the broader institutional involvement, yet such recognition is hurried and peripheral given the framework that the legislation operates within. As will be further explored in Chapter 6, the Court of Protection and the MCA are constrained from the outset in terms of their remit – the judiciary cannot demand particular services are provided. This necessarily constrains the analysis through pushing for a narrow lens focused upon the individuals involved, rather than broader institutional practices and behaviours. There is little scope to engage with what support is provided to enable the relationship and support those within it. Background conditions here which can enable particular care practices are then left out of the frame. It will be seen through the remaining chapters that to include them and acknowledge them runs the risk of unravelling the broader logics of mental capacity law, and liberal legalism more broadly.

There have been critiques of new materialist and post-humanist approaches to responsibility, with suggestions that recognising the interwoven webs of relations in tandem with agential understandings which are not built on humanism (rationality, logic, etc.) but that include non-human agents reduces the capacity to hold actors responsible for occurrences within particular assemblages (see e.g. Häkli, 2017). Yet, what such a critique misses is the importance not just of looking topologically at the different relations and flows within an assemblage, but also of looking topographically at the different peaks and troughs – at the power relations which form and sediment over time and *how* these occur. As seen above, for example, the agency of some within a caringscape is formed and shaped through a number of wider forces, including policy trajectories and material and institutional shifts which may, for example, entail a 'rolling back' of provisions. This can significantly weaken the power of such actors, yet at the same time does not render them as passive objects within these flows. The subjectivity which is shaped through these broader social and political processes – i.e. of the 'carer', of the 'incapacitous individual', of the 'disabled person', of the 'autonomous man' – plays an important role in recursively shaping and defining the role of the state. What is missed or actively hidden through such processes, however, is the fallacy of these static identity categories and the logics which flow from them. In terms of responsibility, this recognition calls for a tracing of the genesis of such relational formations and sedimentations, recognising the ways in which power flows through these, and pinpointing the multiple roots of responsibility through responses which have occurred over time. Moreover, this entails a challenge to received ideas about responsibility as something belonging to an individual agent (such as a person or institution). Rather than seeing it as something that one has, as something that can be determined and delineated, as perhaps law likes to do, it becomes necessary to view it as diffuse and distributed. This illuminates both responses which occur at the interpersonal level (i.e. through the provision of care) but similarly where responses involve an active retreat from care, as well as where state and institutional responses have created particular spatial and discursive context.

Conclusion

This chapter has engaged with the care/disability dichotomy that is prevalent in mental capacity law and a framework within which individuals are sorted into fixed categories. In bringing discourses of care and disability together through the spatial and relational lens, the discussion has offered a critical lens within which scholars working on issues of care and disability can utilise and build alliances to take forward progressive social justice concerns. In terms of the mental capacity legislation, this lens has exposed the struggles faced in maintaining separate legal identities and avoiding recognition of interdependence and complexity. Drawing attention to the carescape, or landscapes of care, brings vital attention to issues of responsibility and causality, and the role of other actors and processes in shaping the care relationship, or caringscape. As seen in the previous chapters, the ideal of the legal subject and liberal subjectivity are bound up with ideas of individualism and privatising responsibility, hiding or obscuring the role of the state and other actors. As is becoming clear, the nature of legal subjectivity and legal responsibility are intimately bounded in the mental capacity framework and in liberal legalism more broadly. In the next chapter, the role of the state and binaries structuring this at present (state/individual, empowerment/protection, autonomy/paternalism) will be brought to the fore. It will more closely consider what thinking in terms of the assemblage, processes, and boundary making means for confronting the role and responsibilities of the state.

References

Back, L. 2015. 'Private Dependence, Public Personhood: Rethinking "Nested Obligations"' *Hypatia* 30(1), 115–31.

Barnes, M., Brannelly, T., Ward, L. and Ward, N. 2015. *Ethics of Care: Critical Advances in International Perspectives*. Bristol: Policy Press.

Beasley, C. 2017. 'Beyond Care and Vocabularies of Altruism: Considering Sexuality and Older People' in R. Harding, R. Fletcher and C. Beasley (Eds), *Revaluing Care in Theory, Law and Policy*. Oxon: Routledge. 233–50.

Bernardini, M. G. 2018. '"Dangerous Liaisons" Critical Reflections on Vulnerability, Disability and Law' *Sociologia Del Diritto* 1, 101–23.

Bowlby, S. 2012. 'Recognising the Time–Space Dimensions of Care: Caringscapes and Carescapes' *Environment and Planning A: Economy and Space* 44(9), 2101–18.

Braidotti, R. 2011. *Nomadic Subjects: Embodiment and Sexual Difference in Contemporary Feminist Theory*. New York: Columbia University Press.

Bridgeman, J. 2007. 'Accountability, Support or Relationship? Conceptions of Parental Responsibility' *Northern Ireland Legal Quarterly* 58(3), 307–24.

Clement, G. 1996. *Care, Autonomy, and Justice: Feminism and the Ethic of Care*. Boulder, CO: Westview Press.

Clifford Simplican, S. 2015. 'Care, Disability, and Violence: Theorizing Complex Dependency in Eva Kittay and Judith Butler' *Hypatia* 30(1), 217–33.

Clough, B. 2014. 'What About Us? A Case for Legal Recognition of Interdependence in Informal Care Relationships' *Journal of Social Welfare and Family Law* 36(2), 129–48.

Cooper, D. 2007. '"Well, You Go There To Get Off": Visiting Feminist Care Ethics Through a Women's Bathhouse' *Feminist Theory* 8(3), 246–62.

Daly, M. and Lewis, J. 2000. 'The Concept of Social Care and the Analysis of Contemporary Welfare States' *British Journal of Sociology* 51(2), 281–98.

Fine, M. and Glendinning, C. 2005. 'Dependence, Independence or Inter-Dependence? Revisiting the Concepts of "Care" and "Dependency"' *Ageing & Society* 25(4), 601–21.

Gilligan, C. 1982. *In A Different Voice*. Cambridge, MA: Harvard University Press.

Guest, C. and Corrigan, O. 2018. 'Extraordinary Normalcy: Home, Relationships and Identities in Narratives of Unpaid Care' *Health and Place* 53, 71–8.

Häkli, J. 2017. 'The Subject of Citizenship – Can There Be a Posthuman Civil Society?' *Political Geography* 67, 166–75.

Hall, E. and Wilton, R. 2016. 'Towards a Relational Geography of Disability' *Progress in Human Geography* 41(6), 727–44.

Hanrahan, K. 2020. 'The Spaces in Between Care: Considerations of Connection and Disconnection for Subjects of Care' *Area* 52(2), 244–50.

Hanrahan, K. and Smith, C. 2020. 'Interstices of Care: Re-imagining the Geographies of Care' *Area* 52(2), 230–4.

Hasler, F. 2003. 'Philosophy of Independent Living' *Internet Publication*. www.independentliving.org/docs6/hasler2003.html last accessed 26/6/2021.

Herring, J. 2007. 'Where Are the Carers in Healthcare Law and Ethics?' *Legal Studies* 27(1), 51–73.

Herring, J. 2014. 'The Disability Critique of Care' *Elder Law Review* 2.

Ho, A. 2008. 'Relational Autonomy or Undue Pressure?' *Family's Role in Medical Decision Making Scandinavian Journal of Caring Science* 22, 128–35.

Hughes, B., McKie, L., Hopkins, D. and Watson, N. 2005. 'Love's Labours Lost? Feminism, the Disabled People's Movement and an Ethic of Care' *Sociology* 39(2), 259–75.

Imrie, R. and Edwards, C. 2007. 'The Geographies of Disability: Reflections on the Development of a Sub-Discipline' *Geography Compass* 1(3), 623–40.

Kayess, R. and French, P. 2008. 'Out of Darkness into Light? Introducing the Convention on the Rights of Persons with Disabilities' *Human Rights Law Review* 8(1), 1–34.

Kittay, E. F. 2001. 'When Caring Is Just and Justice Is Caring: Justice and Mental Retardation' *Public Culture* 13(3), 557–579.

Klaver, K., van Elst, E. and Baart, A. 2014. 'Demarcation of the Ethics of Care as a Discipline: Discussion Article' *Nursing Ethics* 21(7), 755–65.

Lawson, V. 2007. 'Geographies of Care and Responsibility' *Annals of Association of American Geographers* 97(1), 1–11.

McEwan, C. and Goodman, M. 2010. 'Place Geography and the Ethics of Care: Introductory remarks on the Geographies of Ethics, Responsibility and Care' *Ethics, Place and Environment* 13(2), 103–12.

Molyneaux, V., Butchard, S., Simpson, J. and Murray, C. 2011. 'Reconsidering the Term "Carer": A Critique of the Universal Adoption of the Term "Carer"' *Ageing & Society* 31, 422–37.

Morris, J. 1997. 'Care of Empowerment? A Disability Rights Perspective' *Social Policy & Administration* 31(1), 54–60.

Nedelsky, J. 1990. 'Law, Boundaries and the Bmassounded Self' *Representations* 30, 162–89.

Noddings, N. 1984. *Caring: A Feminine Approach to Ethics*. Berkeley: University of California Press.

Price, J. and Shildrick, M. 2002. 'Bodies Together: Touch, Ethics and Disability' in M. Corker and T. Shakespeare (Eds), *Disability/Postmodernity: Embodying Disability Theory*. London: Continuum.

Shakespeare, T. 2013. *Disability Rights and Wrongs Revisited*. London: Routledge.

Simpson, P. 2017. 'Spacing the Subject: Thinking Subjectivity after Non Representational Theory' *Geography Compass* 11(12), e12347.

Spring, J. 2011. 'On the Rescuing of Rights in Feminist Ethics: A Critical Assessment of Virginia Held's Transformative Strategy' *Praxis* 3(1), 66–83.

Tronto, J. 1993. *Moral Boundaries: A Political Argument for an Ethic of Care*. New York: Routledge.

Ward, N. 2011. 'Care Ethics and Carers with Learning Disabilities: A Challenge to Dependence and Paternalism' *Ethics And Social Welfare* 5(2), 168–80.

Watson, N., McKie, L., Hopkins, D. and Gregory, S. 2004. '(Inter)Dependence, Needs and Care: The Potential for Disability and Feminist Theories to Develop an Emancipatory Model' *Sociology* 38, 331–50.

Williams, F. 2001. 'In and Beyond New Labour: Towards a Political Ethics of Care' *Critical Social Policy* 21(4), 467–493.

Williams F. 2012. 'Care Relations and Public Policy: Social Justice Claims and Social Investment Frames' *Families, Relationships and Societies* 1(1), 103–19.

5 State/individual

Situating the state

Disrupting the idea of static legal subjectivity in the way outlined in the previous chapters invites (or perhaps requires) us to scrutinise more carefully the role of the state. As Davies puts it, "Everything, in other words, is up for re-analysis and the scholarly imagination must be attentive to new types of objects not seen, or perhaps sometimes seen and marginalised, at the level of state law" (Davies, 2017, 106). This chapter engages with the various processes and overlapping institutional and jurisdictional landscapes which form parts of the assemblage, and the particular experience of agents within this. Moreover, it explores more fully the claim that such dynamic processes can be reconfigured to enable different assemblages. This will provide an important opportunity to develop the importance of spatial and relational theories and the implications of these for disability and mental capacity, but also more broadly for the liberal legal framework in terms of situating the state and considering the idea of responses and interventions.

The idea of the state (through its interacting institutions and structures, but also in its ostensible *absence*) being always already there will emerge from this discussion. The UN Convention on the Rights of Persons with Disabilities (CRPD) and its potential will be critically discussed through this more situated, dynamic approach, drawing attention to the way in which all of the articles interact and feed into each other and so offering a necessary reimagination of the spatio-temporality of the state. An example of this potential will be the way in which Art 12 (legal capacity) and Art 16 (freedom from abuse) have been approached in the mainstream literature so far. It will be shown that this has been disappointingly narrow and sees the articles as 'in tension', reflecting the autonomy/paternalism, empowerment/protection language which has historically afflicted the mental capacity literature. It will be seen that even the more critical literature on relational autonomy, for example, has struggled around the margins set up by the liberal legal framework.

In particular, drawing from and building on insights from feminist geography and geolegality, and from political ecology, opens up new ways to bring insights on scale into legal analysis in this context. Seeing scale as "socially constructed, relational, contingent and contested" (Neumann, 2015, 475) enables a more nuanced and granular exploration of the role and site of the state, as well

DOI: 10.4324/9781351067881-5

as ideas of intervention and responses, in the context of mental capacity law. Moving away from seeing scale as "distinct and hierarchical" (Faria et al., 2020, 1098), often perpetuated in analyses of mental capacity law which separate the individual, the family, the community, and the state, the argument is made for a more fluid understanding of scale as interweaving "circuits of power" (Faria et al., 2020, 1014) across various sites such as the local, regional, national, and international. Challenging the bounded ideas of the state and the individual, and the powerful fictions rooted in current ideas of scale in this context, acts as an antidote to an individualistic methodology and opens up new ways to think about responses (when, where, how, who responds) in mental capacity law, for implementing the CRPD, and for broader social justice debates.

The chapter will first explore the ways that mental capacity law currently forecloses recognition of the role of the state and other institutions as part of the assemblage, primarily through the dynamics of the autonomy/paternalism and empowerment/protection binaries. It will then outline the current limits of our legal imaginary here and the perceived inevitability of this framework, even within more critical theoretical approaches (including vulnerability, relational autonomy, and capabilities approaches) and reform proposals. Following this, the role and site of the state will be complicated in this context through engaging with geographical literature on spatialising the state through assemblages, drawing out the productive potential for enabling us to rethink responses. Cautionary notes will be sounded, however, to ensure that such responses do not problematically reproduce or reassert the binaries currently shaping the theoretical and doctrinal terrain.

Autonomy/paternalism; empowerment/protection

The previous chapters have begun to open up ways to rethink the legal subject and subjectivity as well as the role of the state, which is entangled within this. The interwoven nature of the subject and the state in mental capacity law, and in liberal legalism more broadly, is perhaps most starkly evident in the binary framing of autonomy/paternalism and empowerment/protection. This binary framing has to date served to draw almost impenetrable boundaries in scholarly and policy debates around capacity legislation and reform. Using a more spatial and relational lens allows us to bring to the fore otherwise hidden elements which shape and constitute experience, challenging the individualistic lens currently perpetuated. So far the chapters have demonstrated the strength of autonomy as (ostensibly) a driver of the capacity legislation, and the situating of autonomy as in contrast to paternalism, broadly equated with unwanted state interference in the lives of individuals. The liberal legal subject is embodied in this logic, with an autonomous being seen as separate from the state, pursuing their own ends without unnecessary interference. This is a central part of a "matrix of ideas that links law to the self" (Davies, 2017, 136). Davies expands on this, explaining the connection through a liberal political imaginary of the bounded body and the bounded state:

> The edges of the body are a legal barrier, the body is imprinted with law, and even still given a legal status ... These physical boundaries – the law of the person in liberal legality – are metaphorically tied to the state as persona.
>
> (Davies, 2017, 137)

This framing pervades the logics of the Mental Capacity Act (MCA) and its application in case law. As has been discussed, the mental capacity legislation creates a framework in which if somebody is deemed to lack mental capacity, a decision then must be made in their best interests, taking into account a range of factors as outlined in section 4 MCA. On the other hand, if somebody is deemed to have mental capacity then they are seen as free to make their decision without state interference. What is presupposed within this framework is an idea of freedom or liberty as non-interference, which enables autonomy and self-determination to flourish unimpeded. This is evident in many Court of Protection judgments, including this statement by Eldergill J in *Westminster City Council v Manuela Sykes* [2014] EWHC B9, which was encountered in Chapter 2:

> Society is made up of individuals, and each individual wills certain ends for themselves and their loved ones, and not others, and has distinctive feelings, personal goals, traits, habits and experiences. Because this is so, most individuals wish to determine and develop their own interests and course in life, and their happiness often depends on this. The existence of a private sphere of action, free from public coercion or restraint, is indispensable to that independence which everyone needs to develop their individuality, even where their individuality is diminished, but not extinguished, by illness. It is for this reason that people place such weight on their liberty and right to choose.
>
> (para 20)

Even if somebody is deemed to lack mental capacity, the best interests framework reinforces this importance through section 4(6) MCA, which states that the decision maker must consider the person's past and present wishes and feelings, beliefs, and values. This is a much-lauded aspect of the best interests assessment, which many see as preventing unwarranted or paternalistic interferences. Cases such as *Wye Valley v B* evidence the importance of s4(6). The case involved a man with a chronic foot ulcer, and the treating clinicians applied to the Court of Protection for declarations that it would be in Mr B's best interests to have the foot amputated. Jackson J agreed that Mr B lacked capacity in relation to treatment decisions, and the case concerned the weight to be placed on his wishes, feelings, beliefs, and values. The judgment emphasised the importance of Mr B's wishes, despite the gravity of the decision, and it was held that it was not in his best interests to undergo the amputation. These statements as to the importance of autonomy and respecting individual wishes, feelings, and values are generally welcomed as positive developments in cases such as this, purportedly demonstrating respect for the autonomy and rights of those deemed incapacitous, however there is a sense in which they can serve to mask broader processes and contingencies that form the background of these cases, which remain unsaid and invisibilised in the judgments. The responses open to judges and other decision makers in these cases again centre on the individual, and presume and reinforce the idea of a 'zone of non-interference' as key to what is to be protected. What is missing here however is the way in which these individual wishes and values are often intertwined with those of others, including institutional constraints and prior state processes. If the facts of the case can be aligned with these norms, such as autonomy and non-interference (as opposed to paternalistic interference), then they can be stated with confidence in a way which reinforces and cements them.

Yet, often hidden underneath the strong assertions of respecting autonomy or self-determination are a number of contingencies – a range of professional intra-actions and actors shaping the context, which allows the case to be framed in such a way. In contrast to *Wye Valley v B*, we have other cases which do not align neatly with these norms, and in which responses cannot be framed in a way that is supportive of autonomy. There is a line of case law which will be explored more fully in Chapter 7 in which it is evident that the possibility of respecting wishes and feelings through best interests decisions is foreclosed by the institutional decision making processes earlier on, such as where doctors or social care professionals are not willing to provide certain treatments or services.[1] In such cases, dividing lines are drawn by judges between public law and private law, and their lack of jurisdiction is deployed to prevent what are said to be public law questions from muddying the waters of mental capacity law. This overlooks the centrality of the interaction of the 'public' and 'private' spheres in enabling the autonomy and empowerment said to be central to the legislative framework. It ignores, or deliberately obscures, the ongoing historicity, power relations, and processes which contribute to decision making and wishes over time.

The static framing of a decision is also bound up in the autonomy/paternalism dichotomy which underpins the limits of state responses and responsibility in mental capacity cases. We saw this reflected in Chapter 3 in relation to the case law on consent to sex, where McFarlane LJ stated in *PC, NC v City of York Council* [2013] EWCA Civ 478,

> The Court of Protection does not have jurisdiction to act to "protect" these women if they do not lack the mental capacity to decide whether or not to be, or continue to be, in such a relationship. The individual's

1 *N v ACCG* [2017] UKSC 22; *North Yorkshire County Council v MAG* [2016] EWCOP 5; *NYCC v MAG* [2015] EWCOP 64; *Re MN* [*2015*] EWCA Civ 411; *ACCG v MN* [2013] EWHC 3859 (COP).

> decision may be said to be "against the better judgment" of the woman concerned, but the point is that, unless they lack mental capacity to make that judgment, it is against their better judgment. It is a judgment that they are entitled to make. The statute respects their autonomy so to decide and the Court of Protection has no jurisdiction to intervene.
>
> (para 53)

This (re)produces boundaries around the state and state responsibility. Such an approach is supported and rationalised further in *A Local Authority v TZ* [2013] EWHC 2322 (COP) by Baker J, that a low threshold for capacity here is "more consistent with respect for autonomy in matters of private life" (para 23). To intervene would be paternalistic.

Yet, this ignores the interventions which have already been occurring prior to the questioning of the individual's mental capacity. Paternalism and its dangers thus appear to be understood in terms of one-off interventions, rather than as part of ongoing processes and practices shaping the events involved here. The narrow framing of autonomy and paternalism (via interventions) here mutually reinforce each other and work to cement both the problematic rendering of the legal subject *and* the corollary bounded nature of the state. It ignores the varying ways in which interventions might occur, and that concerns as to paternalism are inherently relational; at the core of concerns about paternalism are issues of power relations, not 'intervention' or responses in a broad sense. Viewed through this lens, we can see the fiction of 'not interfering' as in itself paternalistic if it works to reduce the power or agency of an individual in a particular set of relations. Not intervening or responding is itself an active intervention. Power, as has been highlighted, is transformed through professional and judicial engagements with these issues in the Court of Protection, with effects rippling far beyond the individual case in hand and cementing or reinforcing power relations in different contexts, as will be discussed further in Chapter 7.

Importantly, paternalistic power relations can be reinforced through these judicial processes in a way which current models of autonomy/paternalism cannot capture. The reliance on expert knowledge, or the knowledge of certain professionals, in the course of capacity and best interests assessments, can work to reinforce power relations between professionals and those whose capacity is in question. This is evident through case law on anorexia in the Court of Protection, in which we see the debate framed in terms of autonomy and paternalism, yet this hides the subtle undercurrent of professional expertise and institutional resources which impact such cases. This works to obscure other means through which agency can be undermined, through professional epistemological knowledge claims which become reinforced through the judgments (Clough, 2016). This is not to deny professional expertise or to suggest that such knowledge is 'false'; instead it is to query the over-determining nature that such knowledge acquires through Court of Protection processes, working to cement power relations at the same time as such cases are purportedly built on concerns as to autonomy and paternalism. Again, the concept of paternalism in this binary takes on a very narrow hue and becomes shorthand for state intervention, all the while ignoring or actively hiding the problematic interventions stemming from its deployment. Moreover, it is common through this framework to think of 'intervention' by the state or other institutions as taking place only when capacity is called into question, but this often ignores or deliberately overlooks the ways in which they play a role before this 'event'.

These problematic logics have also become woven into the norms underpinning social care policy and safeguarding, which provide further evidence of the shaping of the subject and consequent boundaries drawn around the state. We saw in Chapter 2 some of the processes through which the binary framing threaded these logics into the policy developments in this context. Stark examples from serious case reviews in adult social care provide ample illustration of the problems borne out in exalting a particularly thin understanding of autonomy. One often cited example is that of Steven Hoskin, a man with learning disabilities who was murdered in 2006 following a long history of problematic engagement with services. He had cancelled his adult social care services in 2005, and this was deemed to be a capacitous choice. It then became apparent that neighbours, Darren Stewart and Sarah Bullock, had moved into his bedsit and were subjecting him to manipulation and abuse. He was horrifically murdered by them and others in 2006.

What is striking about this Serious Case Review is the way that Steven's disengagement with services had been respected as his 'choice', an aspect that has since faced heavy criticism. Whilst the presumption of capacity underpinning the Mental Capacity Act is seen as positive in terms of preventing widespread and unrestrained interventions into people's decisions, it can prove to be problematic in practice, precisely in cases such as this. In the Serious Case Review, it was stated that "it is essential that health and social care services review the implications of acceding to people's 'choice' if the latter is not to be construed as abandonment" (Flynn, 2007, para 5.13), and further that,

> While no service, whether health or social care, which support adults with learning disabilities advertises its aims in terms of "admit no restraints … adopt an attitude of non-interference … promote unfettered independence" (Keywood et al. 1999), effectively, this is what happens when "choice" is advanced as a rationale for setting aside a duty of care and/or discontinuing a service.
>
> (para 5.16)

Indeed, the police report following Steven's murder expressed it thus,

> Steven Hoskin had lost all control of his own life within his home. He had no say, choice or control over who stayed or visited the flat. He had no voice or influence over what happened within the premises. Darren Stewart had recognised the clear vulnerability of Steven Hoskin and had

> "moved in" on him ... he recognised the opportunity for accommodation and removed from Steven Hoskin the little ability he had to make his own choices and decisions. Darren Stewart was fully aware of Steven's vulnerability and learning difficulties and took advantage of those facts to control both Steven and the premises.

The starkness of this dividing line between capacity and incapacity, entangled as it is with autonomy, is particularly evident in this case. What is also interesting about such serious case reviews is that they demonstrate the way in which the parallel trajectories in adult social care and safeguarding policies map onto practice and intersect with the capacity/incapacity dualism. Reflected in this is the idea of the state as non-interfering in the service of autonomy, given Steven's placement in the conceptual space of a capacitous and thereby autonomous adult.

In the same way that we have seen the concept of autonomy in medical law and mental capacity law being subject to criticism in relation to its almost parochial individual and narrow deployment, the concepts that resonate with it in the social policy literature – choice, control, independence, and empowerment – are facing similar charges. These are set up against (negative) ideas of intervention and protection, echoing the concerns of paternalism seen above. However, many commentators point to the empty rhetoric that surrounds these terms in policy, and the way in which they tend to ignore or overlook the context which adult social care policies occupy. As Rushing discusses,

> empowerment is easily reduced to aesthetic self-expression and individual choice, in a way that not only neglects but fully invisibilises the relational and structural conditions of "choice" and "freedom".
>
> (Rushing, 2016)

There is also a concern here that, particularly in light of policy developments which actively promote service users as 'consumers' and aim at responsibilising engagement with services, ideas of empowerment and choice may work in practice to individualise responsibility for needs and to overlook the ways in which these needs can be structurally produced. As with the idea of autonomy and capacity above, this may translate into seeing liberty and freedom as respected in the absence of outside interference, overlooking or actively obscuring the ways in which the agency required for meaningful empowerment is produced through relations. This can have the effect of depoliticising inequalities and disadvantage and paradoxically subverting the professed aims of empowerment, choice, control, or independence. Again, the boundaries that are drawn and maintained between the individual and the state here work to prevent critical engagement with this broader spatio-legal context.

A bounded legal imaginary: hitting up against the binary

Despite the moves in some parts of the mental capacity and social policy scholarly literature toward more relational approaches, and the increasing recognition of the bind that this binary framing creates, the purported inevitability of the parameters of responses seems to repeatedly stymie transformative approaches. Concerns about paternalistic interventions and unwarranted interference abound. This is evident, for example, in the social policy literature where there is a concern that an increased focus on 'vulnerability' in the context of welfare can invite policies that reinforce notions of acceptable behaviour (Fawcett, 2009; Brown, 2014) or of those deemed vulnerable as being passive recipients of care or services (Daniel, 2010). This is echoed in the context of disability, with commentators such as Hollomotz expressing concern that framing disabled people as vulnerable can reinforce the powers of professionals and allow people to be subjected to paternalistic or protective actions (Hollomotz, 2009, 2011). It is crucial to recognise that this has been the case in the past, and that casting people with disabilities as vulnerable has enabled disempowerment, disavowal, and differential responses through law and policy. Yet these concerns tend to reflect the way in which vulnerability (as opposed to invulnerability) *has* been deployed in law and policy to effect particular ends and as part of a broader policy landscape of responsibilisation and cost-cutting, rather than on the productive potential that rethinking subjectivity will entail. Similarly, in the capacity context, Series stresses that

> if mental capacity assessments did take into account the deleterious effects of particular relationships *this could permit more paternalistic interventions*, evoking similar controversies to externalist constitutive approaches to autonomy ... which permit coercive interventions on the basis of the properties of oppressive relationships.
>
> (Series, 2015, 83; emphasis added)

Similarly, Dunn, Clare, and Holland argue that in the context of mental capacity, "substitute decision making" based on the idea of vulnerability as situational (perhaps due to an abusive partner being deemed to be dominating a person's decision making ability) may allow courts to step in with actions that are "potentially infinite in scope and application" (Dunn et al., 2008, 241) and effect a course of action that is protective. The inevitability of 'protection' as a response to recognising certain forms of vulnerability was echoed more recently in *CH v A Metropolitan Council* [2017] EWCOP 12. This case involved a man who was assessed as lacking capacity to consent to sex, whose partner was then told not to have sexual relations with him as she would then be potentially subject to criminal sanction. Here, whilst damages were awarded for breach of CH's Art 8 rights for a part of the period during which this was ongoing, Hedley J provided some interesting reflections, stating that,

> Many would think that no couple should have had to undergo this highly intrusive move upon their personal privacy yet such move was in its essentials entirely lawful and properly motivated. As I have said, perhaps it is

> part of *the inevitable price that must be paid* to have a regime of effective safeguarding.
>
> (para 25; emphasis added)

Here, there is a clear sense that the recognition of relationships or vulnerability in the context of assessing decision making ability *must* result in some form of paternalistic and individualised interference.

There is an inevitability about all of this – as though these sorts of individualised responses are all that law or policy can (ever) offer. What is missed in these critiques is the opportunity to reframe the discourse by seeing our ontology and epistemology differently. The potential for responses or intervention is narrowly framed both in terms of scope and purpose. There is a tendency then to reinforce the binary through disavowing vulnerability and dependency, in turn leaving the broader framework that structures these debates intact.

As well as relational and vulnerability approaches to mental capacity law, the capabilities approach and capabilities theory, stemming from the work of Amartya Sen and Martha Nussbaum, is also becoming more prevalent as a way for rethinking responses in this context. Jaime Lindsey and Rosie Harding (2021) discuss this in the context of capacity to consent to sex case law, suggesting that the capabilities approach "provides conceptual tools to support arguments for additional resources to help disabled people to realize their rights to sexual intimacy" (60). Capabilities theory essentially developed from Sen's critique of the tendency of mainstream economic and political theories to ignore the context that an individual is situated within, and he instead foregrounded the need to focus on what individuals are able to actually be and do, given this context (1999, 285). This approach has been taken up by political theorists such as Nussbaum, who developed a core taxonomy of capabilities that are central to the human condition and which states are obliged to facilitate. The approach broadly draws on a more positive approach to the state and the role of the state in facilitating freedom – freedom to, not freedom from.

However, capabilities theory is not without its criticisms. Nussbaum's approach in particular has been seen to be problematic from the perspective of disability, with the taxonomy proposed essentially being based upon ableist ideals which can exclude disabled people from the theory (see Harnacke, 2013, and Baylies, 2002, for discussion of this). However, at a more fundamental level, the theory has been criticised for perpetuating an individualist lens and methodology (Dean, 2009; Robeyns, 2005) being concerned with individual freedoms (albeit 'positive' freedoms) and being constrained by positivist and liberal structures and approaches to reality (Kremakova, 2013). As Dean suggests, "[i]n the space of capabilities, the individual is one step removed; she is objectively distanced from the relations of power which her identity and her life chances must be constituted" (2009, 266). In this regard, the approach may fall into the static, linear, and abstract spatio-temporality that the Social Model and vulnerability approaches have been critiqued for in earlier chapters. As such, legal responses which apply the capabilities approach may reinforce the normative legal subject and structures. In the consent to sex cases, for example, the provision of sex education is often lauded as a suitable response to facilitating capabilities; it provides information to bring an individual into line with a particular threshold of knowledge and understanding, yet purportedly avoids directing the individual or becoming overly interfering with their sexual choices. The result then is a reinforcement of a particular normative legal subject (one who is educated and informed yet making decisions freely without undue influence) as well as the inevitability of an individualised response.

The limits of the legal imaginary here, and the given-ness of responses which focus on, where possible, bringing the individual up to a particular normative threshold (as seen in *WMA* in the previous chapter), thus appears to mitigate against fully engaging with relationality in the spatial, dynamic, and ubiquitous way proposed in this book – the binary is thus constraining itself. As McKnight puts it, "the tool defines the problem rather than the problem defining the tool" (McKnight, 1977, 79): the individualised lens of capacity and best interests assessments thus diagnoses the problem as an internal, individual problem to be fixed, obscuring broader relational and spatial dynamics as part of the picture.

These limitations of current critical literatures similarly play out in debates as to broader legal reform in this area. In the context of Article 12 of the CRPD, whilst discussions often begin by problematising the binaries around disability/non-disability and capacity/incapacity, questions inevitably arise around appropriate responses and state obligations. Disability neutrality is often mooted as a potential way forward, as seen in Chapter 3. Such discussions attract concern that this would enable 'paternalistic interventions' in people's lives and widening the 'net' of these. This was unambiguously evident in the Law Commission's justification for limiting the legislation to those with cognitive impairments.

One of the suggestions stemming from Article 12 in the literature stems from Flynn and Arstein-Kerslake's proposal for what they term a "narrow disability-neutral legislative framework for state intervention in the lives of all adults" (Flynn and Arstein-Kerslake, 2017, 39) in which they define state intervention as "unwanted state involvement in the lives of adults" (Flynn and Arstein-Kerslake, 2017, 39). This they envisage would be triggered on the basis of "risk of imminent and serious harm for the individual's life, health or safety" (39), which they argue would result in *less* rather than *more* state intervention in the "private lives of all adults" (39).

Such proposals tend to problematically abstract decisions or actions rather than situating them within a temporal, spatial, and relational historicity which recognises the range of different actors involved over time. It perpetuates the idea that atomistic individuals are progressing through their lives along individual trajectories, uninterrupted by the state or others, but then encountering some potential harm which can thus, in certain circumstances, invite external interference. In many ways, this suggestion perpetuates many of the problems with the mental capacity legislation and the framing of incapacitous/

autonomous, interference/non-interference, which has begun to be problematised in previous chapters. Moreover, the idea that such a framework can be disability neutral at the outset is itself a problematic epistemological claim. At one level, this ignores the ableism that is built into the very structures and foundational assumptions of the liberal framework such proposals are balanced upon, which we have engaged with in earlier chapters. Moreover, it erases the actual lived experiences of disabled people within particular assemblages by reifying a static autonomous subject. Even if these proposals were built upon a more relational subject, the reification of the liberal concept of the state (as present yet separate; over-seeing yet not interfering), which is evident here and which the proposals rely on, mitigates against any meaningful depth to this relationality. As has been suggested and will be reiterated, the legal subject and the role of the state are mutually reinforcing features of the broader legal logics, with a number of binaries which they rely upon to frame the boundaries of these logics. Moreover, Steele rightly suggests that such purported neutrality can result in "legitimating the subtle and hidden ways in which law is complicit in violence against disabled people" (2017, 397). What is seemingly missing then is a more spatially and temporally sensitive appreciation of the ways in which law and legal responses can reinforce particular discourses and material iterations of the role of the state and ideals of the subject, which are themselves built on problematic foundations.

Similar debates around disability neutrality and CRPD compliance have begun to circulate around the potential of the inherent jurisdiction of the High Court to potentially attend to the relationality which the MCA can currently overlook. For example, if it cannot be shown that the impairment or disturbance in the functioning of the mind or brain is causally linked to the inability to make a decision under the mental capacity legislation, there may be latent concerns that some other force – often another individual – is preventing somebody from exercising their autonomy. There has been a recent resurgence in the use of the inherent jurisdiction to fill the gaps left by the legislative framework provided in the MCA (see Herring and Wall, 2015). Often, the use of the jurisdiction is premised upon responses which are facilitative of autonomy – one of the core ideas which underpins the jurisdiction – at least in theory – is that it is facilitative rather than dictatorial (*LBL v RYJ and VJ* [2010] EWHC 2665, per Macur J). This in some ways mitigates against some of the concerns that the mental capacity legislation can enforce interventions which are not necessarily in tune with the wishes and feelings of the individual whose capacity is questioned and can do little to enable or facilitate their autonomy. Moreover, the inherent jurisdiction route is seen by some as a more CRPD-compliant mechanism for responding to individuals whose decision making may be constrained. In particular, it is seen as enabling a disability neutral framework (although the concerns outlined above with purported neutrality must be borne in mind here) and also as resulting in interventions which are aimed at supporting decision making, rather than substituting decision making. However, what is interesting for our purposes here is to focus on the ways in which jurisdiction is deployed by the judiciary to rearticulate particular norms. Historically, the inherent jurisdiction can be seen as an outmoded historical antecedent and not in line with more modern approaches to autonomy, decision making, and the role of the state. Such reserved, seemingly unlimited powers for the state, with shaky legal foundations, went against the very idea of rights, proportionality, legal certainty, and individual freedom. Yet the increased recourse to inherent jurisdiction in this context demonstrates the way that jurisdiction is not static, and is often invoked to "remedy the internal contradictions and failures of modernist legal knowledge formats" (Valverde, 2015, 128). Moreover, the judicial reshaping and rearticulation of the scope of this jurisdiction are evident through the introduction of the logics of the MCA into the realm of the inherent jurisdiction. The inherent jurisdiction had been differentiated from the MCA in earlier case law, such as *A Local Authority v A* [2010] EWHC 1549 (Fam) on the basis that it was about enabling people to make autonomous decisions through being "facilitative" rather than "dictatorial". In many ways it was seen as allowing the judiciary to be more responsive than the MCA, given the broader range of responses that it could facilitate besides simply making best interests declarations. According to Parker J in *XCC v AA and Others* [2012] EWHC 2183 (COP),

> The protection or intervention of the inherent jurisdiction of the High Court is available to those lacking capacity within the meaning of the MCA as it is to capacitous but vulnerable adults who have had their will overborne, and on the same basis, where the remedy sought does not fall within the repertoire of remedies provided for in the MCA 2005. It would be unjustifiable and discriminatory not to grant the same relief to incapacitated adults who cannot consent as to capacitous adults whose will has been overborne.
>
> (para 54)

Yet, more recent case law suggests that the logics of the MCA are being transposed in order to reshape the inherent jurisdiction in the likeness of the more modern framework. For example, whilst we saw in *XCC v AA* that the court in invoking the inherent jurisdiction is not bound by the need to make an assessment of best interests on the basis of s4 of the MCA, it is purportedly able to exercise powers which may amount to a deprivation of liberty, or may make orders which err more on the side of dictatorial than facilitative.

An important recent case demonstrating the reach of the inherent jurisdiction and its potential as a purportedly disability neutral framework is *Southend-on-Sea v Meyers* [2019] EWHC 399 (Fam). This case involved a 97-year-old man, Mr Meyers, who had been living in his bungalow with his son. The conditions in the bungalow and the abusive, neglectful behaviour of the son toward Mr Meyers had been brought to the attention of the local authority, which in turn sought to discharge their safeguarding obligations. It became increasingly difficult for care and support to be delivered, particularly because of the obstructive behaviour of the son, but also because Mr Meyers began to refuse intervention. The local authority had sought declarations that they had discharged their duties and done all they could to assist Mr Meyers, and this was granted. However, a number of calls to the service from Mr Meyers over the subsequent months demonstrated an escalation in the severity of the living conditions, and Mr Meyers was persuaded to leave the bungalow to stay in a care home. However, he then expressed a clear wish to return back to the bungalow. The question then arose as to whether there was a legal basis upon which Mr Meyers could be prevented from doing so.

It was agreed that Mr Meyers had mental capacity, there being no cognitive impairment to bring Mr Meyers within the reach of the MCA. The inherent jurisdiction however was seen as the route in – not because of his physical disabilities (blindness) but because of the behaviour of his son, described by Hayden J as,

> needy, irrational, frequently out of control as well as manifestly emotionally dependent on a father who, despite the alarming history of this case, he obviously loves. KF's influence on his father is insidious and pervasive. It triggers Mr Meyers's sense of duty, guilt, love and responsibility. These, in my assessment, are pronounced facets of Mr Meyers's character, reflected in a different way in his sense of duty, love for his country and pride in his medals. In this particular context however, these admirable features of his personality have become confused and distorted in a relationship in which the two men have become so enmeshed that the autonomy of each has been compromised. In reality, KF exerts an influence over his father which is malign in its effect if not in its intention. The consequence is to disable Mr Meyers from making a truly informed decision which impacts directly on his health and survival.
>
> (para 41)

It was also held that, as a result of the authority provided by invoking the inherent jurisdiction, Mr Meyers could be prevented from living with his son. There was a concern as to whether such an order would deprive Mr Meyers of his liberty, yet Hayden J was careful to suggest that this was not the case as Mr Meyers would be free to live wherever he wanted, including the bungalow, so long as his son did not also live there (see paras 45 and 56). The point regarding deprivation of liberty will be returned to in the next chapter, yet for now the case is a clear example of the way that the inherent jurisdiction operates in an ostensibly disability neutral way, but that the responses flowing from being brought within the jurisdiction are individualised and suffused with ideas of 'fixing' the individual to gain or regain autonomy.

Despite the seemingly separate logics of the MCA and the inherent jurisdiction, we see that it does reinforce the powerful norms of the MCA as well as demonstrate the judicial shaping and reshaping of jurisdiction and consequent reinscription of particular norms. The key point here however is to recognise that the proposals or frameworks put forward to attend to the relationality which is increasingly being recognised in mental capacity scholarship, and/or to make the legal framework more 'CRPD compliant', still adhere to the boundaries of the liberal legal framework in terms of both subjectivity and the role of the state. There is an inevitability and a given-ness to these broader structural norms. They become seen as static background conditions, rather than active agents within ongoing processes and relations, resulting in responses and interventions being premised upon altering the individual, often in the service of enabling them to reach a particular normative threshold. As part of this, the state becomes seen as something which is there but is separate – it hovers over but does not interfere except in carefully circumscribed situations.

Complicating the state

Despite the significance of critical literatures and reform proposals in critiquing autonomy and disability, the other side of the binary – paternalism – and the ideas and role of the state which are bound up in this have thus far escaped critical interrogation. One of the key insights from the understanding of experience, of ontology and epistemology as being entangled with other agents, constantly becoming and being made and remade, is the recognition of the importance of these wider agents. As we have already seen, this requires a relational rather than an individualistic methodology. It also implicates agents such as the state and institutions as part of the making and unmaking of particular assemblages, in contrast to the more conventional legal analysis seen above, which situates the state and institutions as there but not interfering. We see that state and its institutions are not 'absent' at any point and have *always, already* been (intra-)acting, responding, and shaping in particular ways.

The assemblage analysis enabled through closer consideration of spatial dynamics and relationality allows us to complicate not just subjectivity as in the previous chapters, but also offers important tools for challenging these static ideas of the state: what it is, where it is, and how it operates. Geographical ideas of the state offer important insights here for legal analysis to build on. As Allen suggests, writing from a political geography perspective, it is important to locate the state, rather than repeating "centred" notions of the state and power, i.e. that see the state as a "unitary actor capable of controlling and commanding a particular territorial space" which "fail to consider how power and its commands are translated rather than transmitted across space" (Allen, 1999, 196). Building on geographical literatures on the assemblage (Anderson et al., 2012) and state power as part of this (Allen and Cochrane, 2010; Sassen, 2006) enables us to be attentive to the state as part of spatial and relational dynamics – to acknowledge the role of the state and institutions and, importantly, to think about ways that these dynamics could be shifted. The state is always historic and contingent. Moreover, through bringing this literature into conversation with geographical and political ecological ideas of scale, it is possible to more closely interrogate this translation through space, and to draw attention to the various different levels, times and locations at which 'interventions' or 'responses' can and do already take place, and their diffuse effects. What emerges is an understanding that responses are not and do not have to be seen at the individual level – indeed, the individual level or scale is multiply figured through "structural processes that span scales, across the body, family, community, nation and globe" (Faria et al., 1098). These insights, as well as offering important new approaches to mental capacity law and socio-legal scholarship more broadly, also enable a closer interrogation of legal processes and responses, which can, in turn, enrich the spatial and relational literature across critical geographies, geolegality, and political ecology. Moreover, complicating the state in this way, and being attentive to this socio-political ecology, offers a potential means to develop political theoretical approaches such as the capabilities approach discussed earlier, by providing a more critical understanding of the various processes and dynamics involved.

A number of points of clarification are important here before we go into more detail as to the precise critical tools for mental capacity law which flow from this theoretical lens. Firstly, this analysis does not seek to suggest that the state is a monolithic actor. Instead, being attentive to the various forces, flows, and dynamic processes enables us to take a more careful approach to how the state reveals and obscures itself, and the various iterations and forms which state involvement can take. The role of different institutions, entangled to varying degrees within the state apparatus, for example, becomes an important target for analysis, and we can trace the historicity of the shaping and framing of such institutions through the extent of perceived and actual state involvement.

Linked to this is the challenge posed by the assemblage analysis to the binary understanding of being inside/outside the state. As seen in Chapter 2, there is longstanding debate in law and political activism that has been focused on the extent to which critical and progressive movements should situate themselves either within state machinery or outside of it (Lobel, 2007). Yet, such debates can become problematic. At one level, it takes a static and monolithic view of the state and of law. As seen in Chapter 1, new materialist approaches have been drawn upon by legal scholars such as Davies in order to more fully expand our understanding of the concept of law and to highlight the pluralistic processes and relations involved in law as a practice. To unlimit law in the way that Davies calls for suggests a need to avoid positivist approaches to law such as those that underpin the inside/outside binary and calls for extra-legal routes for change. Moreover, at a deeper level, the inside/outside binary also overlooks the role that the state and institutions, including legal institutions, play even in their purported absence. As critiques of neoliberalism highlight, for example, often it is not the rolling back of the state which is occurring, but the *active shaping* by the state and institutions of a role for other forces – primarily, the market. Yet this space for the market requires active construction and reinforcement or reproduction over time, which occurs through a number of linked state and institutional processes. This 'absence' here is, paradoxically, creative and productive of new norms and spaces of regulation in itself. What emerges is the sense in which the state is always already there in particular forms and is already responding in particular ways. Thinking in terms of ongoing intra-actions and connections and the processes of entanglement over time challenges ideas of causality, responsibility, and intervention, which has important repercussions for the concepts underpinning mental capacity law.

In a similar vein, then, the purported extra-legal spaces in which activism is deemed to be able to occur are similarly shaped by state and institutional processes over time, including in their supposed absence. Being attentive to the ways in which such processes occur and are entangled with other actors, including the state, provides a much richer account for enabling change and transformation over time. Similarly, to ignore or overlook the role of the state in these processes can work to paradoxically reinforce the very position that activists seek to push against – that the state has no role or responsibility in relation to social justice (Lobel, 2007). The inside/outside binary which becomes perpetuated through such an approach also reinforces the idea of the state and the individual as separate and separable finite entities, with individuals working along a particular trajectory unimpeded and without interference from the state. As we have seen, such an approach reinforces problematic norms around responsibility, placing it upon the individual and obscuring the tangible role of the state in the material and discursive production of experience. Instead, in highlighting the role of state and institutional processes, in relation to other actors and forces, we can be more attentive to such responsibility but also, more importantly, how these dynamics can be reconfigured to produce different effects. As Cornwall puts it, the "legal arena is both a state of oppression and an important means of social transformation" (2013, ix). As will be seen below, this allows us to think more carefully about the scale and types of intervention that are currently occurring and which can occur, as well as how current responses or interventions may reinforce and reinscribe problematic norms and effects.

A further concern to be addressed here is the idea that such an account may presume a benign or benevolent state in a context in which critique has suggested, on the contrary, that the state is often acting in ways which (re) produce epistemic and material violence. This concern tracks a similar debate in legal scholarship as to whether we should look to the law to solve problems highlighted through critical work, if law is itself creating and/or reproducing these problems (see Munro, 2007, 64). Yet, as Munro questions, "why, if law can be powerful in entrenching, expressing and maintaining women's oppression, legal critique and reform cannot hold out at least some prospect of progress" (Munro, 2007, 69). To reiterate the discussion from Chapter 1, law is not a fixed or static entity. As Davies reminds us, law is not superstructural and abstract, but is (always, already) responsive and relational (Davies, 2017, 157–8). If we turn away from this, and turn away from law and state processes, then we leave this power and these processes unchecked, yet still occurring outside of the margins of our debate.

Yet concerns still abound in the critical literature. Delaney, for example, views the turn to the state as a limiting factor in critical theory.

> under current institutional conditions in much of the world, even those projects that we might comfortably identify as counter-hegemonic are strategically compelled to go through 'the state' or state institutions in order to even compete effectively. That fact alone – a fact which implicates the centrality of statist legalism, legal positivism, ideologies of sovereignty, and the presumptive legitimacy of state (that is 'authorized') violence – necessarily imposes severe limitations on what kinds of worlds can even be imagined, much less brought into being.
>
> (Delaney, 2010, 149)

It is important then to recognise that the point here is not to argue that the state, or law, alone should be the source of change or transformation. It is to draw attention to the role that the state and institutions currently *do* play in order to consider ways in which these processes can be changed, and to consider the productive effects of such changes in terms of reconfiguring assemblages. Neither is this to situate the state as the ontologically prior or primary actor in an assemblage, or as the sole force for change. Reconfigurations between different actors are, of course, multidirectional and multimodal, occurring at different temporalities and scales. Different institutional relations will affect and be affected by state responses, for example. However, law does have a particularly important role in terms of drawing boundaries around responsibility and different actors, as well as working to foreclose the responsibilities of others. In this vein, it is important to focus on the particular role that law does play in mediating, creating, framing, and reshaping these different relations between actors and the productive material and discursive effects of these.

Rethinking responses

Rethinking the state through the assemblage analysis offers novel ways to approach ideas of responsibility, responses, and interventions. In the remainder of this section, what this analysis means specifically in the mental capacity context will be considered, but this analysis provides important insights for other areas of critical legal analysis focused on social change and oppressed groups. Attention will be drawn to the non-linear and diffuse nature of change over time and at different levels. The idea of scale will be particularly important here for recognising that changes at different scales in the topography of an assemblage will impact elsewhere in the assemblage but also in other linked spaces. In this sense, scales are not fixed and hierarchical, but "socially constructed, relational, contingent and contested" (Neumann, 2015, 475). Rather than an individualistic lens premised on interventions taking place as isolated events, in response to a particular crisis or concern as to an individual's welfare, we can trace the ongoing involvement and responses that have occurred over time in the creation of a particular phenomenon. These do not need to have taken place at a purely individual level but take into account the ways in which interventions or responses at a more macro scale will impact at the micro scale. To add here, however, the idea of macro and micro scales as separate and separable planes is problematic and is not supported by this approach, and it is important to see scales as closely interwoven. As Davies puts it, scales are not fixed; they are not like "Russian dolls" (Davies, 2017, 95) but are the "product of normative environments and analytical choices" (95). She goes on to add,

> it is also possible to see that a change in scale involves (by definition) a change in frame of reference, and also in the modes of authority, the definition of a legal subject, the sources of normativity, the affective ties between norms and subjects, and so forth. Certain elements are made visible, while others recede.
>
> (Davies, 2017, 106)

Temporality similarly emerges as an important consideration in the framing of the debate here, with recognition given to the ways in which processes and relations fold, unfold, and reshape over time, and with different temporalities evident in different legal and governance logics occurring in relation to a particular issue. Moreover, power will be seen to be an important factor in the analysis of the role of the state and law here. However, contrary to more conventional analyses of power (particularly in debates as to autonomy and empowerment), this spatial and relational approach, drawing on the idea of the assemblage, critiques what Allen terms "centred" views of power (Allen, 1999). Instead, and in contrast to this, power becomes a much more diffuse force, which is both creative and potentially dominating, but also one which shifts and transforms as it moves through different relations. In this sense, power is "actively constituted through space" (Allen, 1999, 197), and attentiveness to this will provide an important rejoinder to linear and static ideas of power and empowerment through state interventions in the lives of individuals.

What this emphasis on relationality, scale, temporality, power, and jurisdiction enables is a clearer articulation of the connections between subjectivity and the role of the state in the framing and shaping (and recursive reinforcement) of responsibilities and responses. Moreover, we can see how such processes challenge the given-ness and common sense nature in which such boundaries are currently deployed, providing the tools with which to imagine – and ultimately to construct – them otherwise. When recognition is given to the way in which the state and structures/institutions have been involved in shaping contexts and norms over time, these binaries start to dissolve. The structural embeddedness that instead becomes central illuminates the impact of particular modes of governance and law and policy over time which have shaped and defined current problems. Brown and Halley, for example, cautioned that "legalism has ways of hiding its presence, or providing background rules so backgrounded that we can forget they are there" (Brown and Halley,

2002, 12). This echoes the insights from some of the vulnerability theorists who similarly point out the way in which certain structural supports which enable people to function in line with particular norms – such as being autonomous and self-determining – are invisibilised in liberal discourses. This brings into focus the social, economic, political, and structural vulnerability faced by all citizens in a society or community who are dependent on a network of background supports and structures. Leach Scully suggests that "permitted dependencies are naturalised and normalised. They are met and supported without question" (Leach Scully, 2014, 217). The current invisibilty (or, perhaps, deliberate obfuscation) of this has harmful consequences when those who need support are then categorised as different, or 'other'. Recognition of the shared embeddedness within networks enables us to change the perspective; the question becomes not "should we respond or intervene?" as it often is in current debates in mental capacity and adult social care, but "what is the *current* response or intervention *doing*"?

Intervention

This recognition invites us to change the way in which we conceptualise interventions. Interventions tend to be seen as one-off 'events' with a linear trajectory between the intervener (a social worker, a doctor, for example) and the intervened (such as a person deemed to lack capacity who is given a treatment in their best interests). Yet this tends to detemporalise interventions and ignore their historic roots and potentially diffuse ongoing impacts. This is particularly evident in *A Local Authority v H (No 2)* [2019] EWCOP 51, in which the Court of Protection was concerned with best interests decision making in relation to contact. In the case, H was assessed as having capacity to consent to sex, but lacking capacity in relation to contact. Aside from the framing of the case as being about "an inherent conflict between its desire to promote the autonomy if the protected person – in other words to give H such freedom as reasonably she can have – and a need to protect the relevant person" (para 25), we can also see the conceptualisation of responses here as being self-contained and not encroaching beyond legitimate boundaries. Hedley J stated that,

> The next general observation is that in my view any coercive powers should always be framed within the limitations of the area where the party lacks capacity; that is particularly important in a case like this because the coercive powers must not make any mention of the question of how sexual relations or anything else are exercised. They are simply not the court's business. The court's business is simply to deal with best interests arising out of the fact that H lacks capacity to decide with whom she should come into contact.
>
> (para 32)

In doing so, Hedley J was also at pains to state that (again, reaffirming the importance of autonomy and individual liberty),

> It is not the function of the court, it is not the function of the local authority to ensure that H lives a moral life. That is her business. It is only the function of the court and the local authority to regulate who it is she comes into contact with.
>
> (para 33)

Such statements attempt to put such decisions into silos, carefully containing the effects of such decisions within the correct boundaries. Yet this overlooks the broader consequences flowing from interfering with such decisions and their inevitable leakage and impact in other areas. These interventions play an active role in reconfiguring broader relations far beyond purportedly singular decisions, portrayed as a brief interference and then retreat by the state. Moreover, the overarching presence of the MCA and the power relations its spectre will inculcate in H's everyday decision making, beyond the confines of decisions as to 'contact' is left unsaid here. This careful separation of different decisions and their location is given a starkly material illustration in the following paragraph from Hedley J's judgment,

> I think this is probably best illustrated by considering the position within the property in which H currently lives. The local authority have and will retain the power to maintain or monitor the list of welcomed visitors to H's flat. Whilst of course they cannot impose on H anyone she does not want, they do have a veto in relation to anyone that H might want. They may further provide for those times at which a visitor is to be in the flat and the times when that should end. But once that visitor lawfully enters the flat and the front door is shut, the local authority have no further responsibilities for what then takes place. Those are matters entirely for H and the person who is in the flat with her.
>
> (para 34)

Thinking in terms of assemblages and entanglements of actors illustrates the various different levels, scales, and locations that interventions can take place at, and the repercussions that this can have in other locations. Interventions and responses are not linear, and the way in which we conceptualise responses in this context needs to be rethought so that they are not – or not only – located at an individual level. Responses are already occurring – through legal iteration and reiteration in judgments and in professional deployment of norms; through the administration of adult social care policy and the discretionary powers around service provision; through the differentiation and categorisation occurring in the day-to-day practices and applications of the legal framework (i.e. through jurisdictional debates, as will be seen in Chapter 7); through the policy shifts occurring 'outside' of the context of mental capacity law which shape the idea of the state; through bureaucratic processes in care and service provision in hospitals; and so on. Moreover, these ongoing responses are not linear. Recognising the interwoven nature of scale allows us to see that changes in one scale or at what is seen as a macro level have a diffuse impact across an assemblage (and, likewise, shifts at micro levels similarly resonate through the assemblage). Responses which are seen as being individually focused, such as a best interests decision or a decision to provide access to a particular service, ripple outwards and have topological impacts across the terrain. At the same time, those which are seen as purely political shifts will similarly impact at the interpersonal level. Yet it is important to note that this is not a linear process, despite the way it is often presented in mental capacity debates. Aside from the differing temporalities of these responses and their effects over time, we must also be attentive to the productive effects of these in terms of power relations. Power, in this vein, is not a static entity which is "transmitted" between different agents, but must instead be seen as a productive, generative, and shifting force which is "transformed" as it travels across spatial relations (Allen, 1999, 197). Again, the effects of this are diffuse rather than linear and generative rather than entailing a zero-sum game of power/powerlessness.

Empowerment

If empowerment is a goal in law and policy, as it is claimed to be in the MCA, then it ought to be recognised that this is not a product or quality of an individual, but a result of processes over time. As Rushing has argued previously,

> the problem is not how to empower pre-existing citizen-subjects who experience themselves as powerless in the face of those who exercise power over them. The problem is diagnosing precisely how 'technologies of citizenship' function in microlevels of day to day activities to produce subjects of empowerment.
>
> (Rushing, 2016)

This draws attention to the impact of broader rules and practices and professional relations, and how these processes impact on individuals. At present, there is a danger that we locate empowerment in a uni-directional relationship between the professional and the person who is to 'become empowered', which ignores the way in which this power is often created by and (re)produced by professional knowledge practices.

Locating empowerment at an individual level and seeing somebody as 'being empowered' through an individualised intervention emanating from a particular professional is also problematic as it reinforces the idea that the source of the problem, and consequently the location of change, is the particular individual. This can in turn reinforce problematic binaries that see people or categories as 'other' and in need of 'fixing' to reach a particular norm – in this context, an able-bodied, self-determining norm. Similar cautionary tales have been levelled at the focus on resilience in vulnerability theory. As Lotz argues,

> it is of vital importance, therefore, that the significance and role of resilience in human wellbeing and flourishing not be interpreted in an individualistic and voluntaristic manner, to be an individual project or 'boot strapping' exercise ... The development of resilience in individuals must therefore be acknowledged to be a fundamentally social and collective task and achievement, and not the responsibility solely of individuals themselves, nor a function purely of individual will and determination.
>
> (Lotz, 2016, 57)

This emphasises the importance of the structural bases and processes enabling empowerment. Whilst this is said to be a policy goal or value at present, the ability for this to be realised is constrained by the binaries shaping the legal and policy frameworks. Rather than seeing the state as 'responding' once a lack of agency or capacity is 'diagnosed', focusing on the role of the state and institutions and their historicity, and the ongoing spatial and temporal processes, signals alternative sites for responses, and routes for empowerment. Such empowerment is seen not as an individual achievement or attribute, but as produced and enabled through interactions within the assemblage.

In this way, rethinking the role of the state through the assemblage, complicating hierarchical approaches to scale and signalling the need for new approaches to responses and interventions has the potential to enrich capabilities approaches. Some of the problems with current applications of capabilities approaches were highlighted earlier in the chapter and cohere around the individualistic and liberal norms that it perpetuates, and the limited utility of the approach as "a normative rather than an explanatory tool suited to critical social theory" (Kremakova, 2013, 394). At the heart of these critiques is the concern that capabilities theory and applications of it have often been "combined with inadequate theories of society, particularly regarding the external conditions enabling or limiting capabilities" (Sayer, 2012, 580). The spatial and relational account however may offer a more nuanced way to consider the dynamics, historicity, and contingencies within which exclusionary norms and social arrangements are reproduced through assemblages. In doing so, it might provide a way to move away from an individualistic approach to capabilities and to think about alternative sites of response and intervention which enable agency.

It is central to this rethinking that the need for protection is not seen as an exception or as a stand-alone obligation for those who fail to meet the characteristics of the autonomous norm. As discussed in previous sections, ideas of empowerment and protection ought to be seen as ongoing and interwoven processes which do not emanate in linear ways – they are products of complex and entangled relations between various forces and actors. Questions of empowerment, protection, and paternalism become issues for all when it is recognised that we are all dependent upon and embedded within particular material, discursive, technological, institutional, economic, environmental, and cultural configurations. Empowerment and protection become similarly embedded concepts, rather than abstract ideals which stem from one-off interjections into individual lives. They are ongoing, mutually interwoven consequences of an array of entangled forces and processes. Exposing this dense scaffolding that we are all entangled in sits uneasily with the Law Commission's justification highlighted in Chapter 2 for having a 'diagnostic threshold' in the mental capacity legislation. There was a fear central to this that they did not want to enable paternalistic interventions into the lives of those who were 'merely eccentric' – yet there was a shrouding here of the interventions and responses that all in society are already embedded in. What this also ignored is the sheer scope for creativity that faced the Law Commission in terms of what responsibilities, responses, or interventions *could have* been created by the legislation.

This is of particular importance for those seeking to craft progressive legal approaches in the wake of the CRPD. The previous discussion has highlighted some of the problematic approaches to Article 12 which have circulated in the literature and reinforced ideals of the state and the legal subject. We see this entrenched further still in debates as to Article 12 and Article 16 of the Convention, whereby discussion has become mapped onto the autonomy/paternalism, empowerment/protection dichotomy. Art 16 is concerned with freedom from exploitation, violence, and abuse and contains obligations to protect persons with disabilities from these both within and outside the home. Yet, again, some have been concerned that this somehow 'jars' with Article 12 and enables paternalistic interference in decisions, potentially undermining the Convention as a whole (Dawson, 2015). However, such a view problematically maintains the idea of the free and unencumbered subject as well as seeing Article 12 as simply equating to autonomy and non-interference by the state. It is important that progressive reform proposals do not fall back into the well-worn empowerment/protection binary here, given the language of protection in Art 16. If Art 12 and Art 16 are viewed in terms of this binary approach then the much-lauded paradigm shift in thinking will not occur. Rethinking the paradigm and effecting the 'shift' requires that questions of causality, responsibility, and interventions are rethought in the ways offered here, through locating the state as part of assemblages.

Scale: state-community-individual

Moreover, as discussed above, the concept of the assemblage, when interwoven with work on scale (as contingent and relational, rather than hierarchical), offers an important challenge to critical work which seeks to locate responses either in the community (at a local level) or at the level of the state. Recognising that these are not separate or separable sites enables more nuanced arguments for legal change, particularly in the context of Article 19 of the CRPD. This

Article is particularly important in challenging the current spatio-temporality of the current legal framework. It is concerned with living independently and being included in the community, stating that:

> States Parties to the present Convention recognize the equal right of all persons with disabilities to live in the community, with choices equal to others, and shall take effective and appropriate measures to facilitate full enjoyment by persons with disabilities of this right and their full inclusion and participation in the community.

At one level, it places clear obligations upon States Parties to actualise the right. It is not simply about negative non-interference. When read alongside and through Articles 12 and 16, the concern as to whether these mean the state should take a 'hands-off' approach and simply leave people alone (putting to one side the fallacy inherent in this view, given the state's ubiquitous presence) become less pressing as it is clear that the state is conceptualised as having an active role in actualising the Convention.

As seen in previous discussions, however, there is a danger that ideas of independence, choice, and control can take on a particularly (neo)liberal flavour through policies which are actually premised upon reducing state resources to enable these. There has been the initial shaping of such an approach in England and Wales through the Care Act 2014 and case law which engages with it. The case of *Davey v Oxfordshire CC* [2017] EWHC 354 (Admin) is particularly instructive here. The case involved Luke Davey, a disabled adult who had been supported by a team of personal assistants almost 24 hours per day. This support was vital to his independence. However, following the closure of the Independent Living Fund, the local authority assessed his needs and felt that his eligible needs could be met for less, essentially resulting in a significant cut to his personal budget and, in turn, to the amount of support he would be able to access.

In endorsing this decision, and the assessment of needs that this was premised upon, Morris J stated that,

> the relevant need to which spending more time alone is addressed is the need to "develop independence and reduce anxiety". Spending more time alone is the means of achieving that … and this will be developed by spending time without his carers present … [I]n her witness statement, Ms Lovelock accepted that the Claimant does experience anxiety when left alone, but that she assessed that the need, and the way to reduce that anxiety, was to develop greater independence rather than a need never to be left alone.
>
> (para 120)

The assessment that Luke's independence would be enabled by a *reduction* in his support, with more time spent alone, is particularly striking in relation to the discussion above as to the idea of the state as not interfering, and as autonomy or empowerment stemming from the individual as a silo. It is also a matter of concern that this deeply problematic reasoning has been enabled by the application of the Care Act which, at least facially, purports to be about facilitating wellbeing; moreover, that it was endorsed through a judicial process. Those seeking to leverage Article 19 as a progressive site for legal change need to be wary of reinforcing this constrained idea of independence as located in the individual, placing state intervention as antithetical to it.

Moreover, a broader issue emerges as to how the community is understood and framed as part of legal responses. There is a risk that the community may be viewed as a separate entity, as distinct from the state, and overlook the myriad ways in which the state plays a role in the shaping of the community even in its claimed absence. As Shepherd puts it,

> A faith in the therapeutic power of the community is part of what Dean and Villadsen refers to as "fetishizing the local" that accompanies an aversion to the state ... When we think of society in terms of a withered state replaced by "an emergent field of contestation and experimental self-creation", it becomes very difficult to even think about broader social structure.
>
> (Shepherd, 2019, 344)

As part of this, there is also a need to be attentive to the problematic spatialisation of 'the community', which may occur through the deployment of legal and policy developments. Jarrett, for example, suggests the need to be aware of the historically contingent nature of the term and how ideas of "inclusion" can emanate differently from these shifts (Jarrett, 2015, 112). He points to the very recent history of segregation and isolation of disabled people, contrasting this to the previous position in the 18th century where "their status as community members was never strongly questioned" (Jarrett, 2015, 111). We have moved now, through this trajectory, to a position where discussion of inclusion within the community,

> suggests a notion of a community that people with intellectual disabilities visit, or to which they are 'acculturated', from a liminal service space neither fully within nor fully outside it. When 'community' is talked about in this way it refers to a space to which 'we', the non-intellectually disabled, belong, and which 'they', the intellectually disabled, are given support to 'access', a process managed and negotiated through a series of quality of life assessments, risk profiles, funding decisions, and personalized plans.
>
> (Jarrett, 2015, 108)

Recognising this, there is a need to tread carefully in conceptualising the community and spaces within/without it, and the different actors and norms involved in shaping and constructing it. Such concerns will be returned to in the next chapter, which considers the static materiality of institutions and the boundaries drawn around them through law and policy.

Thus Article 19 *can* provide an important challenge to current ways of viewing the state and its role in relation to enabling inclusion within the community. This 'inclusion' may be problematic, however, if situated within a framework built on the ideal of the autonomous liberal norm and wider logics of this, and work is to be done to facilitate the idea of the transformation of the community itself, and recognition of the state's role within it, as part of the broader potential of the CRPD. Thinking through the assemblage offers the tools to do this, and to avoid reifying a hierarchical or bounded scalar structure of state-community-individual.

Conclusion

This chapter has highlighted the bounded nature of the role of the state, which is interwoven, and mutually dependent on, the liberal legal subject. This has worked to produce and reproduce a binary frame of autonomy/paternalism and empowerment/protection in legal and policy debate and, at the same time, has resulted in the obscuring of the ongoing role of the state and institutions in varying ways as part of the "distributions of meaning and modes of exclusion practiced by law" (Davies, 2017, 141). This negative interference model, based on the importance of a zone of self-determination, has naturalised existing boundaries of debate, furnishing them with a given-ness which forecloses alternative trajectories. This is particularly evident in the scholarly discourse around the CRPD at present, which problematically reinforces norms of legal subjectivity and the role of the state through the binary deployment of Article 12 (and, similarly, Article 16). The thin conceptualisation of responsibility and responses which inhabits these logics works to prevent recognition of broader processes implicated in the constitution and representation of legal problems and as such stymies transformative thinking. Rethinking the state and being attentive to issues such as responsibility, power, jurisdiction, scale, and temporality provides critical tools to begin to challenge these binary frames and to disentangle these broader boundaries.

This foreclosure of transformative potential is not a new phenomenon: Sheppard, citing Krieger, points to the ways in which "entrenched norms and institutionalized practices, operating as taken-for-granted background rules, systematically skew the interpretations of transformative legal rules so that those rules increasingly come to resemble the normative and institutional systems they were intended to displace" (Sheppard, 2010, 486). The assemblage analysis offered through a more relationally and spatially situated approach to law allows us not just to be cognisant of the role of the state in spaces in which it claims to be absent, but also to draw attention to the processes occurring in the production and reproduction of these exclusionary legal norms around the subject and the state. In the remaining chapters, closer attention will be drawn to these ongoing processes and to the issues of jurisdiction, scale, and responsibility which have been introduced here, particularly in the context of the pervasive public/private divide and freedom/

interference. It is important to pay close attention to these processes if we want to engage with the potential disruption and transformation or reconfiguration of these logics.

References

Allen, J. 1999. 'Spatial Assemblages of Power: From Domination to Empowerment' in D. Massey, J. Allen and P. Sarre (Eds), *Human Geography Today*. Cambridge: Polity Press. 194–218.

Allen, J. and Cochrane, A. 2010. 'Assemblages of State Power: Topological Shifts in the Organization of Government and Politics' *Antipode* 42(5), 1071–89.

Anderson, B., Kearnes, M., McFarlane, C. and Swanton, D. 2012. 'On Assemblages and Geography' *Dialogues in Human Geography* 2(2), 171–89.

Baylies, C. 2002. 'Disability and the Notion of Human Development: Questions of Rights and Capabilities' *Disability & Society* 17(7), 725–39.

Brown, K. 2014. 'Questioning the Vulnerability Zeitgeist: Care and Control Practices with "Vulnerable" Young People' *Social Policy and Society* 34(3), 371–87.

Brown, W. and Halley, J. 2002. *Left Legalism/Left Critique*. Durham: Duke University Press.

Clough, B. 2016. 'Anorexia, Capacity, and Best Interests: Developments in the Court of Protection Since the Mental Capacity Act 2005' *Medical Law Review* 24(3), 434–45.

Daniel, B. 2010. 'Concepts of Adversity, Risk, Vulnerability and Resilience: A Discussion in the Context of the "Child Protection System"' *Social Policy and Society* 9(2), 231–41.

Davies, M. 2017. *Law Unlimited*. Oxfordshire: Routledge.

Dawson, J. 2015. 'A Realistic Approach to Assessing Mental Health Laws' Compliance with the UNCRPD' *International Journal of Law and Psychiatry* 40, 70–9.

Dean, H. 2009. 'Critiquing Capabilities: The Distractions of a Beguiling Concept' *Critical Social Policy* 29(2), 261–78.

Delaney, D. 2010. *Nomospheric Investigations: The Spatial, The Legal and The Pragmatics of World Making*. Oxfordshire: Routledge.

Dunn, M., Clare, I. and Holland, A. 2008. 'To Empower or Protect? Constructing the Vulnerable Adult in English Law and Public Policy' *Legal Studies* 28(2), 234–53.

Faria, C. et al. 2020. 'Embodied Exhibits: Toward a Feminist Geographic Courtroom Ethnography' *Annals of the American Association of Geographers* 110(4), 1095–113.

Fawcett, B. 2009. 'Vulnerability: Questioning the Certainties in Social Work and Health' *International Journal of Social Work* 52, 473–84.

Flynn, E. and Arstein-Kerslake, A. 2017. 'State Intervention in the Lives of People with Disabilities: The Case for a Disability-Neutral Framework' *International Journal of Law in Context* 13(1), 39–57.

Flynn, M. 2007. *The Murder of Steven Hoskin: A Serious Case Review*. Cornwall Adult Protection Committee. https://www.scie-socialcareonline.org.uk/the-murder-of-steven-hoskin-a-serious-case-review-executive-summary/r/a11G00000017tmDIAQ last accessed 26/6/2021.

Harnacke, C. 2013. 'Disability and Capability: Exploring the Usefulness of Martha Nussbaum's Capabilities Approach for the UN Disability Rights Convention' *The Journal of Law, Medicine & Ethics* 41(4), 768–80.

Herring, J. and Wall, J. 2015. 'Autonomy, Capacity and Vulnerable Adults: Filling the Gaps in the Mental Capacity Act' *Legal Studies* 35(4), 698–719.

Hollomotz, A. 2009. 'Beyond "Vulnerability": An Ecological Model Approach to Conceptualizing Risk of Sexual Violence Against People with Learning Difficulties' *British Journal of Social Work* 39, 99–112.

Hollomotz, A. 2011. *Learning Difficulties and Sexual Vulnerability: A Social Approach*. London: Jessica Kingsley.

Jarrett, S. 2015. 'The Meaning of "Community" in the Lives of People with Intellectual Disabilities: An Historical Perspective' *International Journal of Developmental Disability* 61(2), 107–12.

Keywood, K., Fovargue, S. J. and Flynn, M. 1999. *Best Practice? Health Care Decision-Making By, With and For Adults with Learning Disabilities*. Manchester, UK: National Development Team.

Kremakova, M. 2013. 'Too Soft for Economics, Too Rigid for Sociology, or Just Right? The Productive Ambiguities of Sen's Capability Approach' *European Journal of Sociology* 54(3), 393–419.

Leach Scully, J. 2014. 'Disability and Vulnerability: On Bodies, Dependence and Power' in C. Mackenzie, W. Rogers and S. Dodds (Eds) *Vulnerability: New Essays in Ethics and Feminist Philosophy*. Oxford: Oxford University Press, 204–21.

Lindsey, J. and Harding, R. 2021. 'Capabilities, Capacity, and Consent: Sexual Intimacy in the Court of Protection' *Journal of Law and Society* 48(1), 60–83.

Lobel, O. 2007. 'The Paradox of Extralegal Activism: Critical Legal Consciousness and Transformative Politics' *Harvard Law Review* 120(4), 937–88.

Lotz, M. 2016. 'Vulnerability and Resilience: A Critical Nexus' *Theoretical Medicine and Bioethics* 37(1), 45–59.

McKnight, J. 1977. 'Professionalized Service and Disabling Help' in I. Illich (Ed), *Disabling Professions*. London: Marion Boyars. 69–92.

Munro, V. 2007. *Law and Politics at the Perimeter: Re-evaluating Key Debates in Feminist Theory*. Oxford: Hart.

Neumann, R. P. 2015. 'Political Ecology of Scale' in R. Bryant (Ed), *The International Handbook of Political Ecology*. Cheltenham: Elgar. 475–86.

Robeyns, I 2005. 'The Capability Approach: A Theoretical Survey' *Journal of Human Development* 6(1), 93–117.

Rushing, S. 2016. 'What's Left of "Empowerment" after Neoliberalism?' *Theory and Event* 19(1).

Sassen, S. 2006 *Territory, Authority, Rights: From Medieval to Global Assemblages*. Princeton: Princeton University Press.

Sayer, A. 2012. 'Capabilities, Contributive Injustice and Unequal Divisions of Labour' *Journal of Human Development and Capabilities* 13(4), 580–96.

Sen, A. 1999. *Development as Freedom*. Oxford: Oxford University Press.

Series, L. 2015. 'Relationships, Autonomy and Legal Capacity: Mental Capacity and Support Paradigms' *International Journal of Law and Psychiatry* 40, 80–91.

Shepherd, N. 2019. 'Governing through Freedom: Mental Health Care in the Age of Empowerment' *Critical Policy Studies* 13(3), 328–44.

Sheppard, C. 2010. *Inclusive Equality: The Relational Dimensions of Systemic Discrimination in Canada*. Montreal: McGill-Queen's University Press.

Steele, L. 2017. 'Temporality, Disability and Institutional Violence: Revisiting In re F' *Griffith Law Review* 26(3), 378–400.

Valverde, M. 2015. *Chronotopes of Law: Jurisdiction. Scale and Governance*. Oxon: Routledge.

6 Freedom/deprivation of liberty

The logics of liberty in mental capacity law

This chapter traces the boundaries that are created around spaces, the subject, and the state through legal processes and discourses of liberty. Again, this is an area heavily steeped in the organising binaries which have been explored in previous chapters. Here, these will be seen to be mutually dependent upon the ideal of liberty, which manifests itself in the current mental capacity legal framework through distinctions between freedom/restraint (or deprivation of liberty) as well as negative/positive ideas of how liberty is realised. Jennings suggests that concepts such as liberty should be understood as "forming a semantic web of mutual implication" (2015, 10) and calls for a contextualised look at the work that such concepts can do and are doing in particular localised sites, as well as the discursive webs within which they are entangled. As seen throughout this book so far, liberal legal concepts such as autonomy, self-determination, capacity, and liberty do form (and are recursively formed by) such a semantic, discursive, and agential web and these effects are produced through a number of different legal mechanisms and techniques. This chapter engages with the need to understand and, in turn, dismantle these webs in relation to the idea of liberty in mental capacity law. There is a need to more carefully trace relations between different concepts and the practices and effects which these produce and the historical context of their production. Law's (re) production of boundedness – of selves and spaces – will be again seen as central to the workings of these processes.

Liberty is a heavily contested ideal, however debates in social theory and political philosophy tend to range between liberal and republican accounts of liberty. At the same time, these positions often reinforce the image of the bounded self and spaces, and the either/or absence/presence of the state. Rather than seeing liberty as something which is a property of an individual, to be wielded against the state or an institution, liberty will instead be understood as a relational dynamic, through the spatial lens of the assemblage. Whilst the materiality of liberty is indeed important, spatial approaches expose the more fluid nature of materiality and the boundaries which impact on the agentic abilities of individuals. Considering the webs of relations which shape agency and experience, including the institutional inter-relations, will move the focus away from debates as to when the state should intervene and whether the state

DOI: 10.4324/9781351067881-6

has or will transgress certain material or ideological boundaries in doing so. A focus on relational dynamics instead allows us to trace and acknowledge the various relations and their effects, as well as shifting the focus away from securing these imagined borders and towards facilitating and generating new relations. In this way, the assemblage approach goes beyond current purportedly progressive literatures which engage with ideas of republicanism or capabilities, offering a new perspective on freedom which is not entangled with liberal logics.

After outlining the current conceptual terrain around liberty and progressive approaches, the legal landscape will be introduced in order to orientate the reader to some of the current challenges taking place for the concept of 'liberty' in mental capacity law, demonstrating why this is a particularly opportune moment to introduce new conceptual approaches. The chapter then considers in more depth the underlying logics of liberty residing in this legal framework, tracing this through the mental capacity jurisprudence. The critical analysis built in previous chapters will be further developed in order to engage with the centrality of 'freedom from interference', the very static materiality of liberty underpinning the Deprivation of Liberty Safeguards (DoLS), the shaping and rendering of the legal subject through the legal dynamics of liberty, and uncovering the state through such processes. It will be seen that there is a real physicality, materiality, and boundedness to current legal approaches to liberty which belies the broader sources of control, constraint, and domination that inflect and shape the everyday experiences and empowerment of individuals. Thinking more relationally about liberty offers ways to expose what is currently hidden in legal and conceptual frameworks, as well as new ways to think about responses. Whilst the focus is on mental capacity law, these insights engage with and take forward current debates in geography, political theory, and philosophy, as well as providing critical legal tools for other social justice movements which engage with ideas of liberty.

Critiquing the liberal logics of liberty

This section offers an outline of how focusing on relationality and the dynamic, shifting processes and intra-actions between a number of agents provides an alternative critical vantage point to the traditional debates around liberty. It is not possible within the confines of this book to give a full account of the various instantiations of the linked concepts of liberty and freedom in political liberalism. Indeed, as Kapur points out, liberalism is an "elusive and paradoxical concept" (2018, 27) with extensive debate over its meaning. Yet, as Kapur goes on to suggest, we can trace common assumptions through key liberal political theorists (such as Mill and Berlin, for example); "first, that freedom is a progressive, external pursuit, which is owned or possessed; second, related to the first, that freedom originates or is accessed through the consciously exerted will of a finite, thinking, individual subject" (2018, 27). Central to this is the idea of freedom *from* the state, or, alternatively, the idea of non-interference by the state in the individual pursuit of freedom. Through this lens, the liberty of the subject is threatened by external constraints such as state interference or interference by others. Berlin's famous *Two Concepts of Liberty* broadly align to this. The first, negative liberty, is manifested through the idea of the absence of constraint. The second, positive liberty, is concerned with self-mastery or self-realisation, as opposed to being acted upon by external forces: to be "moved by reasons, by conscious purposes, which are my own, not by causes which affect me, as it were, from outside" (Berlin, 1969).

The centrality of such a rendering of liberty in political liberalism has been heavily criticised by many, with republican scholars in particular posing some of the more potent challenges to this framing. As Shnayderman outlines, central to republican accounts of freedom is the idea that it "should not be conceived of as the absence of interference, but rather as the absence of domination, that is, the absence of arbitrary power to intervene" (2015, 241). Republican political theorists such as Phillip Pettit and Quentin Skinner have given a number of examples of why the liberal account of negative liberty (i.e. the non-interference account) fails to capture the complex realities of freedom (Pettit, 2001, 1997; Skinner, 1997). Such theorists have drawn on examples such as the "contented slave" who has a benign master – one who possesses the arbitrary power to interfere in the slave's life yet chooses not to. In the mental capacity and social care context, this might be seen in situations in which those in a domiciliary setting are dependent on services to enable them to go out and engage with community. Such scenarios, according to republican theorists, draw attention to *domination* as opposed to the freedom espoused in liberalism, and expose the ways that such domination creates dependency – a more critical harm to freedom than the interferences which liberalism can capture. Pettit, for example, argues that, in situations of domination,

> The person who is dominated will tend to second-guess the wishes of the dominator, wanting to keep him or her on side and to restrict their own options accordingly. In the traditional language, they will tend to toady and fawn, bow and scrape, placate and ingratiate – in a word, abase themselves; furthermore, they will censor everything they say and do, tailoring it to an assuaging effect.
>
> (Pettit, 2002, 348)

The threat to freedom in republican accounts is thus from domination, seen to be the arbitrary power held over individuals. The harm stems from the latent potential in the arbitrary power which one yields over another, and the effects that this then consequently has upon behaviour and choices.

There has been increasing interest in republican approaches and the utility of the concept of freedom as non-domination, particularly among those seeking to draw attention to relationality (Wenner, 2020; O'Shea, 2018a, 2018b; Garrau and Laborde, 2015). Danielle Wenner, for example, suggests that republicanism can offer productive insights for relational autonomy, particularly in terms of focusing on economic redistribution, identifying freedom-limiting aspects of structural oppression, and allowing for responses that avoid interfering with individual agency (2020). Moreover, Wenner suggests republicanism is more attentive in this way to the role of relations and social context.

However, there are a number of difficulties with the republican reconceptualisation and reorientation of freedom which begin to emerge when it is scrutinised through the lens of the assemblage. At the heart of both liberal and republican accounts of liberty and freedom is an individualised focus; both see the locus of concern as the individual, and tend to see freedom therefore as an attribute of the individual, or at least as a descriptor of their situation. As Greg Scherkoske contends (2020), republicanism is still often weighed down by individualistic baggage in the same way that liberalism is. As a result of this individualised focus on the subject, and the conceptualisation of an external 'threat' to liberty stemming either from the state (in liberalism) or arbitrary power (in republicanism), the broader community becomes framed as the source of potential danger. As Jennings outlines in his discussion of the Millian paradigm, both Mill and Berlin see individual liberty as trumping community solidarity, and moreover, they set up a conflict or antithesis between the individual and the community (Jennings, 2009). He goes on to suggest that

> The framework that Mill establishes in *On Liberty*, and that Berlin sharpens and refines with his rejection of developmental and perfectionist accounts of human nature, is remarkably devoid of the web of interdependencies, culturally meaningful roles, styles and self-identities and shared values, rituals or practices. In short, it is a world of atomistic individuals each with their own interests, idiosyncrasies, projects and life-plans.
>
> (130)

Importantly, this is not to suggest that the community is absent or ignored in these accounts. It is that their role is seen as a potential threat to individual freedom. As Jennings goes on to argue,

> the Millian paradigm leads us to discuss virtually all issues in morality and politics, including issues of public policy and public health, using the assumption that community is inherently confining and restrictive; that individuals require an expansive and unencumbered environment within which to grow and flourish; that it is more in keeping with the human good to hustle rather than to huddle.
>
> (130–1)

Here there are clear echoes of the separate, bounded scales of the state, community, and individual which were encountered in the previous chapter – a central technique and logic of liberalism. Whilst the republican tradition does not perpetuate such a stark divide between the individual and the community and state, there is still a sense in which a particularly individualistic stance is retained. For republicans, there is a sense in which interferences can occur without any diminishment in the freedom of individuals – for example non-arbitrary interferences such as properly enacted laws and taxes would not fall foul of the republican concern with domination and arbitrary power. There is a problematic confidence in the rule of law and democracy here to prevent arbitrary power. Yet, as discussed in earlier chapters, this overlooks the complexities of law (Davies, 2017). Writing on republicanism and disability, Tom O'Shea does recognise that this account of law is problematic for republicanism and suggests that when focusing on discretionary power in decisional regimes (such as that contained in mental capacity law, for example), it cannot be assumed that domination will not occur through the administration of these. However, as noted above, the locus of concern is still the individual, with liberty (or freedom) seen as an attribute. Indeed, the source of the freedom-limiting domination in republican theoretical approaches also tends to follow the linear, interpersonal route that is also seen in political liberalism. As Garrau and Laborde suggest, there still appears to be a need in republicanism for a tangible "agent" with the arbitrary power to wield (2015). This misses the long-term structural processes and other relations which occur beyond this linear wielding of arbitrary power (Hirschmann, 2003). Moreover, and perhaps more importantly here, dependency is seen as a negative and avoidable state – in itself the result of relationships of domination. Yet, as will be discussed further below, such dependency and entanglement with other actors is a central and – importantly – unavoidable feature of the assemblage analysis and is not something which can be escaped in the sense that republicanism or liberalism suggests.

Some scholars working in the area of mental capacity law and policy have begun to engage with republican political theory in order to provide a richer conceptualisation of liberty and freedom and to inform more substantive legal responses. Arstein-Kerslake and Flynn, for example, suggest that, in the context of disability, there is a dependence on others which creates the risk of domination (2017) and drawing on Frank Lovett's republican approach, which sees laws, rules, and procedures as potentially constraining arbitrary power (Lovett, 2010, 96), they argue that an effective way to challenge this potential domination of disabled people is to oblige institutions to recognise their legal capacity, or agency (in line with Art 12 of the UN Convention on the Rights of Persons with Disabilities (CRPD)). O'Shea similarly turns to the law and bolstering legal agency (through rights and voice and in advanced care planning and in influencing decisions about access to services) as a way to counteract domination in the lives of disabled people (2018a). However, these engagements with republicanism demonstrate the individualised focus that it perpetuates, seemingly being trapped within the same liberal frameworks that the authors seek to avoid. Leveraging consent or individual agency in this way, as a way to counteract domination, ignores the broader structural constraints and the logics that these are entangled with. As discussed in the previous chapter, 'empowerment' in this way is often problematically individualised.

Focusing on the individual diverts attention from the broader dynamics which impact upon agency.

The capabilities approach has similarly been seen as potentially offering a more progressive approach to freedom and liberty, as seen in the previous chapter. For example, the focus on freedom to be and do (Sen, 2009) potentially offers a more positive framing of freedom, drawing attention to obligations of the state to enable freedom, rather than seeing the state as a threat to freedom and prioritising non-interference. Rosie Harding has outlined the potential for the capabilities approach to provide a productive frame for rethinking liberty in the mental capacity law context (2021) and as a way to leverage support to enable freedom. However, as has been discussed, the capabilities approach is often seen as being shackled by a liberal, individualist focus, and as perpetuating problematic ideals of the individual and the state. As Josh Miller discusses, the capabilities approach follows the liberal philosophy of starting with the individual and *then* bringing in social influence, rather than starting out with the onto-epistemology of the community (2018, 141). The state is seen as a "responder", which "ignores how injustices manifest" (142).

The assemblage account developed through this book, drawing on spatial and relational dynamics, offers new ways to uncover the productive effects of current conceptual framings of liberty in law, as well as new perspectives for progressive legal and political theories seeking to disentangle themselves from these liberal logics. Jennings suggests that concepts such as liberty should be understood as "forming a semantic web of mutual implication" and calls for a contextualised look at the work that such concepts can do and are doing in particular localised sites, as well as the discursive webs within which they are entangled. An assemblage approach allows a focus upon such practices and patterns. This is important in the context of disability and mental capacity in particular, where, as will be discussed below, there has long been recognition of the carceral logics which infuse care and treatment practices, and which tend to become normalised and sanctioned through a justification of their necessity for disabled people.

The lens which has been articulated through the earlier chapters provides a distinct challenge to the concept of liberty which has underpinned the broader liberal legal framework (through political liberalism) and which has permeated the jurisprudence in the mental capacity context. The alternative critical lens used to view the current legal framework provides a way to reconsider liberty outside of what Kapur has termed the "liberal fishbowl" (2018), as well as ways to bring these broader questions into legal purview. After outlining the current legal landscape, the discussion will turn to highlighting what the current boundaries of liberty in this context do – what they produce and what they hide – as well as suggesting ways to reconfigure legal responses.

Navigating the legal landscape

At the time of writing, the framework governing the right to liberty in the context of mental capacity law is the DoLS, however, it is important to note that these are currently undergoing reform following a tumultuous implementation period. This in itself is testament to the real difficulties faced by legislators and policy makers in grappling with the concept of liberty and its legal materialisations. The replacement Liberty Protection Safeguards (LPS), contained in the Mental Capacity (Amendment) Act 2019, were due to come into force in October 2020, however this has been delayed until at least 2022, given the ongoing impacts of COVID-19 on the social care context. In essence, the DoLS provide a legal process for the authorisation of what would otherwise amount to an unlawful deprivation of liberty of somebody deemed to lack mental capacity. They were enacted following a landmark Strasbourg ruling in *HL v UK* 45508/99 [2004] ECHR 471 in which the lack of a legal process for authorising or enabling a challenge to the deprivation of liberty of an individual lacking mental capacity was held to breach Article 5 of the European Convention on Human Rights (ECHR). As a result of this ruling, there was found to be a significant breach of the UK's Art 5 obligations, and the UK government responded by enacting the DoLS. The DoLS then, at heart, are about ensuring that there is a process by which the deprivation of liberty of those deemed to lack capacity under the Mental Capacity Act (MCA) can be authorised and challenged, in accordance with Art 5 of the ECHR. Art 5, the right to liberty and security, states that:

> 1. Everyone has the right to liberty and security of person. No one shall be deprived of his liberty save in the following cases and in accordance with a procedure prescribed by law …
>
> (e) the lawful detention of persons for the prevention of the spreading of infectious diseases, of persons of unsound mind, alcoholics or drug addicts or vagrants.

Here there is a clear statement that whilst ordinarily, everyone has the right to liberty, there are exceptions to this, one of which is the detention of persons of unsound mind. Yet such detentions must comply with Art 5(4), which states that:

> Everyone who is deprived of his liberty by arrest or detention shall be entitled to take proceedings by which the lawfulness of his detention shall be decided speedily by a court and his release ordered if the detention is not lawful.

In this sense, the DoLS provide for compliance with Art 5 by ensuring there is a legal process in place to enable the lawfulness of the detention to be challenged.

The DoLS have had a turbulent existence, with criticisms levelled at their complexity and the subsequent lack of meaningful engagement with them by those working in different settings (House of Lords Select Committee, 2014). Their replacement, the LPS, have sought to address some of the more problematic aspects of the DoLS, but it is anticipated that this will have varying degrees of success (see Series, 2019, for a discussion of this). It is not the purpose of this chapter to provide an analysis of the LPS and the extent to which they will improve authorisation processes or access to justice in this context. However, it is notable that, as with the MCA more generally and the DoLS, the LPS can be seen as a legal tool to justify and legitimate existing practices and to ensure that they are compliant with Article 5. The focus here is on the underpinning normative ideas of liberty (bound up with broader logics of capacity and the role of the state) and how these materialise through the legal framework.

Yet, one of the central problems with the schemes is the very meaning of 'deprivation of liberty', and this is not something which the LPS have addressed. A definition of 'deprivation of liberty' has been subject to almost continuous challenge through the courts, with some very revealing notions about what liberty means in the current legal framework – particularly in the context of disability and mental capacity – emerging through the jurisprudence. This will be illuminated through the discussion in later sections on the emphasis on freedom from interference, the static materiality of liberty, the shaping of the subject, and the role of the state. In doing so, the assemblage account will provide an important critical perspective, revealing what is currently overlooked or hidden in the legal framework.

The current definition of deprivation of liberty, or "acid test" as it has come to be known, comes from the Supreme Court decision in *Cheshire West* (*P v Cheshire West and Chester Council and another; P and Q v Surrey County Council* [2014] UKSC 19). This case involved two linked appeals from the Court of Appeal ([2014] A.C. 896) relating to whether individuals had been deprived of their liberty in their respective living arrangements. The case of *P* involved a then 38-year-old man with cerebral palsy and Down's syndrome, residing in a shared bungalow known as 'Z House'. In the bungalow, which he shared with two other residents, there were generally two members of support staff, with P also entitled to one-to-one support for 98 hours each week. He regularly left the bungalow with support staff, attending a day centre and hydrotherapy pool as well as a club, shops, and the pub in the community. In the first instance, Baker J held that P was being deprived of his liberty at Z house due to the continuous control of the staff as well as the practices being utilised to deal with his "challenging behaviour". However, he went on to say that this deprivation of his liberty was in his best interests. On appeal, the Court of Appeal ruled that the arrangements did not constitute a deprivation of P's liberty. A key component of Munby LJ's reasoning was the idea of a "relevant comparator" whereby he suggested that P's life must be compared with other people like him, with the same disabilities, and the types of lives they might be expected to lead. On this basis, P was not deprived of his liberty.

MIG and MEG (previously known as P and Q) were sisters who had been taken into care due to neglect and concerns as to sexual abuse in 2007 when they were 16 and 15 respectively. MIG was placed with a foster mother and went to a further education unit daily. She never attempted to leave the foster home by herself but would have been restrained from doing so had she tried. MEG was moved from foster care to a residential home for learning disabled adolescents with complex needs. She sometimes required physical restraint and received tranquillising medication. In both the Court of Protection and the Court of Appeal, the arrangements for both MIG and MEG were held not to be deprivations of their liberty, based on the "relative normality" of their situation, as well as the idea that the limits to their freedom stemmed from their disability, rather than an imposition by those caring for them.

In the Supreme Court, both appeals were allowed, and it was held that P, MIG, and MEG were being deprived of their liberty. Here, Lady Hale stated that in assessing whether or not somebody is deprived of their liberty, we must ask (1) Is the person subject to continuous supervision and control? And (2) Is the person free to leave? If the answer to these questions is "no", then they are being arbitrarily deprived of their liberty and this must be authorised and subject to the procedural safeguards entailed in Art 5(4). It is important to emphasise, however, that a finding that P is being deprived of their liberty does not necessitate a change in their living arrangements. It simply requires that procedural safeguards are in place and adhered to.

The decision by the Supreme Court, and the "acid test", whilst welcomed for recognising the rights of disabled people not to be arbitrarily deprived of their liberty, has attracted criticism and has also significantly increased the reach of the DoLS and the number of people who are now defined as being deprived of their liberty, imposing a heavy administrative and bureaucratic burden in an already stretched adult social care context, and widening the reach of the need for legal oversight outside of more traditional institutional settings and into the home. As will be seen in the remainder of the chapter, the blurring of some of the central organising boundaries that this has affected has disturbed the foundations of the MCA and DoLS, and in turn unsettles some of the liberal logics. Yet, before more fully engaging with the logics of liberty in the context of capacity and the effects of *Cheshire West* upon them, it is important to note a much stronger challenge to the DoLS, and the very foundations upon which it is built, stems from the CRPD.

Article 14 of the CRPD poses a fatal challenge to many current care practices which take place in this context. It states that:

> 1. States Parties shall ensure that persons with disabilities, on an equal basis with others:
>   (a) Enjoy the right to liberty and security of person;
>   (b) Are not deprived of their liberty unlawfully or arbitrarily, and that any deprivation of liberty is in conformity with the law, and *that the existence of a disability shall in no case justify a deprivation of liberty.*
>
> (Emphasis added)

This is a stark challenge both to Article 5 of the ECHR, which *does* permit (but not *require*) deprivation of liberty on the basis of disability (i.e. unsoundness of mind), and consequently to the DoLS and the LPS. Article 14 thus seemingly proscribes *any* framework which allows for detention or deprivation of liberty on the basis of disability. As will be seen, whilst *Cheshire West* can be seen to begin to blur some of the boundaries of the liberal legal framework, particularly in the recognition contained in Lady Hale's "acid test" that deprivations of liberty can occur within the home, the judgment also reiterated and reaffirmed the broader point that deprivation on the basis of disability is sanctioned, so long as it is underpinned by procedural safeguards in line with Art 5(4) ECHR. Art 14 then potentially poses a much more potent challenge to these logics. However, the progressive potential in Art 14 is dependent upon how liberty and deprivation of liberty is understood. The assemblage account offers an important lens to complicate the logics of liberty, revealing processes and practices going beyond liberal and purportedly progressive republican approaches.

Complicating the logics of liberty

The static materiality of liberty

The materiality of the spaces in which deprivations of liberty are seen to occur is particularly striking and provides a useful lens through which to consider the static and bounded ideas which pervade in this context. The corollary of this is that those outside of such spaces are ordinarily seen as 'free' and as embodying the autonomous legal subject, given the lack of external constraint upon them. The logics here are deeply rooted in the policy developments throughout the 19th century and leading to the present day, where the closure of large institutions and moves into the community was seen as enabling 'deinstitutionalisation'. What this then forecloses, however, is attentiveness to the ongoing carceral logics which permeate beyond the walls of such 'classic' institutional settings, and the ways in which such logics can work alongside and through other spaces in order to constrain and dominate. Rather than perpetuate this static materiality in liberty discourse, this section builds on the ideas of scholars such as Moran (2015), and Ben-Moshe, Chapman, and Carey (2014), in order to enable a more critical consideration of the carceral as "spatial, emplaced, mobile, embodied and affective" (Moran, 2015).

This static materiality is initially evident in the structure of the DoLS and the settings in which the statutory authorisation process applies. The DoLS statutory authorisation process applied only to those who are deprived of their liberty in care homes and hospitals. Outside of those settings – such as in supported living, shared lives, or domiciliary settings – if somebody was considered to be deprived of their liberty then this needed to be authorised by the Court of Protection. It is striking here that there is a clear, and potentially arbitrary, distinction in terms of the application of the legal and regulatory framework based upon the status of the setting. In terms of justifying this exclusion of other settings from the DoLS authorisation process, the Department of Health stated that

> The Government did not include supported living because it considered it less likely that severe restrictions would be placed on people in supported living arrangements, who would tend to lead more independent lives.
>
> (Department of Health, 2005)

This betrays a very strong sense in which particular settings are viewed as more institutional, perpetuating a view of institutions and institutionalisation as tied to a static space. Moreover, it suggests that deprivation of liberty is an exception, occurring only in certain spaces, with those outside of this leading the independent, free life of the autonomous norm. In contrast to this, an assemblage understanding, in conversation with emerging literature on carceral logics, provides a more nuanced view of the relational dynamics which occur in different spaces beyond 'the institution' and the ways in which different spaces can be shaped by – and shape – such logics. As Gill et al. discuss,

> Geographers have critically discussed Goffman's (1961) notion of the 'total institution' in order to call attention to this interconnectedness of prisons and other carceral spaces ... Their intention has been to counter the imagination of a closed-off and sealed carceral institution, discussing instead the liminal spaces "betwixt and between" the inside and outside of prisons (Moran, 2015: 90) ... carceral geographers have already been at pains to emphasize the continuities that stretch across institutional boundaries.
>
> (Gill et al., 2018, 184)

As Chapman suggests, there is a need to be attentive to the "continuities of structural violence" and "the historical political rationalities that still haunt us today" in contexts where populations who were previously confined continue to be confined in the present day, despite purported shifts in policy (2014, 38). Together these insights draw attention to the "causes and consequences of the increasingly interconnected, more-than-institutional landscape of carceral spaces and practices" (Gill et al., 2018, 185). Often, this literature has tended to focus on the prison as a carceral space, or punitive settings and purposes underpinning the interventions, yet such ideas have particular resonance in the context of 'care' settings and practices. As already noted, rather than seeing the institutional practices as ending at the asylum or institution walls, this lens allows a focus on the enduring and shifting patterns of control, coercion, and domination which take place in other settings and, importantly, the processes through which this occurs.

The status of home and private settings occupies a similarly revealing status in the legal framework at present. As already seen, such settings are outside of the administrative authorisation process in the DoLS and instead require authorisation via the Court of Protection. So, theoretically then, somebody can be deprived of their liberty in a home setting. However, it is evident that there is unease about such a notion, with jurisprudence in cases involving the home setting illuminating both the static divide between the institution and the community, but also the public/private binary. This is hardly surprising, given the quintessential construction of the home as a private domain, outside of the realms of the state, in traditional liberalism. As discussed above, however, *Cheshire West* has affected a destabilising influence on the boundaries of the home. In recognising that deprivation of liberty can occur in domestic settings, such as Z House, and as such need to be subject to procedural safeguards, the judgment is seen as opening up legal oversight of care practices in the home. The focus of the reasoning in Lady Hale's acid test – continuous supervision and control, and not being free to leave – are tied not to the location, but more to the practices occurring within them. This theme and the tensions evinced by it are traceable through the judgments in the individual cases which culminated in the Supreme Court decision, as well as through the robust dissenting judgments.

The High Court decision in *Re MIG and MEG* [2010] EWHC 785 (Fam), demonstrates the difficulty that the judiciary has in holding that a small group home, which was portrayed as like a home environment for MEG. Parker J gave a number of reasons for finding that MEG, a 17-year-old residing in a small group home, was not deprived of her liberty. Parker J suggested that because each is under the continuous supervision and control of her carers so as to meet her care needs rather than to restrain her in any way, and that in neither of these homes are they principally there for the purpose of being "treated or managed", rather they are there to receive care (para 230), then there is no deprivation of liberty. The framing of the situation of both MIG and MEG in the High Court is very much built on the idea of 'home' – "The 'concrete situation' is that each lives exactly the kind of life that she would be capable of living in the home of her own family or a relative" (para 229); "In relation to both girls, the primary intention is to provide them each with a home" (para 230); "Those circumstances are in my judgment very far from the 'paradigm' example of imprisonment" (para 235). It is telling that Parker J here draws on the "paradigm of imprisonment" to contrast to the conceptualisation of the living arrangements of MEG as being akin to her home. Moreover, the reliance upon the family-like nature of the setting, as well as the purpose as being about 'care', is drawn upon to tip the balance away from deprivation of liberty. Statements from the dissenting judgments of Lords Carnwath and Hodge (and endorsed by Lord Clarke) are instructive here;

> It is notable that all the cases cited in the court's review related to people living in institutions of some kind, not in ordinary homes.
>
> (para 97)

> We are concerned that nobody using ordinary language would describe people living happily in a domestic setting as being deprived of their liberty.
>
> (para 99)

Again, the strong boundaries being drawn between different settings are evident, but also through these judgments the state and family begin to emerge as heuristics, as well as 'care' being opposed to the purportedly more controlling or constraining logics of 'treatment or management'.

Following *Cheshire West* and the challenge to the institution/home distinction it provokes, there has been further judicial wrangling on this issue. The case of *Rochdale Metropolitan Borough Council v KW* [2014] EWCOP 45 involved a 52-year-old woman who had suffered brain damage as a result of surgery in 1996. She was discharged from hospital into rehabilitation, and then eventually into her own home with 24/7 support. The case followed quickly from the Supreme Court decision in *Cheshire West*, and the broadening of the definition of deprivation of liberty which stemmed from the "acid test". In terms of the question as to whether or not KW was being deprived of her liberty in her home, Mostyn J refused to define such a situation as a deprivation of liberty. What Mostyn J seemed to really object to here was the view that a purportedly beneficent arrangement in somebody's home could amount to deprivation of liberty. He went on to say that

> I find it impossible to conceive that the best interests arrangement for Katherine, in her own home, provided by an independent contractor, but devised and paid for by Rochdale and CCG, amounts to a deprivation of liberty within Article 5 … In my opinion this is arbitrary, arguably irrational, and a league away from the intentions of the framers of the Convention.
>
> (para 7)

Again, a divide is drawn between the family and the state here, mapping onto the home/institution divide and the public/private divide which emerges through this discussion. What this meant then in practical terms (until the successful appeal of the case in [2015] EWCA Civ 1054) was that those not deemed to be deprived of their liberty, such as Katherine here, would be left without the procedural oversight of their care that Article 5 and the DoLS afford. The responsibility of the state is thus erased. In this way, care becomes seen as a 'private' act, contained within the walls of the home. Thinking back to the 'carescape' introduced in Chapter 4, this rendering of the boundaries between the home and the state works to exclude the broader institutional, structural, and historical processes shaping the context. Mostyn J's approach can be seen as an attempt to sustain the logics of liberty that have traditionally underpinned this framework, and to contain (or restrain?) the consequences that could flow from recognising deprivations of liberty unshackled from material boundaries, and the types of questions this might open up.

As already highlighted, the policy of deinstitutionalisation and care in the community did not put an end to 'care' practices which were dominating, and which suppress the agency of individuals. In many cases, it equated to shifting responsibility from the state to families without ensuring the resources to facilitate meaningful engagement and participation in the community. The logics of the provision of care and treatment, through statutory obligations on local authorities or through clinical decision making, often simply escaped the walls of the institution, and instead took place through the same professionals in the community. As discussed in Chapter 4, under the guise of choice and independence, these institutional and carceral logics could persist through this shifting of responsibility, and through diminished provision of services and support. These policy choices actively pervade the walls of the home and the ideological boundary of the public and the private (Guest and Corrigan, 2018). Human geographers have long highlighted the role that policies can have in shaping and co-constituting the experience of space and place (Massey et al., 1999; Bowlby, 2012). Rather than an abstract, static, and empty container, the material and discursive work together to shape the experience of place.

The static framing, such as of home/institution, has leveraged the concept of 'care' to demarcate carceral or punitive logics from those that are caring and, as such, benevolent. Yet again this attempt to shift care outside of the boundaries of the political and of state responsibilities belies the effects that purportedly caring practices and policies can have. As discussed in Chapter 4, seeing care as shifting, mobile, and relational helps to challenge this legal separation and impermeable boundedness of care and punishment. Focusing on the ways in which policy decisions, such as the decision whether or not to provide particular services, shape the relationships within the domestic sphere is crucial to recognising the affective impacts that such decisions have on the agency of both carer and disabled person. This enables us to move away from only recognising the interpersonal, direct, and immediate constraints on people's liberty, and instead to bring into view the broader structural and systemic factors which have real and tangible institutionalising effects. Rather than reinforcing these potentially damaging logics of the separateness of home and other settings, the public and the private, and the family and the state, recognition of the shifting nature of such spaces, and the shaping of them through shifts in embodied needs and policy discourses, points to rethinking the prior and ongoing role of the state and the ways in which responses should and could be reconfigured.

Interestingly, the Law Commission's proposals in relation to reforming the DoLS sought to challenge some of the static materiality of the DoLS by ensuring that their replacement applied to *any* setting, including supported living, shared lives, and domestic settings to ensure that any deprivation of liberty was able to be challenged and provided with external scrutiny (Law Commission, 2017, Chapter 7). This attracted criticism, with responses to their consultation expressing concern about the unwarranted intrusion of the state into the private realm (para 7.9). This amendment has made its way into the LPS framework. These safeguards will now apply to a range of settings including domestic settings, which means that these can now be subject to the authorisation and review process rather than needing to be authorised through the Court of Protection.

It is important however to recognise the real concerns emanating from suggestions that people are being deprived of their liberty in the community, and particularly in family homes. As Series puts it, it may be "political dynamite" to suggest that families are detaining loved ones (Series, 2019). If the current logics of liberty persist then there is an understandable concern that this could translate to a blaming of the family for depriving their family member of liberty. Indeed, given the parameters of the liberal legal logics, it is unsurprising that this may seem the logical corollary. Here, spatial and relational dynamics offer ways to avoid this framing and to rethink responses. Without a broader understanding of the complex, non-linear causality circulating in such contexts, and the ways in which constraints and institutionalising effects occur, these problematic boundaries will persist through the shifting of responsibility away from the state. Much depends on the purpose and legal response to recognising when somebody is being deprived of their liberty. If it is about allocating 'blame' and viewing interferences with liberty as a direct (and necessarily negative) consequence of an individual's actions, requiring bureaucratic state interference to authorise it, then of course this is problematic. However, if there is a shift from an interpersonal idea of interference and recognise the various sources impacting on an individual then there is no necessary attribution of blame to families. Drawing on the carescape and attending to practices and processes rather than material settings enables a closer focus on institutional and structural forces shaping the care arrangements, and avoids situating 'blame' for deprivations of liberty on family members. Responsibility, as discussed in previous chapters, becomes much more diffuse and historically contingent. Often, a lack of services and resources are the cause of people being effectively detained in their own homes, despite the best will and efforts of those caring for them. By not being driven by material boundaries, there is more scope to be attentive to what Milligan (2000) refers to as the "institutionalization of the home" through, for example, routines, practices, and formal care visits. Moreover, the legal response need not simply be an authorisation and consequent legitimation of detaining practices but can instead be oriented towards facilitating liberty, and options for new relations, taking into account the multiple interacting sources that currently foreclose this as part of the assemblage. As Miller puts it, "assemblages have the capacity to act and influence and change constituent components" (2018, 145) and different sources or sites can be pinpointed to allow change to occur. This sort of approach to responses is often foreclosed in the current framework however, given the constrained discursive space in which liberty is situated and through which threats to liberty are recognised/obscured.

Shaping the subject

The analysis so far suggests not that space has been absent in debates as to liberty and freedom; instead, it has been central to it. However, this often goes unsaid, or a static, bounded, and impermeable idea of space is deployed to draw rigid material and ideological boundaries. Freedom or liberty has been framed as an attribute of an individual, with their spatial setting as a potential container. It is also important to reflect on how this materiality of the regulatory framework also works to shape the legal subject through these processes. As Ford has argued, in the context of a discussion of rights as a particularly liberal institution,

> These walls of liberalism do in fact define liberty, but they do much more than this – they create the very entity that is to enjoy liberty. Both individual rights and the formal rules of jurisdiction are 'technologies of the self', they are discourses and concrete acts that define political selfhood and provide the model for biological individuals to 'perform themselves' as (autonomous, rational, profit-maximising, god-fearing, desiring, willful, raced, sexed) selves.
>
> (Ford, 2000, 208)

Similarly, the concept of "governing *through* freedom" (Rose, O'Malley, and Valverde, 2006, 91) is useful here for exposing the way in which liberal governance, far from creating spaces of freedom for individuals in which to cultivate their own self-mastery, actually and actively *creates* the subject through particular practices. This is starkly evident in the context of the right to liberty and its role in shaping the identities of those subject to mental capacity law and the regulatory frameworks aligned to it. The materiality of the living arrangement is tightly bound up in the resultant framing of the resident. As already seen, whether a setting is defined as a hospital or care home matters for the reach of the DoLS. Yet, the status of a setting as residential care or supported living, for example, has equally pernicious effects on the regulatory framework applied and, importantly, on the rendering of the legal subject who inhabits this setting. This was evident in the Inquest and Serious Case Review of Richard Handley. Richard was 33 years old when he died following serious complications resulting from constipation. The Serious Case Review and Inquest both note that Richard resided at a council-run residential care home, Goshawk Close, until July 2010, when it was de-registered. It then became classed as a supported living arrangement, delivered through Suffolk County Council's supported living contract with United Response, who then ran Goshawk Close. According to the Serious Case Review, Richard's family associate this shift with a reduction in the support offered to him in the arrangement (Flynn and Eley, 2015, para 18). Notably, the shift in the spatial designation also altered the portrayal of those within it. The Review further notes that

> [D]uring the consultation with families about the change to supported living, there was no suggestion that this would in any way diminish or change the support to people living at Goshawk Close. The emphasis of the consultation was on increased income and control over finances, tenancy rights and choice of activities. James' family wrote that the log of this process clearly shows that he had no understanding of the implications of the transition and that he was erroneously deemed to have capacity to

> make this decision and his family were denied the opportunity to contribute to a best interests decision.
>
> (Flynn and Eley, 2015, para 26)

The language of choice, control, and independence, discussed in earlier chapters, is here heavily infused in the very materiality and regulatory landscape of a particular space. Those occupying such spaces become the capacitous, autonomous, and self-determining subject which is central to the liberal legal structure. This shifting of Richard into the realm of the self-determining liberal figure, freely expressing his wishes and being left alone to do so then becomes central to the trajectory of the Review and Inquest, with his refusals to engage with certain services framed as his choice and independence in action.

> At an unknown date during 2010 United Response notes concerning James' appointments state: Stop seeing the Chiropodist! The family confirmed that this means that he was refusing to see the chiropodist.
>
> (Flynn and Eley, 2015, 26)

What is important to reflect on here is the ways in which the policy aims of independence, choice, and control can become entangled with particular spatial and material arrangements in order to shift the rendering of the subject within it and the responsibilities of others.

Through such processes, ideas of bounded materiality and subjectivity become reproduced, foreclosing attentiveness to the particularities of the relational assemblage in which individuals are situated, and the various forces and relations which prevent this assigned agency from manifesting. Furthermore, such processes work to reinforce boundaries around different types of physical settings, and the types of subjects who reside within them. Space or materiality emerges as an active agent within these processes, not simply a static and fixed object within which subjects are contained. It is thus important through this assemblage lens not to reinforce these boundaries or to view those outside of particular settings as the embodiment of the liberal legal subject, or as an ideal to aim for in legal and policy interventions.

What is also evident in the wrangling around the meaning of liberty in domestic jurisprudence is the shaping of the disabled subject as 'other' and outside of the 'normal' confines of liberal logic. In a sense, despite material moves of deinstitutionalisation, the legal framework itself provides a tool by which to segregate, acting as a discursive institution. Again, very static ideals of disability and the givenness of particular living arrangements for disabled people can be traced here. In liberal theory, political theorists such as Hobbes and Mill have long justified this relegation of disability to a separate realm. Hobbes, for example, reasoned that immobility due to disability was not in any sense a denial of liberty, stating that "a stone [that] lyeth still" is no more unfree than "a man fastened to his bed by sicknesse" (Hobbes, 1651). Mill similarly suggested that the account of liberty only applied to those who are "in the maturity of their faculties" (para 14). What we see here is both the reinforcement of the idea of the constraint upon liberty as having to necessitate from a concrete, external object or barrier (reflecting again a binary between internal and external forces and the problematic framing of antagonism) but also the imposition of a static disabled subjectivity. This ignores the broader context and historicity of the individual's positioning, as well as seeing impairment as being intrinsic and internally created.

Such an understanding is also evident in some of the jurisprudence around the DoLS and the definition of liberty to be applied. In the Court of Appeal judgment in *Cheshire West*, Munby LJ (as he then was) propounded the "relevant comparator" test as part of the calculation of whether or not somebody is being deprived of their liberty. Munby LJ contended that while in most contexts, the relevant comparator is "the ordinary adult going about the kind of life which the able bodied man or woman on the Clapham omnibus would normally expect to lead" (para 102), such a comparison ought not to be made in the context of cases arising under the DoLS framework. He pointed out that the Court of Protection in such cases is dealing with adults with "significant physical and learning disabilities" whose lives are "inherently restricted" or "dictated" by their own "cognitive limitations" (para 102). As a result of this, he reasoned that the relevant comparator ought to be "an adult of similar age with the same capabilities as X, affected by the same condition or suffering the same inherent mental and physical disabilities and limitations as X". The court must focus on "the kind of lives that people like X would normally expect to lead" (para 102). Similarly, statements by Mostyn J in *KW* demonstrate this idea of disability as an inherent, static feature of an individual, taking them outside of the realms of the liberal concern within which liberty can persist. Drawing explicitly on John Stuart Mill, he stated that

> For Mill, human liberty has three essential strands or components ... Each of these components requires a positive and reasoned intellectual function which is hard to ascribe to a person of unsound mind, which is why Mill qualified his doctrine as applying only to those human beings in the "maturity of their faculties".
>
> (para 14)

This endorsement of Mill demonstrates not only the strong liberal underpinning of the jurisprudence, but also the very problematic nature of Mill's views on rationality and "unsoundness of mind" in relation to liberty. He further went on to say that Katherine was

> not in any realistic way being constrained from exercising the freedom to leave, in the required sense, for the essential reason that she does not have the physical or mental ability to exercise that freedom.
>
> (para 29)

Mostyn J's "causal" idea – that arrangements ought to only be recognised as a deprivation of liberty if they stem from constraints imposed by others, and not if they stem from the disability itself – has been influential to an extent in debates surrounding the LPS. In his response to the Joint Committee on Human Rights Inquiry into the right to freedom and safety, Sir Nicholas Mostyn suggested again that the focus of the "acid test" be on differentiating the cause of the deprivation of liberty – "Is it the 'real cause' that P is not free to leave the continuous supervision and control, or is it the underlying condition, for which the state is not responsible?" (Mostyn, 2018, para 12). This was further taken up by the Joint Committee on Human Rights in their report as part of their suggested definition of deprivation of liberty (Joint Committee on Human Rights, 2018, Chapter 5).

Aside from the problematic ways in which such statements reinforce an individual model of disability, they also ignore the contingency of the experience of impairment and entrench a static subject position, overlooking how this experience is constantly shifting, spatially mediated, and open to change. Importantly, as has been reiterated through the spatial and relational tools laid out at the start of this book, this is not something that is unique or exceptional to disability. As Delaney suggests

> we, each of us, are always multiply figured (positively and negatively), but the pragmatic significance of any given figuration may be contingent on our position on the nomosphere, or on our location vis-à-vis the lines of meaning and lines of force that constitute our life-worlds.
>
> (2010, 75)

This poses a distinct challenge to the causal rationality evidenced in Mostyn J and Munby LJ's thinking around the disabled person as a static subject. It further challenges the causality inherent in these ideas and the ways in which they obscure the contingencies and roles of other actors in institutions in the lived experience of impairment.

Moreover, these judicial statements sediment particular service or care arrangements as 'common sense' or pre-given, rather than recognising that they could be otherwise, and responses could be different. They see material arrangements as stemming from the internal inabilities of the individual, rather than as produced through particular webs and experienced through particular material and discursive contexts. As Weller highlights, the strength of more governmental understandings is that they refuse to "contemplate the concepts of 'freedom' and 'disability' as fixed ontological categories" (Weller, 2014, 505). Furthermore, and as will be discussed in the next section, individualising disability in this way serves to obscure the role of the state in the production of particular arrangements and relations, in turn closing down mechanisms for accountability and recognising responsibility.

Obscuring the state

The shaping of the subject through these legal processes performs an important function for liberal legal theory – as well as constructing the state and the community as an existential threat to liberty, it also hides the very interventions which already take place via state and institutional mechanisms. Liberty is portrayed as a zero-sum game, in which rights are framed in negative terms (i.e. freedom from) and an increase in rights for individuals is seen to signal a reduction in the power of the state or institutions (Kapur, 2018, 32). Moreover, there is an emphasis on a direct, immediate, and tangible relation between the state and the individual, through a particular concrete interference, to enable any claim that an individual's liberty is being impacted. Such a vision actively obscures the role of the state and the historicity of institutional shaping of the present.

The case of *RK* (*RK v BCC, YB & AK* [2010] EWHC 3355 (Fam)), is a useful example of how these constraints are rendered outside of the concern of liberty. The case involved the question of whether RK, a minor, was deprived of her liberty in a care home in which she had been placed pursuant to an agreement between her parents and the local authority. The complexity here stemmed from the fact that under s20 of the Children's Act 1989, the parents could, legally, remove her from the care home. Thus, the local authority has not, in the eyes of the statute or – more importantly – in the eyes of liberty – removed RK from the care of her parents. As such, there was held to be no deprivation of liberty taking place in RK's care setting. The parents had sought to argue however that the main obstacle to caring for RK at home is the lack of support to enable them to do so, seeking to suggest that the purported right to withdraw consent to the care arrangement in s20 Children's Act is meaningless and that, as such, she is being deprived of her liberty. Mostyn J, however, gave such an argument short shrift, stating that

> I do not believe that the means of the parents can as a matter of logic or principle inform the answer to the question of whether RK's liberty is being deprived. The whole point of Article 5 is to prevent arbitrariness, not to foster it.
>
> (para 35)

He goes on to say that as such the arrangement is not "imputable to the state" and is entirely at the behest of the parents. Having a *legal* right to bring RK home should they wish was a strong factor in establishing that she was not being deprived of her liberty. The *practical* impossibility of doing so was not something which the vision of liberty here was prepared to engage with – it is foreclosed through the need for a direct and linear interference by the state. The lack of a tangible direct interference, by an individual or a legal process, was seen to negate any claim by the parents as to the impossibility of removing her, notwithstanding the (invisibilised) role of the state in the creation of the conditions for access to support to enable individuals to care for family members at home, as well as the broader conditions which actually enable informal carers to perform such care work. The situational impacts on liberty – of both RK and her parents – are outside of the boundaries of liberty in this framework.

The case of *Meyers* which was discussed in the previous chapter is another particularly stark example here. In relation to the directions of the court that Mr Meyers is not allowed to reside with his son, it was held by Hayden J that this did not constitute a deprivation of Mr Meyers' liberty,

> Properly analysed, the ambition here is not to confine Mr Meyers to the Care Home, but to protect him from the grave danger that living in the bungalow with his son has already been demonstrated to represent. To safeguard him, by invoking the inherent jurisdiction of the High Court, it is necessary to restrict the scope and ambit of his choices, not his liberty. It is important to highlight that there remain a range of options open to him. The impact of the Court's intervention is to limit Mr Meyers's accommodation options, but it does not deprive of his physical liberty which is the essence of the right guaranteed by Article 5.
>
> (para 56)

The 'concern' of liberty then is not in facilitating or enabling choice or agency, but in ensuring procedural checks on paradigmatic physical containments. Constraints upon agency caused by structural barriers or delegitimating practices that entrench disavowed subject positions, and problematic institutional relations that perpetuate these, are rendered 'outside' of the liberal gaze. Remember that agential cuts such as judicial statements as to what is or is not the concern of liberty, creating this 'outside', do not erase these constraints but serve instead to invisibilise them. As Hesse discusses, such foreclosure is often built into the very structures of a particular hegemonic discourse (such as liberty here) and as a result, "certain redacted themes or objects become unsayable, lacking in preferentiality because they are routinely prohibited by the conventions or rules of what can be formulated in a particular discourse" (Hesse, 2014, 290).

This emphasis on the tangibility and immediacy of state involvement is typical of the carceral logics which infuse the liberal concern with liberty we started with at the outset of the chapter. It is echoed further in the broader case law on the extent of state obligations to provide health and social care, where there is again an institutional logic underpinning the divide drawn in the case law on Article 3 (freedom from torture and inhuman and degrading treatment) between the prison settings and the community (see, Clements, 2011, and Clough, 2018, as well as case law on positive obligations in relation to prisons or the community, *Price v UK* (2001) 34 EHRR 1285; *R (on the application of McDonald) v Royal Borough of Kensington and Chelsea* [2011] UKSC 33). Here, again, the prison is presented as a paradigmatic space of deprivation of liberty, and the community as a space of freedom. As has been seen, these logics play an important part in hiding the always, already nature of state 'interference' and work to shift responsibility for the diffuse consequences of this in the everyday lives of disabled people. Instead, an assemblage analysis allows us to focus "less on the visible lines of legal force and more on how those lines are bent and directed by the law's geometry" (Tribe, 1989, 16). This is not a call for more law or less law – i.e. a binary decision between deepening legalism or manufacturing a retreat by the state. Importantly, it is not about valourising the state as a site and source of reform, but instead calling attention to the current place of law and its material effects.

Unbounding liberty in the assemblage

As has been seen, the logics of liberty in the mental capacity framework are rendered workable upon certain assumptions about the bounded spaces of liberty, tied to ideas of the role and reach of the state and of legal (and disabled) subjectivity. Even when boundaries are tested or blurred in one of these realms (such as we have seen in the wake of *Cheshire West*), the broader problematic boundaries tend to remain intact and undisturbed – or, problematically, further shored up in order to maintain the broader structure. In *Cheshire West*, for example, despite the unsettling of the previous static materiality of liberty, and Lady Hale's statement that whilst it is "axiomatic that people with disabilities, both mental and physical, have the same human rights as the rest of the human race" (para 45), she did then go on to qualify this: "[i]t may be that those rights have sometimes to be limited or restricted because of their disabilities" (para 45). Despite the positive intentions behind such a statement, it still reinforces the idea of disability as static and as necessitating different treatment, outside of the boundaries of the universality that liberalism promulgates. As such, legal reforms and suggestions for these are often constrained by this bigger picture and broader liberal framework, and it becomes somewhat of a 'lawyers game' to find or create ways to comply with the law, whilst at the same time leaving this broader framework intact (see Clements, 2021). Instead of trying to work within these confines, it is perhaps more important now to confront the problematic effects of our current approaches to liberty and to find productive ways to rethink it.

Challenging the bounded concepts of subjectivity and space emerges as an important starting point for this, building instead on the importance of relational dynamics and processes through the assemblage. In calling for a more relational approach to freedom, Jennings suggests that

> just as there are certain kinds of practice or activity that by their very nature cannot be done alone, so there is a kind of freedom that subsists not in separation from others but through connection with them – not in protections but in pacts of association; not in locked futures but in open ones; not in sharp elbows but in outstretched hands. This is the located, the emplaced or in-placed freedom of a person who dwells and acts in a here and now, a person who is somebody, somewhere.
>
> (Jennings, 2015, 10)

This signals both the importance of place and connection to a relational understanding. As Gilson suggests, "if relations are primary, then our notions of security and safety should turn on the nature of relations, rather than on carving out fictitiously enclosed territories" (Gilson, 2018, 240). Rather than seeing relations as a potential threat to liberty and, in turn, autonomy, relations are recognised as ontologically prior. Rather than proceeding from a vision of the self and spaces as impermeable and bounded, recognising them as affective and entangled with other relations shifts the concern with liberty towards being about

> being able to sustain a range of relations and a variety of modes of relation, which would compromise flourishing, rather than being impeded from relating or compelled to relate only in a limited way...[and] being able to forge new relations rather than being limited to a pre-existent or pre-established range of relations or modes of relations.
>
> (Gilson, 2018, 240)

In other words, it entails being attentive to and acknowledging the full range and effects of different relations and the conditions that make these possible or impossible. This provides a distinct challenge to the concept of liberty, which has underpinned the broader liberal legal framework (through political liberalism) and which has permeated the jurisprudence in the mental capacity context. There are clear echoes here of Foucault's work on governance and his consideration of dense networks of power, which exposes the ways in which these relations are not causal or linear, but are always historical, contingent, and shaped by a number of different discursive forces. Ivison sums up Foucault's stance on freedom as,

> I am free to the extent that I can actually exercise my capacities in such a way as to modify the actions of others on my actions. Freedom is tied very closely to action. But that corporeal freedom is itself conditioned by various social, political and historical forces, as well as the interpretive frameworks within which the agent understands himself … It is not merely a natural body seeking to maintain itself in motion and satisfy whatever desires it happens to possess. Instead, it includes a dynamic account of the capacities and perspectives that enable a particular kind of natural body to respond to and reflect on those actions acting on it, however much it is always acting within a dense field of relations of power.
>
> (2008, 25)

Unlike republican approaches, the ideas of power here are not based on arbitrary/non-arbitrary wielding of power. Moreover, further engagement with Foucault's governance account exposes the ways in which these relations are not causal or linear, but are always historical, contingent, and shaped by a number of different discursive forces. Far from the liberal ideal of the "external, linear, progressive pursuit by a universal, finite, thinking subject" (Kapur, 2018, 30), the account of freedom becomes more complex as multifarious relations and practices are exposed, within which the 'individual' is located and entangled. As Ivison suggests,

> Freedom, in the end, is what must be practised, and it will always be a function of the relations of power within which one is always enmeshed and against which one always reacts … Individuals are not to be understood as free as such, or free in some non-specific sense, but free to do particular things and pursue particular ends.
>
> (2008, 18)

The understanding of freedom which emerges here is one as a practice and/or a process, rather than an attribute of an individual. The relationality central to this account resonates with the work of Jennings in his call for a conception of "freedom *through*". In his relational account, Jennings calls for a more relational interpretation of ethical concepts including liberty, and a move away from our understanding of such concepts as "givens" (Jennings, 2015, 8).

However, it is important to reflect on what this relational and contextual account of freedom within the assemblage might mean. Does it entail, for example, that, given the ubiquity and universality of 'interference' in the shaping of everyday experience, we ought to abandon freedom or liberty as an ethical concern? Do we then turn away from situations in which we are concerned that somebody is being deprived of their liberty, on the basis that *everyone*, through the lens of governmentality and the assemblage, is similarly deprived of their liberty? Or, alternatively, the argument could be interpreted as suggesting that as nobody is free, and we are all entangled in these onto-epistemological webs, then the focus now needs to be on ensuring that we *do become* free, in the liberal image of liberty. It is important to make clear here that this is not the logical corollary of these critical perspectives. The purpose of such perspectives is to expose the caricature of 'freedom' and the uncomplicated picture that it paints, but also, more importantly, what the tangible effects of this fiction are. The 'harm' which can occur through particular coercive or dominating power and relational dynamics then is still important to these accounts, however this is not because of the ways that such dynamics deny the individual the ability to be self-determining but rather through the ways that they deny agency via the suppression or closure of relational engagements and opportunities to be otherwise. This denial of, and consequent suppression of, agency is captured in the words of Rusi Stanev, who was at the centre of one of the key European Court of Human Rights cases involving liberty in the context of guardianship laws (*Stanev v Bulgaria* [2012] ECHR 46 (Application no. 36760/06)). In a chapter with Sheila Wildeman before his death in 2017, Rusi stated that, "I am not an object, they can't move me where they want. I am a human being and I need my freedom and people to communicate with" (Stanev and Wildeman, 2018). Here there is a real sense in which the denial of agency and subjectivity reduces individuals to objects, whereas the assemblage account offered here and throughout the book recognises the agential nature of interactions, and of alternative sites and routes to respond.

Turning to responses, the assemblage account avoids the need to start with the individual, instead focusing upon the various different actors and relations which are interacting and shaping or foreclosing alternatives. The focus is instead upon enabling flourishing or the opening up of new relations and flows, recognising where these are currently being constrained. Thus, attentiveness to the various sources and contingencies enables new sites for change to be explored, not just at the individual level. As discussed above in relation to recognising deprivations of liberty in family settings, causality is not linear here, and responses and responsibility can be located in, for example, legal and policy shifts, changes to service commissioning practices, and broader systemic changes around how disability is understood and responded to. Moreover, the focus and temporality of state intervention also shifts away from being simply about recognising and authorising deprivations of liberty and reacting to a legal concern. What is interesting currently is that law only begins to *question* liberty or freedom in situations in which there is the possibility of a particular force being employed to constrain it. In law, and in the context of mental capacity law particularly here, this tends to be in situations where institutions seek to impose a particular care or treatment arrangement. The historically situated assemblage account enjoins us to challenge and question the prior relations and interactions leading to this moment or legal 'event', troubling the contingency and purportedly linear causality of the situation. This can then disrupt the perceived necessity or inevitability of disabled people being deprived of their liberty. In this way, the assemblage account, underpinned by a focus on spatial and relational dynamics, acts as both a critical analytical tool but also a way to reimagine legal and policy responses. Unlike the republican approach, the focus of response here is not at the level of the individual, and recognises multiple sources of domination or power imbalance which arise through historic, entangled processes beyond simply the arbitrary exercise of power. Law, and the state here, are much more complex, and issues cannot simply be resolved by a democratic legal process to avoid arbitrariness. Dependency similarly is not something that is or ought to be avoided but is central to the very assemblages that we are all part of. Moreover, this approach goes beyond capabilities theory, again in the shift away from the individual as the prior concern, and a complicating of the separate and linear relation between the individual and the state. It provides a more nuanced look at the contingencies and processes involved in the shaping of the current situation, highlighting important critical junctures and, importantly, points of disruption.

Conclusion

The chapter has highlighted the problematic ways that liberty is understood in the mental capacity framework and the broader effects of this, linked to ideals of static materiality, liberal legal subjectivity, and the bounded state that have been shown to feature across the liberal legal landscape. Progressive literatures, including some which have been engaged with by mental capacity scholars, have been seen to be constrained by the broader liberal logics, and the spatial and relational approach, through the lens of the assemblage, offered as a way to rethink understandings of, and responses to, liberty.

One of the key themes emerging from the assemblage approach, and from utilising the conceptual tools offered by spatial and relational dynamic approaches, is the ways that practices can sediment and congeal, and become seen as givens through certain relations and processes. In the context of liberty and freedom, Iveson suggests that

> As these relations of power and the forms of subjectivity they engender stabilize and become normalized, they act to constrain some range of actions (and thus persons) more than others, and identify some actors for particular forms of governance and interference rather than others. To the extent that this ends up severely constraining the capacities of particular individuals or groups to act on the actions of others acting on them, they congeal into relations of domination as opposed to relations of power.
>
> (Ivison, 2008, 11)

The approach offered here allows a focus upon such practices and patterns and, importantly, ways to resist them. This is important in the context of disability and mental capacity in particular, where there has long been recognition of the carceral logics which infuse care and treatment practices, and which tend to become normalised and sanctioned through a justification of their necessity for disabled people. Rather than reinforcing these logics and the boundaries they produce, it is instead important to challenge the very foundations of this ideal of liberty.

This is particularly important when responding to the challenge posed both by *Cheshire West* and, more broadly, Art 14 of the CRPD. Current debates as to how mental capacity law, and linked frameworks around liberty, can be made to be compliant with the CRPD tend to focus on leveraging consent as a way to make the law compliant with Art 12 *and* Art 14. For example, the Joint Committee on Human Rights, in their report on the reform of the DoLS, endorsed an approach suggested by Ruck Keene which sought to avoid the DoLS/LPS route for those who were validly consenting to their arrangements (Ruck Keene, 2018, also see Series, 2020). Some have suggested that this approach – seeing consent to the arrangements as vitiating any deprivation of liberty – is more in tune with Art 12 of the CRPD, as *not* basing the analysis of whether someone is being deprived of their liberty on their subjective wishes reinforces the capacity/incapacity binary (Series, 2020). However this is a potentially problematic approach, as in reality, and without sustained change to other vectors of the binary logics we have seen throughout the book, this would conversely reinforce the binary framework. Those who are said to have capacity would be 'moved' into the realm of the capacitous and autonomous adult, obscuring state responsibility for their situation or options available to them. Those deemed not to have capacity would occupy the realm of DoLS/LPS. Far from moving us away from the binary framework, such an approach seems instead to reinforce it, and the other problematic consequences which flow from this, most worryingly enabling societal and institutional factors to be obscured and privatised. Like the engagements with republican theory discussed in the chapter, such approaches fall into the trap of seeing autonomy and individual choice as the lynchpin for change, reinscribing the problematic consequences of this that we have seen in previous chapters. As noted earlier, this has become a 'lawyers game', tweaking individual concepts yet leaving their broader, mutually sustaining, concepts intact, or inadvertently shoring them up. There is a need for a wholesale rethinking, unshackled from the current legal armoury of MCA, DoLS/LPS, and the European Convention on Human Rights. Rather than reinscribing this tendency to individualise the concern with liberty, the focus ought to shift to facilitating and enabling freedom *through* – by unbounding liberty and being attentive to the relational and spatial dynamics and what they allow or foreclose. In tracing the processes and the maintenance of the boundaries of liberty through jurisprudence, this chapter has provided this contextualised exploration of the logics of liberty and its effects, as well as offering critical tools to enable this unbounding of liberty. The next chapter continues this thread and takes a more focused look at the public/private divide and how it is deployed as a means to actively entrench disempowerment and foreclose scrutiny of broader disabling structures and processes.

References

Arstein-Kerslake, A. and Flynn, E. 2017. 'The Right to Legal Agency: Domination, Disability and the Protections of Article 12 of the Convention on the Rights of Persons with Disabilities' *International Journal of Law in Context* 13(1), 22–38.

Berlin, I. 1969. 'Two Concepts of Liberty' in I. Berlin (Ed.), *Four Essays on Liberty*. Oxford: Oxford University Press. 118–72.

Ben-Moshe, L., Chapman, C. and Carey, A. 2014. *Disability Incarcerated – Imprisonment and Disability in the United States and Canada*. New York: Palgrave Macmillan.

Bowlby, S. 2012. 'Recognising the Time–Space Dimensions of Care: Caringscapes and Carescapes' *Environment and Planning A: Economy and Space* 44(9), 2101–18.

Chapman, C. 2014. 'Five Centuries' Material Reforms and Ethical Reformulations of Social Elimination' in L. Ben-Moshe, C. Chapman and A. Carey (Eds), *Disability Incarcerated: Imprisonment and Disability in the United States and Canada*. New York: Palgrave Macmillan. 25–44.

Clements, L. 2011. 'Disability, Dignity and the Cri de Couer' *EHLRH* 6, 675–85.

Clements, L. 2021. *Clustered Injustice and the Level Green*. London: Legal Action Group.

Clough, B. 2018. 'Accountability, Social Care Decision Making and Social Justice: Reflections on the Responsive State' in B. Clough and J. Herring (Eds), *Ageing, Gender and Family Law*. (London: Routledge).

Davies, M. 2017. *Law Unlimited*. Oxfordshire: Routledge.

Delaney, D. 2010. *Nomospheric Investigations: The Spatial, The Legal and The Pragmatics of World Making*. Oxfordshire: Routledge.

Department of Health 2005. Bournewood Consultation: The Approach to be Taken in Response to the Judgement of the European Court of Human Rights in the 'Bournewood' Case. https://webarchive.nationalarchives.gov.uk/+/http://www.dh.gov.uk/en/Consultations/Closedconsultations/DH_4113613 last accessed 24/7/2020.

Flynn, M. and Eley, R. 2015. A Serious Case Review: James. Suffolk Safeguarding Adults Board. https://www.scie-socialcareonline.org.uk/a-serious-case-review-james/r/a11G000000CT4OLIA1 last accessed 27/7/2020.

Ford, R. 2000. 'Laws Territory (A History of Jurisdiction)' in N. Blomley, D. Delaney and R. Ford (Eds), *The Legal Geographies Reader: Law, Power, Space*. Toronto, ON: Wiley. 200–17.

Garrau, M. and Laborde, C. 2015. 'Relational Equality, Non-Domination, and Vulnerability' in C. Fourie, F. Schuppert and I. Wallimann-Helmer (Eds), *Social Equality: On What it Means to be Equals*. Oxford: Oxford University Press. 45–64.

Gill, N., Conlon, D., Moran, D. and Burridge, A. 2018. 'Carceral Circuitry: New Directions in Carceral Geography' *Progress in Human Geography* 42(2), 183–204.

Gilson, E. 2018. 'Beyond Bounded Selves and Places: The Relational Making of Vulnerability and Security' *Journal of the British Society for Phenomenology* 49(3), 229–42.

Goffman, E. 1961. *Asylums: Essays on the Social Situation of Mental Patients and Other Inmates*. New York: Anchor.

Guest, C. and Corrigan, O. 2018. 'Extraordinary Normalcy: Home, Relationships and Identities in Narratives of Unpaid Care' *Health and Place* 53, 71–8.

Hesse, B. 2014. 'Escaping Liberty: Western Hegemony, Black Fugitivity' *Political Theory* 42(3), 288–313.

Hirschmann, N. 2003. *The Subject of Liberty: Toward a Feminist Theory of Freedom*. Princeton, NJ: Princeton University Press.

Hobbes, T. 1651. *Leviathan: Or the Matter, Forme and Power of a Commonwealth, Ecclesiasticall and Civil*. Menston: Scolar Press.

House of Lords Select Committee on the Mental Capacity Act 2005 2014. *Report of Session 2013–14, Mental Capacity Act 2005 Post Legislative Scrutiny*. London: TSO.

Ivison, D. 2008. 'Foucault's Hobbes and the Concept of Liberty' *Arts* 30, 9–33.

Jennings, B. 2009. 'Public Health and Liberty: Beyond the Millian Paradigm' *Public Health Ethics* 2(2), 123–34.

Jennings, B. 2015. 'Relational Liberty Revisited: Membership, Solidarity and a Public Health Ethics of Place' *Public Health Ethics* 8(1), 7–17.

Joint Committee on Human Rights 2018. The Right to Freedom and Safety: Reform of the Deprivation of Liberty Safeguards. Seventh Report of Session 2017–19. https://publications.parliament.uk/pa/jt201719/jtselect/jtrights/890/890.pdf last accessed 24/7/2020.

Kapur, R. 2018. *Gender, Alterity and Human Rights: Freedom in a Fishbowl*. Cheltenham: Elgar.

Law Commission 2017. *Mental Capacity and Deprivation of Liberty*. Law Com No 372. London: HMSO.

Lovett, F. 2010. *A General Theory of Domination and Justice*. Oxford: Oxford University Press.

Massey, D., Allen, J. and Sarre, P. 1999. *Human Geography Today*. Cambridge: Polity Press.

Miller, J. 2018. 'On Epistemic Diversity, Ontologies and Assumptions in Capability Approaches' in Comim, Fennell and Anand (Eds), *New Frontiers of the Capability Approach*. Cambridge: Cambridge University Press. 139–52.

Moran, D. 2015. *Carceral Geography: Spaces and Practices of Incarceration*. Surrey: Ashgate.

Mostyn, N. 2018. Written evidence from Sir Nicholas Mostyn (DOL0012). http://data.parliament.uk/writtenevidence/committeeevidence.svc/evidencedocument/human-rights-committee/the-right-to-freedom-and-safety-reform-of-the-deprivation-of-liberty-safeguards/written/78398.html last accessed 27/7/2020.

Milligan, C. 2000. 'Bearing the Burden: Towards a Restructured Geography of Caring' *Area* 32, 49–58.

O'Shea, T. 2018a. 'Disability and Domination: Lessons from Republican Political Philosophy' *Journal of Applied Philosophy* 35(1), 133–48.

O'Shea, T. 2018b. 'A Civic Republican Analysis of Mental Capacity Law' *Legal Studies* 38(1), 147–63.

Pettit, P. 1997. *Republicanism: A Theory of Freedom and Government*. Oxford: Oxford University Press.

Pettit, P. 2001. *A Theory of Freedom: From the Psychology to the Politics of Agency*. Oxford: Polity Press.

Pettit, P. 2002. 'Keeping Republican Freedom Simple: On A Difference With Quentin Skinner' *Political Theory* 30(3), 339–56.

Rose, N., O'Malley, P. and Valverde, M. 2006. 'Governmentality' *Annual Review of Law and Social Science* 2(1), 83–104.

Ruck Keene, A. 2018. Written Evidence from Alex Ruck Keene (DOL0120). http://data.parliament.uk/writtenevidence/committeeevidence.svc/evidencedocument/human-rights-committee/the-right-to-freedom-and-safety-reform-of-the-deprivation-of-liberty-safeguards/written/80869.html last accessed 25/7/2020

Sen, A. 2009. *The Idea of Justice*. London: Penguin.

Series, L. 2019. 'On Detaining 300,000 People: the Liberty Protection Safeguards' *International Journal of Mental Health and Capacity Law* 25. https://www.northumbriajournals.co.uk/index.php/IJMHMCL/article/view/952 last accessed 24/7/2020.

Series, L. 2020. 'Making Sense of Cheshire West' in C. Spivakovsky, L. Steele and P. Weller (Eds), *The Legacies of Institutionalisation: Disability, Law and Policy in the "Deinstitutionalised" Community*. Oxford: Hart.193–206.

Sherkoske, G. 2020. 'Should Relational Autonomy Theorists Embrace Republican Freedom Instead? A Commentary on "Nondomination and the Limits of Relational Autonomy" by Danielle M. Wenner' *International Journal of Feminist Approaches to Bioethics* 13(2), 56–9.

Shnayderman, R. 2015. 'On "Being Forced to be Free" Between Republican and Liberal Freedom' *Ethical Perspectives* 22(2), 247–70.

Skinner, Q. 1997. *Liberty before Liberalism*. Cambridge: Cambridge University Press.

Stanev, R. and Wildeman, S. 2018. 'Freedom: A Work in Progress' in E. Flynn et al. (Eds), *Global Perspectives on Legal Capacity Reform: Our Voices, Our Stories*. London: Routledge. 197–212.

Tribe, L. H. 1989. 'The Curvature of Constitutional Space: What Lawyers Can Learn from Modern Physics' *Harvard Law Review* 103(1), 1–39.

Weller, P. 2014. 'Reconsidering Legal Capacity: Radical Critiques, Governmentality and Dividing Practice' *Griffith Law Review* 32(3), 498–518.

Wenner, D. 2020. 'Nondomination and the Limits of Relational Autonomy' *International Journal of Feminist Approaches to Bioethics* 13(2), 28–48.

7 Public/private

Dichotomies of powerlessness in the Court of Protection

The previous chapters have demonstrated the importance of the recursive and mutually reinforcing connection (or discursive separation) between the legal subject and the role of the state. Challenging the liberal legal ideal through attention to the assemblage has exposed the interwoven, permeable, and differential spaces and sites of state involvement – alongside other forces and actors – posing a challenge to the traditional idea of the state as monolithic and super-structural. Through this, questions of responsibility and responses begin to arise, particularly when the various connections between different actors are exposed. Continuing this call to be attentive to the processes through which particular ideal and material spaces are constructed and maintained, as part of assemblages, the focus of this chapter will turn to the pervasive public/private divide. This binary has been alluded to in various chapters so far and is one of the central organising ideas underpinning political and legal liberalism. It works to delineate the (often impermeable) space around state involvement and individual responsibility, working in tandem with the conceptualisation of the state considered in earlier chapters. Thinking about the public/private divide and how it works through the lens of the assemblage is useful both in terms of an analytical frame and as a way to reimagine legal and policy responses. This chapter considers this challenge to the public/private divide in more depth, exposing the way the distinction is utilised in mental capacity law, and the effects of this, as well as tracing how it is entangled with the other mutually sustaining binaries in the legal framework that have been encountered across the earlier chapters. In a recent case, we can see this stark material impermeability of the private realm by the state in action when Hedley J discusses the responsibilities of the local authority in relation to best interests around contact,

> I think this is probably best illustrated by considering the position within the property in which H currently lives. The local authority have and will retain the power to maintain or monitor the list of welcomed visitors to H's flat. Whilst of course they cannot impose on H anyone she does not want, they do have a veto in relation to anyone that H might want. They may further provide for those times at which a visitor is to be in the flat and the times when that should end. But once that visitor lawfully enters

DOI: 10.4324/9781351067881-7

> the flat and the front door is shut, the local authority have no further responsibilities for what then takes place. Those are matters entirely for H and the person who is in the flat with her.
>
> (*A Local Authority v H (No 2)* [2019] EWCOP 51, para 34)

The flat door here provides a stark image for the demarcation between the public and the private. The public/private divide has long been recognised by critical legal scholars and feminist theorists as a problematic organising idea which has pernicious material and discursive effects, particularly in terms of ideals of responsibility and accountability. As Lacey puts it,

> The ideology of the public private dichotomy allows government to clean its hands of any *responsibility* for the state of the 'private' world and *depoliticises* the disadvantages which inevitably spill over the alleged divide by affecting the position of the 'privately' disadvantaged citizen.
>
> (Lacey, 1993, 97)

This chapter will pick up this concern stemming from this ongoing critical legal scholarly debate around the public/private divide, but will bring this into conversation with new materialisms, disability perspectives, and spatial understandings in order to deepen the appreciation of the broader effects of the binary divide and the logics which it helps to sustain and is sustained by. Again, mental capacity law provides a useful and important case study for such an analysis, given the stark ways in which the divide can be seen to be utilised by the judiciary as a technique for shifting responsibility and obscuring the wider context. Moreover, the day-to-day power relations and locations of decision making will be foregrounded as a crucial context in which attention needs to be focused. The day-to-day and 'mundane' spaces and sites of mental capacity law are often ignored or overlooked – such as the way in which social care assessments are made, or that medical decisions are made. Yet these spaces and practices will be seen to trouble the public/private divide that is being applied by the judiciary, and judicial techniques for managing this expose the ways in which responsibility is carved up. The institutional dynamics and relations here, including the recursive relations between courts and professionals, are important processes in this reproduction of the boundaries of the public/private divide. In particular, judicial techniques will be a prominent focus of the chapter, situating the judiciary not as neutral observers, simply stating or discovering the boundaries of mental capacity law, but as an active part of the process of constructing, defining, and reproducing the public/private divide and legal subject that inhabits it. This public/private boundary will thus emerge as one requiring constant policing and maintenance through the workings of mental capacity law and judicial engagement with it; yet, at the same time, one which is "permeable, dynamic, fluid" (Davies, 2017, 138) and, importantly, open to change.

The public/private divide

The public/private divide has long been the target of critical debate for feminists, unifying debates across law, politics, philosophy, history, sociology, social policy, and geography. The divide has historically been seen as separating the realm of the state from the private realm (including the family). Feminist legal scholars have drawn attention to the problematic effects of this, in terms of entrenching (often) gendered inequalities and disadvantage, by situating them as outside of the realm of state (public) responsibility. Olsen (1985) for example drew important attention to the lack of focus on women's work in the home, and to the ways that violence within the home was privatised and left outside of state regulation. The home, in this sense, was delineated as the private realm, and not to be interfered with. The feminist rallying cry "the personal is political" which reverberated through the work of Mackinnon (1989), Pateman (1983), and care ethicists such as Tronto (1993) similarly sought to draw attention to the problematic privatising of disadvantage and to bring such issues into the realm of the public.

However, this important feminist work has not been without criticism. Rose, for example, has challenged the utility of the public/private divide as a conceptual tool, particularly for progressive or emancipatory approaches (1987). Rose is critical of the ways that the divide was utilised in a way which often reinforced some of the other sources of inequality or disadvantage, such as through uncritical reliance on ideas of law or the state as the site of response. Lacey, similarly, critiques the way that some work which seeks to bring the 'private' to public and political attention then wrongly makes the argument that this then requires a public response through, for example, law or state regulation (1993). In a sense, both of these critiques then point to the problematic ways in which a simplistic analysis of the public/private divide can end up reinforcing it.

However, as Boyd (1997) suggests, the public/private divide does retain utility not as a static marker, but as "indeterminate and shifting, but at the same time connected to identifiable relations of power", and a tool to recognise "the role of the state at particular historical moments, in particular contexts, and in relation to particular issues" (4). In this way, it provides a useful lens to draw attention to the productive effects of the way the divide is deployed. As Lacey puts it, the divide plays a role in the government hiding responsibility and depoliticising disadvantage (1993, 97): "[t]he practical consequence of non-regulation is the consolidation of the *status quo*: the *de facto* support of pre-existing power relations and distributions of goods within the 'private' sphere" (97).

Alongside Rose's call to "fragment, disturb and disrupt" (1987, 66), some of the explanatory categories that the feminist critique of the public/private divide historically relied upon (such as law, the state, and power), the assemblage account underpinned by a focus on spatial and relational dynamics offers a way to trace the deployment of the public/private divide and its effects, and to reimagine responses in a way that do not rely upon or reinforce the problematic explanatory categories. As Rose suggests, "modern societies are shifting networks of agencies, associations, corporations and domestic units, with many distinct and differentiated loci of decisions, criteria of judgment, bodies of knowledge and expertise" (1987, 68). As with the assemblage, this calls for a disruption of static ideas both of the discursive and spatial delineation of the public and private, but also recognition of the shifting nature of relations within networks and different effects of shifts within these. The spatial and relational nature of the assemblage analysis, driven by new materialist insights, draws attention to the inseparability of material and discursive processes of boundary drawing, and the creative, agential nature of these. In this way, the public/private divide is a generative and agential boundary making practice, not a descriptive marker. This offers ways to rethink the role of law, the state, and power within the assemblage, echoing Rose's suggestion of the need to recognise the plurality of law (Davies, 2017), to complicate the state, and to recognise power as diffuse and distributed rather than centralised.

As seen in previous chapters, the assemblage offers a way to complicate the idea of scale, particularly in terms of responsibility and sites for response. It demonstrates the interplay between different scales, rather than seeing them as bounded and hierarchical. This analysis then offers important insights for fields such as political geography, where feminist geographers have been calling for a more nuanced appreciation of scale, power, and space through engaging with the public/private divide (England, 2003; Hyndman, 2008). Moreover, as Valverde suggests, as well as thinking about scale, these insights need to be "supplemented by insights derived from analysing the workings of jurisdiction" (2008). This is particularly evident in relation to issues of jurisdiction and the territories of law or state obligation that are created and bounded through various processes and relations. Davies highlights that the concept of jurisdiction brings together a number of key issues, including

> territorial and conceptual spaces of state based law, personal status, temporality, the power to speak/decide, the universality, particularity and performativity of law, and the numerous contestations that prevent these variable coming into sustained alignment … [Jurisdiction is] the problematic element through which a norm is figured as formal law; where force or repetition becomes authority, where relational beings become interpellated subjects and citizens, and where spatial boundaries become territory. (Davies, 2017, 101)

As Valverde suggests, jurisdiction is often seen as a legalistic or technical issue, uninteresting for critical scholarship, yet it involves "much larger, extralegal issues of power and authority" (Valverde, 2015, 82). Thinking about the deployment of jurisdiction as a judicial technique in the context of mental capacity law, the public/private divide will thus be analysed to see how the boundaries of the public and private are drawn and how this works to obscure responsibility and constrain responses. As Massey, Allen, and Sarre contend, the problems of binary approaches, such as the public/private divide, which are central to the liberal legal structure, are that they are "bound up with ways of spatio-temporalizing the world which are so seemingly 'natural', so habitual, that we have almost forgotten to think about them" (1999, 8). Instead, there is a need to look at the ways in which the spaces of the public and the private, and associated institutional norms that stem from these, do not pre-exist but instead are created and reproduced.

Shaping the public/private divide

The legal subject

The representation of the legal subject through case law provides one key element of the reasoning employed by the judiciary around the public/private divide. It is important to trace the rendering of the subject, and the material impacts of this. As Robert Leckey suggests, juridical processes within the legal system "structure identity and reconfigures the field of social possibilities in ways over which individuals do not have full agency" (Leckey, 2008, 6). These techniques and judicial processes can be seen in the case of *Re MN* and the various judgments as the case moved through the appellate courts (*Re MN* [2017] UKSC 22; *Re MN* [2015] EWCA Civ 411; [2013] EWHC 3859 (COP)).

The case involved a young man with complex disabilities and questions as to his care and residence. He was in residential care as a child, and the litigation stemmed from his transition to adult social care. The parents, prior to the first hearing in 2013, accepted that he could stay where he was for the time being, however they were keen in the long run to be more involved in his care and for him to eventually come to live in the family home. There were arrangements that the parents could go and visit MN in the residential care home if they gave the hospital one hour's notice, as well as periodic arrangements to enable MN to meet his brothers who were also in residential care. At the time of the first hearing in the Court of Protection in 2013, the parents stated that they wished MN to be able to visit them in their family home. The care home was unwilling to facilitate this – they said that trained carers would need to go with him (and that the parents were reluctant to allow professionals into their home), and given that staff feared parents would not co-operate, they were not willing to do this. MN's mother also wanted to be involved in providing intimate care to MN when she went to visit at the residential home. The independent social worker felt this would form an important element of MN's quality of life. However, the care home was not willing to allow this – they argued that the mother wouldn't co-operate and would not undergo necessary manual handling training. Overall, the Clinical Commissioning Group (CCG), who were responsible for funding MN's care, said that it was not in his best interests to have his mother involved in his care or for him to have visits to the family home.

These issues were due to be heard by the Court of Protection; however, the night before the first day of the hearing, counsel for the local authority, at 11.32pm, gave notice to the other parties of her intention to argue that the Court of Protection has "no jurisdiction" to decide these issues – essentially, given that the options that the parents wanted were not "on the table" (i.e. not available options), then they were public law issues which could only be heard in a judicial review claim. Counsel argued then that the Court of Protection could only decide between "available options" and that it was inappropriate to use private law best interests proceedings in the Court of Protection to try to obtain a declaration to influence a public law decision.

King J heard these "jurisdictional issues" and gave her judgment on the basis of these – the best interests arguments then were not discussed. In essence, she agreed with the argument by counsel for the local authority that the Court of Protection can only choose between available options. The court cannot interfere with the decision of public bodies (such as local authorities, clinical commissioning groups, and the NHS). Such matters are for judicial review proceedings given their public law nature, in contrast to the private law nature of the Court of Protection.

> [a]n inevitable consequence of a person lacking capacity is that a public authority will often be providing services to that incapacitated person pursuant to various statutory duties. There is *a danger of a blurring of the distinction* as between the Court of Protection's statutory duties in a private law context (namely to consider the best interests of an incapacitated adult), with public law challenges in relation to the willingness, unwillingness, reasonableness or rationality of the services a public authority is willing or able to provide.
> ([2013] EWHC 3859 (COP), para 34; emphasis added)

The judgment makes it clear that there is no scope for demanding particular treatments or services via the Court of Protection, as this is not a right afforded generally in health and social care (see, for example, *R (Burke) v General Medical Council* [2005] EWCA Civ 1003). In essence then, the Court of Protection must decide between the options which are placed "on the table" by the clinician, local authority, or CCG.

On appeal, in *Re MN* [2015] EWCA Civ 411, Munby LJ upheld and fully endorsed King J's judgment and analysis of the law. He stated that,

> The function of the Court of Protection is to take, on behalf of adults who lack capacity, the decisions which, if they had capacity, they would take themselves.
> (para 80)

This position was cemented by the Supreme Court in 2017 with the leading judgment delivered by Lady Hale. Again, she fully endorsed the approach taken by King J and Munby LJ. There is an interesting focus that emerges through these judgments on situating the legal subject within a static space as either capacitous or incapacitous, the effects of which are problematic in terms of obscuring wider relations. This technique is seen in:

1 The statement in relation to the Court of Protection and appellate courts, that "[t]he function of the Court of Protection is to take, on behalf of adults who lack capacity, the decisions which, if they had capacity, they would take themselves". (Munby LJ, para 80).
2 The definition of the options that a person *with* mental capacity would have if they were in the situation that MN was in.

The first, describing the function of the Court of Protection, is part of a long-running thread in medical jurisprudence and mental capacity jurisprudence more recently. It stems from well-known dicta asserted in *R (Burke) v GMC* [2005] EWCA Civ 1003.[1] This was then reiterated by Lady Hale in the first Supreme Court decision on the Mental Capacity Act 2005, *Aintree v James* [2013] UKSC 67, where she stated that

> This Act is concerned with enabling the court to do for the patient what he could do for himself if of full capacity, but it goes no further. On an application under this Act, therefore, the court has no greater powers than the patient would have if he were of full capacity.
>
> (para 18)

There are a number of problems with this position, however in terms of the rendering of the legal subject here it assimilates the position of an individual deemed to lack capacity with one deemed to have it, creating an illusion of an abstract autonomous legal subject, devoid of context. This obscures the very different contexts in which two such individuals will be embedded in the process of these types of medical or social care decisions. The previous chapter critiqued the focus on the "relevant comparator" in Munby LJ's *Cheshire West* Court of Appeal judgment, which saw disabled people as legally different to non-disabled for the purposes of asking whether they were being deprived of the liberty. Interestingly, we see comparators being used in a different, but equally problematic, way here. Now, the individual deemed to lack capacity (or, more correctly, the Court of Protection standing in their shoes) is placed in a comparable position to a fictitious capacitous individual.

However, when viewed through the lens of the assemblage, drawing attention to the particularity of the relational dynamics which individuals are situated in, which shift as these assemblages transform, the very different situations

1 Also see *R v Cambridge District Health Authority*, ex p B [1995] 1 WLR that a patient has no right to demand a treatment which a medical professional does not think is clinically appropriate.

which those entangled in the mental capacity regulatory landscape will experience in contrast to those ostensibly outside of it becomes clear. The judgment seems to place people in static realms of capacitous and incapacitous. As Keenan suggests,

> Legal geography shows that the ways that law connects space and the subject are often not reflective of the ways that people are actually connected to the spaces where they live, work and otherwise inhabit, however briefly. Through the imposition of its own regime of space–subject connection (via citizenship, domicile, property and other areas of law), law produces spaces in which some subjects belong and others do not. Although the movement of subjects through different spaces is often a privilege and can be a transgressive act, movement does not necessarily mean leaving spaces of oppression behind, and can be used by law to bolster power structures such as those based on race, sex, nationality or anti-state political activity.
>
> (Keenan, 2015, 34)

This is particularly instructive here, as the law can be seen to move individuals into either the space of capacity (and thus seen as an independent, rational actor, freely choosing) or the space of incapacity (the 'other' to this norm). This hides and depoliticises the realities of the situation that people are in and the assemblages which shape and constrain agency.

Yet, as seen in earlier chapters, such an analysis needs to tread carefully and not reinforce an essentialised 'difference' between those deemed to be capacitous and those who are not, which could take us back to Munby LJ (and also Mostyn J's) relevant comparator from Chapter 6. The focus in *MN* on "what an individual with capacity" could do runs the risk of suggesting that those with capacity *are* indeed autonomous, free from external constraints and able to navigate and negotiate these various different forces to facilitate their self-determination in these matters. Instead, a more nuanced understanding of subjectivity as embodied, and recursively constituted by situatedness within complex assemblages of material, discursive, technological, institutional forces prevents the simplistic and harmful rendering of the legal subject as autonomous, unencumbered, and self-determining. We see here what Delaney refers to as the way in which spatial imaginaries (such as the public/private divide) have "productive and constitutive effects on other aspects of social being such as identity, personhood and power" (2010, 15). We can thus begin to explore these effects of "the social spatialisation of difference and the pragmatic effacement, denial or recalibration of difference" (Delaney, 2010, 18), which seems particularly stark in the deployment and assimilation of capacity/incapacity here.

Hall and Wilton have made similar points in relation to the need to spatialise our understandings of relationality and disability. They suggest that a relational sense of space sees

> spaces as made up of relations and, as such, always being "made, unmade, and remade by the incessant shuffling of heterogeneous relations" (Doel, 2007, 810). From this perspective, rather than separating the "oppressive social experience of disability" from the "limitations (and capacities) [of] impairment" (Gleeson, 1999, 52) we can imagine bodies (both impaired and non-impaired), objects and spaces engaged in shifting relations that have the capacity to produce both exclusionary and/or enabling arrangements.
>
> (Hall and Wilton, 2016, 728)

Similarly, Feely engages with an assemblage account in order to provide an understanding of how particular approaches to disability are created and materialise.

> To elaborate, an assemblage account of why a particular service user, diagnosed as having cerebral palsy, cannot currently speak might consider:
>
> - the biology of the particular body and its actual physical capacities (the things it can and cannot do in its current material context);
> - existent communication technologies and current research into communication;
> - technologies;
> - what funding is, or is not, available for this;
> - how the relevant legislation and policies enable and constrain access to speech technologies; and
> - how societal discourses construct speechless subjects and the provision of expensive technologies to them.
>
> The assemblage analyst would seek to map how the complex interaction of all of these elements produces the problem of a body that cannot currently speak.
>
> (2016, 284)

The importance of this attentiveness to the particularities of the situation, and embeddedness within assemblages, is similarly highlighted through an analysis of King J's statements as to what the options are for somebody deemed to *have* mental capacity in the same position as MN.

> If MN had capacity, but required the type of nursing care he currently needs due only to his physical needs, he might wish his mother to assist with his personal care. The care providers (here RCH), may, as here, be unwilling to allow this for whatever reason; perhaps health and safety issues or difficult relationships with the MN's mother. MN with capacity would have the following options: (i) accept the conditions of residence at the care provider's establishment (ii) privately fund his care elsewhere

> or (iii) seek to negotiate with the ACCG in the hope of them agreeing to fund his removal to a different residential unit which would allow his mother to assist with his personal care. What MN with capacity would not be able to do is to force, by way of court order or otherwise, the care providers (RCH) to agree to his mother coming into their facility and "assisting" with his intimate care.
>
> (para 53)

This however overlooks, or deliberately obscures, the realities of the options available here, both for somebody deemed to lack capacity and an individual deemed to have it. It ignores the very material effects of the regulatory frameworks which interact here and impact upon the actual options available to those who come under the gaze of the mental capacity framework. For instance, if MN had capacity, he would – in theory at least – be able to walk out or have a family take him out of the setting in which he was residing and which was felt to be unsuitable. For those who lack capacity, this is simply not an option given the powers that this status then bestows upon professionals to determine decisions in their best interests. The governance frameworks and techniques that circulate within these particular configurations for people deemed to lack capacity thus have material and tangible effects. There is a clear difference between these subject positions that the 'options' provided by King J fails to recognise and which assimilates this difference in a problematic manner. Yet, it is also true that in relation to those who are deemed to *have* capacity, the options set out above may also turn out to be fictional, as seen in Chapter 3. Again, what we encounter here is a rendering of the legal subject *with* capacity as a self-determining individual who can freely negotiate these complex institutional and legal relations, without fear of questioning their capacity to do so. This reinforces the paradigmatic yet unattainable autonomous legal subject. As Simplican states, in relation to traditional Rawlsian theories of justice in the context of disability,

> [i]deal theory promotes two distinct fictions in relation to idealized capacities: it neglects inequalities in cognitive capacities – whether these inequalities are caused by injustice or impairment – and it exaggerates the abilities of the privileged, constituting a class of not just able-bodied but super-bodied agents.
>
> (Simplican, 2016, 94–5)

The picture painted by King J misrepresents the realities for many individuals who are dependent upon the provision of services by local authorities and clinical commissioning groups and the institutionally and systemically produced inequalities in power that these can create between the individual and professionals. This is not to say that individual professionals within these relations are necessarily acting in malign ways – instead it is to recognise the power relations that the legal and institutional configurations produce. What is missing in this explication of the context and options available is an appreciation of, for example, the power relations enabled by and circulating through bureaucratic and discretionary service provision regimes such as adult social care assessments, and the day-to-day engagements with these by service users but also a range of differently situated professionals. The assemblage account allows us to bring these aspects to the fore, and to avoid a static, abstract idea of the individual and their options. We similarly see more clearly the ongoing role of the state in the shaping of this context, through institutional reconfigurations and policy shifts.

The framing of the legal subject in this case law then problematically assimilates very different subject positions, obscuring from legal purview the crucial factors which impede the so-called autonomous decision making of the patient or service-user, regardless of their deemed status as capacitous or incapacitous. It is a crucial technique employed here by the judiciary to avoid unmasking these factors, instead framing the issue as about powers and jurisdiction, and in turn, shoring up the public/private divide. As Ford suggests, "jurisdictional boundary does more than separate territory, it also separates types of people" (Ford, 2000, 201). This is a particularly striking manoeuvre in the context of mental capacity law, given that one of the central techniques and ostensible purpose of this legal framework is precisely to establish the *difference* of those deemed to lack mental capacity in contrast to the capacitous individual. For that difference to then disappear (or, more accurately, be actively concealed) when considering issues of power and institutional responses becomes a technique of individualising responsibility and obscuring institutional and structural involvement (see Garland and Travis, 2020, for discussion of these techniques in relation to intersex issues).

What these approaches seek to foreground are the ways in which subjectivity and embodied experience are produced through these shifting configurations of the biological, the material, the discursive, the technological, and the institutional. This stands in contrast to the static subjectivity that King J espouses through the image she paints of the options available to those with and those without mental capacity. Moreover, the effects of this rendering of the subject by King J, and endorsement of it by Munby LJ and Lady Hale, individualises the issue by placing the locus of responsibility and potential change upon the individual, rather than recognising the institutional role played in the creation and reproduction of powerlessness. Recognition of the relationality of the subject *and* of the production of embodied experience thus has important normative consequences in the field of disability and mental capacity law. Rather than focusing on relationality and vulnerability to simply advocate attentiveness to context, appreciation of the ways in which this embodied experience is always, already produced through particular configurations (institutional, material, discursive) points to the need to consider how such spatial relations can be reconfigured to produce different assemblages.

The role of the court and judgment

The repeated references to jurisdiction (and later, to powers) ignore the always, already, role that the state and institutions, including the court, play. It ignores the historicity and ongoing temporality of institutional relations and interrelations and the ongoing (re)configurations of these that take place. As Blomley, Delaney, and Ford outline,

> law can be understood as constitutive of social reality in the naïve sense that the operation of law as a force in the world causes things to happen. Beyond that, law is constitutive of social relations and relational identities … Law is constitutive of the institutional world within which we act … To some extent each of these domains – and their boundaries – are what they are in large part because of their legal definition.
>
> (Blomley, Delaney, and Ford, 2000, xv)

Institutional powers are as such created and actively constituted as they move through particular institutional relations, including through the interactions between legislation and the courts. In particular, what is evident through the case law discussed above is the active reproduction and reinforcement of the boundary between the public and the private. We see this at a number of points through the judgments, including in this statement by King J in *MN*:

> [a]n inevitable consequence of a person lacking capacity is that a public authority will often be providing services to that incapacitated person pursuant to various statutory duties. There is a *danger of a blurring of the distinctio*n as between the Court of Protection's statutory duties in a private law context (namely to consider the best interests of an incapacitated adult), with public law challenges in relation to the willingness, unwillingness, reasonableness or rationality of the services a public authority is willing or able to provide.
>
> (para 34; emphasis added)

The 'danger' that King J is referring to is not unpacked any further in the judgment, but the fact that the blurring of the distinction is seen as potentially dangerous by the judiciary demonstrates the political importance of the public/private divide and urgency of maintaining it. It has repercussions for the rendering of the role of the state and of the individual. The creation of the realm of the public, in contrast to the private realm, actively produces and reproduces configurations of obligations and responsibilities owed by the state and its institutions, and draws a line over which it is deemed inappropriate for such institutions to transgress. Thinking back to Lacey's work on the public/private divide, this is a clear instance where it is deployed in order to shape the realm of responsibility of the state, and consequently to depoliticise disadvantage, in turn supporting existing power relations (1993, 97).

Turning now to the role of the courts and judgment in this, we will see the importance of dynamic processes, performance, and reinscription for the persistence of these norms. As Tribe puts it, pre-empting in some ways the challenge to atomism which has recently exploded in new materialist and posthuman thought:

> If law is, in fact, best understood through some such post-Newtonian framework, then courts do not have the luxury of deciding who did what to whom, measuring the conduct against pre-existing norms, awarding appropriate relief, and then proceeding as though the relief granted or withheld were all that ultimately mattered. Instead, courts must take account of how the very process of legal observation (i.e. judging) shapes both the judges themselves and the materials being judged. The results courts announce – the ways they view the legal terrain and what they think about it – will in turn have continuing effects that reshape the nature of what the courts initially undertook to review, even beyond anything they directly order anyone to do or refrain from doing.
>
> (Tribe, 1989, 20)

This points to the need to analyse such processes, as well as the spatial and topological consequences and entanglements which stem from them.

While the *MN* jurisprudence unfolded, a further case involving a man referred to as MAG was developing. MAG was (at the time) a 34-year-old man who was born on 2 November 1980. He has autism, ataxic cerebral palsy, hearing and visual impairments, and a learning disability. There was no dispute between the parties that MAG lacked capacity to conduct proceedings and make decisions about his tenancy, where he was to live, and his care needs. There was also no dispute that MAG was being deprived of his liberty in this accommodation. MAG had been in his current placement, a ground floor flat, since 2006. His care package was jointly funded, with 75% of costs being met by the CCG and the balance by North Yorkshire County Council (NYCC). It was not until August 2013 that NYCC accepted that it was responsible for meeting MAGs accommodation needs. MAG's flat is very small with no outside space. He cannot stand independently, and the flat is too small to accommodate the wheelchair; therefore, he moves by pulling himself along the floor and up to his bed and up onto chairs. As a result of pulling himself around like this, MAG has sustained painful bursitis in both knees and he also has calluses to his knees and ankles. If he was not taken out, he was confined to his flat.

The issue before District Judge Glentworth in *NYCC v MAG* ([2015] EWCOP 64) was essentially about the authorisation of the deprivation of liberty that was taking place. Bold attempts were made by Glentworth DJ to circumvent the difficulties facing MAG if the approach taken by King J in the earlier decision in MN was to be followed. Recognising the powerlessness of the court in terms of directing institutional resources through a best interests decision, she instead refused to authorise the deprivation of liberty of MAG. She argued that such a deprivation breached his Art 5 rights, given that the conditions of his accommodation were overly restrictive and not appropriate or justified by his unsoundness of mind. On appeal however, in *NYCC v MAG* ([2016] EWCOP 5), Cobb J allowed the appeal by NYCC delivering a scathing judgment of Glentworth DJ's approach (see paras 22, 24, 36, 52, and

62 for a flavour of this). Essentially Cobb J felt that Glentworth DJ had allowed her frustration at the authorities to cloud an otherwise clear and settled legal issue, and cited with approval the judgment of Munby LJ in *Re MN* (discussed above). It is worthy of note, however, that due to Glentworth DJ's refusal to authorise the deprivation of liberty, alternative and suitable accommodation *had* been found for MAG – something that the authorities had purportedly been unable to do since 2013 (or possibly earlier – see paras 34, 35, and 36 of Glentworth's judgment for an idea as to the wrangling between the authorities on this point). Again, however, Cobb J reiterated the importance of the public/private divide here and the powerlessness of the court to intervene and direct resources.

What is striking about the judgments in the *MN* and *MAG* cases is the *powerlessness* that the judiciary repeatedly state that they have over the situation. The techniques described above, such as likening the court's abilities to an individual who has mental capacity and representing the court's power as simply about standing in the shoes of the incapacitous individual, are key to this. The judiciary are eager to paint themselves as powerless, rather than active and powerful agents within these assemblages. As well as the purported powerlessness of the court, it is striking that these judgments, bolstered by the public/private divide, serve to disempower the individual at the centre, and there is no readily apparent mechanism by which they can challenge this. Moreover, these judgements weave an interlocking thread between each other, with repeated references not just to the court below, but across the cases, carving out a particular space of reasons and reasoning. These intertwine the conceptual framing and relevance of the facts of the cases and create the necessary connections to justify the particular outcomes. The assemblage analysis here allows an exploration of the ways in which the judiciary do this and the productive effects in terms of constructing the conceptual space for understanding and responding to the facts, and reinscribing particular norms. As suggested above and throughout the theoretical engagements in this book, this process is an active and not a passive one, and is equally so in the context of judgments. As Tribe puts it, "[t]he law is thus not simply a backdrop against which action may be viewed – even a 'backdrop' that may be 'curved' by the acting objects themselves – but is itself an integral part of the action" (Tribe, 1989, 10).

One of the core strands of these cases is the matter of jurisdiction. It was seen in the *MN* case that the 'trump card' of jurisdiction was played the night before the hearing in the Court of Protection was due to take place. To recall, counsel for the local authority informed the parties, at 11.32pm, of their position that the Court of Protection has "no jurisdiction" to decide on these issues, given that these were public law issues to be decided by judicial review. This then effectively set the framing for both the judgments in the higher courts, and in the MAG case.

This "game" (Valverde, 2015, 57) of jurisdiction has long been recognised as an important facet of governance techniques, occurring both within and between legal systems. Whilst commonly jurisdiction is discussed in relation to international law and transnational boundaries, as Valverde rightly points out, it is important to focus also on the jurisdictional manoeuvres which occur within a legal system. The public/private divide and its deployment in these cases provide a particularly stark example of this. According to Valverde's characterisation of the game of jurisdiction,

> every legal process comes already classified as belonging to a specific project … The legal facts that are relevant in one type of law are not necessarily relevant in another type, as is the case with features of the terrain, which appear in some types of maps but not others.
>
> (Valverde, 2015, 61)

In the context of this mental capacity case law, the classification of the issue as a private or public law matter thus serves to highlight certain facts yet conceal others. Obscuring the public law processes which ought (legally) to feed into the decisions about the provision of care services by local authorities (through the Care Act 2014) or by clinical commissioning groups (under the National Framework for NHS Continuing Health Care), the designation of these cases as private law reduces the focus to the language of best interests. Interestingly, we see the tacit acceptance of this by Lady Hale:

> The CCG's position was that it was not in MN's best interests for his mother to be involved in his personal care or for him to have visits to the family home. The staff were unwilling to facilitate this and the CCG was not prepared to fund alternatives.
>
> (para 10)

There is a tacit reluctance by the court here to delve into the processes underpinning the decision, again a technique through which these can be depoliticised, as will be discussed in the next section on institutional relations. In terms of explaining why the decision is presented in this way, one could argue that the jurisdictional game is at play here. The framing of the issues in these judgments as being about *private* as opposed to *public* law must necessarily erase the public law processes which are entangled with these decisions. Instead, the language of the purportedly private law framework of the Mental Capacity Act (i.e. best interests) must instead be used to ensure the coherence and separateness of the public and private processes. As Valverde suggests, "jurisdiction … sorts competing powers and knowledges into ready-made, clearly separate pigeon-holes" (Valverde, 2015, 85). Otherwise, blurring this distinction could potentially unravel the boundary that is central to the liberal legal framework. In ignoring *these* processes, the judges here are instead part of a broader, ongoing process of production and reproduction of particular norms, of reinscribing the boundaries between the public and the private, and of reinforcing central frames of liberal legal jurisprudence.

Yet these processes and practices are subtle and do not take place in an overt way. Instead, what we see, and what these cases demonstrate, is the manner in which jurisdiction is carefully *de*politicised (Dietz, 2020). As Valverde argues, the game of jurisdiction occurs, "not through an explicit dialogue about appropriate and inappropriate governance, about the political and ethical issues involved, but rather through the quiet working of the game of jurisdiction, as courts decide apparently apolitical questions" (Valverde, 2015, 85). This is again evident throughout the judgment of Lady Hale in the Supreme Court. Rather than endorsing the view of both King J and Munby LJ that this is a jurisdictional issue, Lady Hale instead sought to frame it as about the 'powers' of the Court of Protection. For example, she sums up by saying that

> This was not a case in which the court did not have jurisdiction to continue with the planned hearing. It was a case in which the court did not have power to order the CCG to fund what the parents wanted. Nor did it have power to order the actual care providers to do that which they were unwilling or unable to do. In those circumstances, the court was entitled to conclude that, in the exercise of its case management powers, no useful purpose would be served by continuing the hearing.
>
> (para 44)

Instead, Lady Hale suggested it is instead about *case management.*

> The court clearly has jurisdiction to make any of the orders or declarations provided for in the Act. The question is not strictly one of jurisdiction but of how cases should be handled in the light of the limited powers of the court.
>
> (para 38)

It is striking that the judgment takes a technical tone covering the history of the Mental Capacity Act 2005, the law relating to children under the Children Act 1989 and its interplay with housing legislation, the Care Act 2014 and eligibility criteria, and the case management powers in the Court of Protection Rules 2007. It reduces the case to issues of technicality and management, a jurisdictional technique which serves to sustain the idea of judges as simply neutral observers applying the law. At the same time as technicalities take precedence in the Supreme Court decision, discussion of MN and his best interests, or the process by which the local authority and CCG reached their best interests decision, is starkly absent.

The recourse to technicalities and powers of case management (a heavy focus of the Supreme Court judgment) serves here to further depoliticise the issues involved and remove the discussion further away from the processes of the residence decision which occur (or should have occurred) on the ground, and away from the impacts of the judgment in terms of both entrenching the powerlessness of those falling under the webs of governance spun by the interaction of the MCA with discretionary powers of local authorities and CCGs, and the inter-institutional relations reproduced by the judgment. The judicial technique of depoliticising through technicalities thus prevents "incommensurable processes from clashing ... and the consumers of legal decisions are kept from asking: how should problem X or Y be governed in the first place?" (Valverde, 2015, 85). Again, King J's warning reverberates throughout the judgments:

> [The] danger of a blurring of the distinction as between the Court of Protection's statutory duties in a private law context ... with public law challenges in relation to the willingness, unwillingness, reasonableness or rationality of the services a public authority is willing or able to provide. (para 34)

The tone of the judgments suggests the powerlessness of the courts to do anything, bound as they are by the technicalities of case management powers and jurisdiction. It presents these powers and jurisdictional boundaries as pre-given, as natural and concrete, and the role of the judiciary simply as observers, outside of these boundaries and simply discovering and revealing where these cases fit within such structures. Yet, the focus on the processes of the game of jurisdiction, and the manoeuvres by the courts in terms of both framing the legal subject and framing the jurisdictional location of the facts and resultant powers of the court, reveals a different story. Instead, we see that the persistence of the boundaries between the public and the private, and the rendering of the legal subject within these locations, depends heavily upon the reinscription and reproduction of legal norms. As Massey et al. suggest, "the assembling of power is part and parcel of social reproduction; it is a spatially active, discursive and representational process" (Massey et al., 1999, 172). It is important to be attentive to the processes and techniques by which this occurs, and the discussion above has demonstrated some of these in action. Far from being external observers, the judiciary are actively engaged in constructing and reproducing the public/private divide, and the material effects of this in terms of stabilising particular social assemblages and arrangements in this context.

The processes of inscription, reinscription and citation here are not static and are ongoing, reliant upon reiteration for their persistence. Jurisdictional manoeuvres can shape and reshape the performance and material effects of these processes. In the first instance decision of Glentworth DJ in the *MAG* case, we saw, for example, the refusal of the judge to endorse the deprivation of liberty of a man in accommodation which was wholly unsuitable for his needs. Despite the discursive reversal of this decision and the judicial telling-off that was delivered in the appeal judgment, Glentworth DJ's judgment had a material impact – albeit short-lived – on the jurisdictional landscape here. Given that the decision rendered the living arrangements of MAG as violating Art 5 of the European Convention on Human Rights, the housing authority quickly moved to find alternative, suitable accommodation for him to avoid having to continue to pay damages for the violation of his Convention rights.

This is despite the fact that, according to the judgment, the housing authority had been unable to find any such accommodation during the previous years. Here, the intervention by the judge had material impacts in terms of facilitating access to suitable housing – a consequence which went unchanged despite the appeal judgment.

Institutional relations

Through these processes of (re)production of boundaries and norms, the judiciary in these cases also play an important role in negotiating the inter-institutional dynamics which take place in decision making in this context. Again, however, this is carefully depoliticised and, as such, invisibilised, through the recourse to the deployment of the public/private divide. In the cases discussed above, there is an entwining of medical jurisprudence into the territory of cases involving social care decision making by the judiciary in order to maintain a boundary between the courts and 'public' matters such as resources. At the same time as bolstering the public/private divide, this can also be seen as also maintaining particular configurations of institutional relations, further serving to entrench and naturalise power relations that have proven problematic for groups in society, including those with disabilities. This enables the problematic constructions of disability, or subjectivity, to persist unchallenged, and to become seen as natural or pre-given.

In this context, for example, in terms of the administration of health and social care decisions, the system pertaining to such decisions is complex, involving a multiplicity of actors, including the government, arms-length agencies, local authorities, NHS bodies, housing associations, and private contractors undertaking public functions (Collingbourne, 2013, 476). There are complex, hybrid forms of governance which permeate well beyond the traditional dividing line between the public and the private (Cooper, 1998). As Carney and Beaupert suggest, "law may be infiltrating relationships better left outside its sphere, or conversely its contribution may be being overlooked; and the innovative private, public, hybrid forms of law deployed may or may not be being correctly entertained or critically reviewed" (Carney and Beaupert, 2013, 175). Moreover, such a stark division of the public and private, and realms of decision making, overlooks the role of the state and institutions, in concert with other forces, in creating the particular conditions for experience which particular theories of justice will render as 'private'. Thus it is important here to draw on the assemblage to think through how judicial responses and legal responses to the public/private can shape the broader terrain of governance and decision making and effects of this.

As discussed in Chapters 2 and 3 and the outlining of the development of the MCA, the roots of the mental capacity legislation are heavily medico-legal, both in the cases which drove the need for the legislation in the first place, and in the prominence of medical concerns in the resulting framework. On one level, the cases discussed in this chapter can be viewed as further reproducing this medicalisation through endorsing the ongoing logics of one of the core (and equally problematic) principles of medical jurisprudence: that the courts cannot force medical professionals to provide a particular treatment against their clinical judgement. We can trace the development of this thread from medical jurisprudence into mental capacity jurisprudence more broadly through the case of *Aintree v James* [2013] UKSC 67 in the leading judgment delivered by Lady Hale. One of the more lauded – and most cited – aspects of Lady Hale's judgment in this case was the statement affirming the centrality of the patient in assessing their best interests (para 45). However, in making this point – which was seen as enabling a more empowering and patient-centred approach to decision making in the medical context – Lady Hale went on to stress that nothing in the judgment changed the law as previously understood (para 47), and that the person's wishes will not always prevail (para 45). She stated that the MCA is concerned with enabling a court to do for the patient what he could do for himself if he had full capacity, but nothing more (para 18). Drawing on cases such as *R v Cambridge District Health Authority, ex p B* [1995] 1 WLR and *R (Burke) v General Medical Council* [2005] EWCA Civ 1003, Lady Hale reminded us that a patient cannot demand that a doctor provide a treatment which he considers is adverse to the patient's clinical needs, nor is it the role of the Court of Protection to demand this.

This line of reasoning is then carefully channelled into the case law on social care decision making in both the *MN* and *MAG* cases. This position was approved by King J in *MN* in which *Aintree v James* was cited in support of the principle that the MCA is only concerned with "enabling the court to do for the patient what he could do for himself if of full capacity, but it goes no further" (para 52). This is then reiterated throughout the *MN* and *MAG* cases in order to align the approach to challenges to medical decisions with social care ones and to maintain the boundaries between the institutions. Such reiteration has productive effects in terms of institutional relations and the relations between different actors within an assemblage, reinforcing power relations in new spaces or territories. Focusing on the historicity of these institutional relations here reveals how these "exclusions tend to build on and reinforce each other, as the availability of alternative interpretations becomes increasingly remote" (Benson, 2004, 234). Yet, at the same time, the jurisdictional techniques at play here are evident, as different decision making contexts are assimilated and abstracted in order to enable the sustention of these boundaries. A contextual appreciation of the realities of medical decision making in comparison to social care decision making reveals very different processes and assemblages which defy the abstracted likeness that these cases portray. However, the realities of social care decision making processes – such as the assessment of needs, the potential for personal budgets and direct payments, and the centrality of the 'wellbeing' principle (in the Care Act 2014) are necessarily concealed in this intersection with mental capacity jurisprudence given the necessity of rendering them as private, rather than public, matters. In this process, the day-to-day processes and mundane spaces in which decisions are made, often entangled in webs of broader decisions, is overlooked. As Delaney suggests, it is important to consider "[h]ow … ordinary/ordering workings of power become invisible, unremarkable" (Delaney, 2010, 49).

Yet, in challenging the parallels drawn by the judiciary with medical decision making, the point here is not to endorse the position taken by the courts there. Rather, the portrayal of the doctor–patient relationship and the processes of decision making in that context too is problematically abstracted and ignores the various institutional dynamics and broader forces which shape clinical decisions. The simplistic sense in which doctors are seen to make decisions solely on the basis of 'clinical judgement' – an objective, neutral process free from external influence, has long been challenged by feminist theorists. As such, it could equally well be argued that even in medical decision making, the discretion and power afforded to individual doctors are inappropriate, particularly when involving relatively powerless individuals such as those deemed to lack mental capacity. There seems to be increasing recognition of this in the medical law literature. Recently, Foster and Miola raised this issue in a paper questioning the relationship between professional judgement and the role of the law. They argued that,

> To state the obvious: healthcare resource funding decisions kill, maim and save. It is perhaps curious (although understandable) that such obviously repercussive decisions are quite so hard to review. In making decisions about healthcare resource allocation, NHS bodies will (effectively non-reviewably) take into account not only data justified by the objective utilitarian tools of Quality Adjusted Life Years per Pound, but also views which can only bear the name of ethical or moral. The courts' reluctance to adjudicate must partly be a distaste for getting embroiled in this ethical/moral battleground – as well as a concern about opening the floodgates to litigation by disaffected patients, so clogging the courts. But precisely because the decisions are so difficult, and so 'ethical', we think that the courts should (with appropriate procedural safeguards to stop tidal waves of litigation swamping the court lists) be prepared to grapple with these life and death funding decisions.
>
> (Foster and Miola, 2015, 523)

Moreover, dicta in *Montgomery v Lanarkshire Health Board* [2015] SC 11 has highlighted the multidimensional aspect of medical decisions, and signals at some potential tools with which to further question the emphasis on professional discretion.

> The treatment which they can offer is now understood to depend not only upon their clinical judgment, but upon bureaucratic decisions as to such matters as resource allocation, cost-containment and hospital administration: decisions which are taken by non-medical professionals. Such

> decisions are generally understood within a framework of institutional rather than personal responsibilities, and are in principle susceptible to challenge under public law rather than, or in addition to, the law of delict or tort.
>
> (para 75)

> Furthermore, because the extent to which a doctor may be inclined to discuss risks with a patient is not determined by medical learning or experience, the application of the Bolam test to this question is liable to result in the sanctioning of differences in practice which are attributable not to divergent schools of thought in medical science, but merely to divergent attitudes among doctors as to the degree of respect owed to their patients.
>
> (para 84)

There is thus increasing acknowledgement of the reality of decision making processes and the dangers of shrouding both medical and social care decisions in a cloak of professional discretion. Yet in the same breath with which Lord Reed in *Montgomery v Lanarkshire* sews the seeds of doubt in relation to the primacy of 'clinical judgement', we also see the hasty reinforcement of the appropriate legal means by which to challenge these and, consequently, the reinforcement of the public/private law divide. Again, the zealous judicial maintenance of the public/private divide is apparent, as to begin to unravel this would have repercussions across the legal framework.

The discussion of the inter-institutional dynamics created and sustained through these cases further demonstrates that these structures and relations are not natural or static, and require constant maintenance and reproduction by the judiciary in order to persist. As Leckey argues, "each judicial intervention in the relationship between individuals and the administration may be regarded as simultaneously an instance of readjustment of the relationship between the courts themselves and the administration" (Leckey, 2008, 144). In a recursive process, through such cases, we see maintenance of (1) the power relations between individuals and professionals, (2) the circulation of power into new professional groups, and (3) the distancing of the judiciary from interference in professional discretion. This focus on inter-institutional dynamics within an assemblage engages with, and adds an important dimension to, literatures on everyday decision making and bureaucratic processes. Whilst much of the early literature on these discretionary decision making processes built upon Lipsky's work on street level bureaucracies (1980) and sought to reign in discretionary power, there has more recently been a shift to thinking instead about these bureaucracies in terms of agency (Maynard-Moody and Musheno, 2012). Thinking in terms of agency, and situating practices and processes within the broader structural context, allows a focus on cultural renderings and practices and processes through which these are created or reinscribed. Situating that shift within the assemblage lens offered here allows a deeper appreciation of this – rather than seeing the judicial level and the bureaucratic or street level as two separate scales or sites of justice/injustice, an assemblage analysis allows a focus on the connections and relations between these and the ways that power flows through these. Reflecting on the logics of the mental capacity legislation and the desire seen in the shaping of the legislation to enable flexibility and professional practice through informality, the inter-institutional relations supported by the judiciary here can be seen as extending these logics, ensuring power remains within the hands of medical (and now social care) professionals and creating the discursive space for their authoritative clinical and professional judgement.

It is important to note here, however, that this analysis does not posit judicial techniques or the game of jurisdiction as the primary driver of the creation or maintenance of a particular spatial configuration. Considering the discussion in Chapter 5 and the critiques of the 'turn to law' or 'the state', it is necessary instead to situate these judicial processes and dynamics within a broader set of institutional relations and actors. Revillard, for example, highlights the problematic lack of focus on day-to-day mobilisations of social movements through navigating bureaucracies, noting instead a tendency for social movements to focus on law and judicial processes (Revillard, 2016). Yet the analysis here enables us to focus on how these dynamics work and relate to each other. It is not an either/or focus on court processes or day-to-day mobilisation, but instead calls for attentiveness to how they feed into and shape each other. As this section suggested, the judicial techniques employed have an impact on the broader institutional relations and shape (or cement) the day-to-day relations in service provision. Likewise, the day-to-day experiences of individuals can shape the framing of cases coming to court, and can be represented (or hidden) through judicial processes in order to effect particular outcomes.

Conclusion

In relation to King J's statement above, about the *danger* of blurring this important divide between the public and the private, it must be asked, for whom is this a danger? It is apparent from this line of cases, and arguments in feminist legal literature more broadly, that the demarcation of the public and the private is central to liberal legal theory and its foundational assumptions about both the legal subject and the role of the state. In this sense, recognition of the porosity of this line (indeed, questioning of its existence) challenges the norms that underpin the endurance of the liberal legal framework and threatens to unravel these.

The chapter has begun to reveal some of the ways in which the public/private divide is problematically sustained through judicial techniques – namely the (shifting) rendering of the legal subject, the technicalities of jurisdiction, and the inter-institutional profession relations reproduced through these dynamics. The public/private divide at the heart of this has been revealed as a dichotomy of powerlessness – powerlessness for those individuals caught within these processes, and the ostensible – yet judicially reinforced – powerlessness of the courts. Drawing attention to these processes and the problematic norms which they actively reproduce demonstrates that these are not natural, neutral, or pre-political but require constant reinforcement. In so doing, this recognition provides the tools with which to consider how such processes can be disrupted and reconfigured. Flagging up the contradictions of the jurisprudence allows us to challenge the prevailing socio-spatial relations through "acts of reorientation of … the outcome of taken-for-granted habitus" (Radcliffe, 1999, 236–7). This again is not simply an exercise in critique. The theoretical lens employed throughout this book is particularly useful for highlighting the contingency of these processes and effects. As Fitzgibbon and Maher put it,

> The premise that the authority of law is inherently unstable and open to remaking actually operates at both the structural and instrumental levels: the law is in effect changed by each new iteration and thus new animating principles can, and should, be mobilised by legal actors within such re-iterations, even if change is slow, uneven and sometimes invisible.
> (Fitzgibbon and Maher, 2015, 268)

Law contains these tools. This more positive and transformative approach contained in these insights will be further discussed in the conclusion, where we turn to consider these binaries in concert, which work to entrench static ideals of the state and the spaces which the state touches. Returning again to survey the legal processes which reassert and reinforce the broader, interwoven logics, we see that the potential for transformative debate and progress tends to be subdued through the acceptance and reproduction of these binaries as pre-given. Disentangling them in the ways suggested in the book provides important reflection on the ways in which laws could be configured otherwise, particularly in light of the CRPD offering scope to engage with such transformative understandings.

References

Benson, M. H. 2004. 'Rules of Engagement: The Spatiality of Judicial Review' in I. Braverman, N. Blomley, D. Delaney and A. Kedar (Eds), *The Expanding Spaces of Law: A Timely Legal Geography*. Stanford: CA: Stanford Law Books. 215–38.

Blomley, N., Delaney, D. and Ford, R. 2000. *The Legal Geographies Reader: Law, Power, Space*. Toronto, ON: Wiley.

Boyd, S. (Ed) 1997. *Challenging the Public/Private Divide: Feminism, Law, and Public Policy*. Toronto: University of Toronto Press.

Carney, T. and Beaupert, F. 2013. 'Public and Private Bricolage: Challenges Balancing Law, Services & Civil Society in Advancing CRPD Supported Decision Making' *University of New South Wales Law Journal* 36(1), 175–201.

Collingbourne, T. 2013. 'Administrative Justice? Realising the Right to Independent Living in England: Power, Systems, Identities' *Journal of Social Welfare and Family Law* 35(4), 475–89.

Cooper, D. 1998. *Governing Out of Order: Space, Law and the Politics of Belonging*. London: Rivers Oram.

Davies, M. 2017. *Law Unlimited*. Oxfordshire: Routledge.

Delaney, D. 2010. *Nomospheric Investigations: The Spatial, The Legal and The Pragmatics of World Making*. Oxfordshire: Routledge.

Dietz, C. 2020. 'Jurisdiction in Trans Health' *Journal of Law and Society* 47(1), 60–86.

Doel, M. 2007. 'Post-Structuralist Geography: A Guide to Relational Space' *Annals of the Association of American Geographers* 97, 809–10.

England, K. 2003. 'Towards a Feminist Political Geography?' *Political Geography* 22, 611–16.

Feely, M. 2016. 'Disability Studies after the Ontological Turn: A Return to the Material World and Material Bodies without a Return to Essentialism' *Disability & Society* 31(7), 863–83.

Fitz-Gibbon, K. and Maher, J. 2015. 'Feminist Challenges to the Constraints of Law: Donning Uncomfortable Robes?' *Feminist Legal Studies* 23(3), 253–71.

Ford, R. 2000. 'Laws Territory (A History of Jurisdiction)' in N. Blomley, D. Delaney and R. Ford (Eds), *The Legal Geographies Reader: Law, Power, Space*. Toronto, ON: Wiley. 200–17.

Foster, C. and Miola, J. 2015. 'Who's In Charge? The Relationship Between Medical Law, Medical Ethics, And Medical Morality?' *Medical Law Review* 23(4), 505–30.

Garland, F and Travis, M. 2020. 'Making the State Responsible: Intersex Embodiment, Medical Jurisdiction, and State Responsibility' *Journal of Law and Society* 47(2), 298–324.

Hall, E. and Wilton, R. 2016. 'Towards a Relational Geography of Disability' *Progress in Human Geography* 41(6), 727–744.

Hyndman, J. 2008. 'Towards a Feminist Geopolitics' *The Canadian Geographer* 45(2), 210–22.

Keenan, S. 2015. *Subversive Property: Law and the Production of Spaces of Belonging*. Oxfordshire: Routledge.

Lacey, N. 1993. 'Theory Into Practice? Pornography and the Public/Private Dichotomy' *Journal of Law and Society* 20(1), 93–113.

Leckey, R. 2008. *Contextual Subjects: Family, State and Relational Theory*. Toronto: University of Toronto Press.

Lipsky, M. 1980. *Street Level Bureaucracy: Dilemmas of the Individual in Public Services*. New York: Russel Sage Foundation.

MacKinnon, C. 1989. *Towards a Feminist Theory of the State*. Cambridge, MA: Harvard University Press.

Massey, D., Allen, J. and Sarre, P. 1999. *Human Geography Today*. Cambridge: Polity Press.

Maynard-Moody, S. and Musheno, M. 2012. 'Social Equities and Inequities in Practice: Street-Level Workers as Agents and Pragmatists' *Public Administration Review* 72, S16–23.

Olsen, F. 1985. 'The Myth of State Intervention in the Family' *University of Michigan Journal of Law Reform* 18, 835.

Pateman, C. 1983. 'Feminist Critiques of the Public/Private Dichotomy' in S. Benn and G. Gaus (Eds), *Public and Private in Social Life*. London: Croom Helm. 281–303.

Radcliffe, S. 1999. 'Popular and State Discourses of Power' in D. Massey, J. Allen and P. Sarre (Eds), *Human Geography Today*. Cambridge: Polity Press. 219–42.

Revillard, A. 2016. 'Social Movements and the Politics of Bureaucratic Rights Enforcement: Insights from the Allocation of Disability Rights in France' *Law and Social Inquiry* 42(2), 450–78.

Rose, N. 1987. 'Beyond the Public/Private Division: Law, Power and the Family' *Journal of Law and Society* 14(1), 61–76.

Simplican, S. 2016. 'Disavowal of Disability in Rawls Theory of Justice and his Critics' in B. Arneill and N. Hirschmann (Eds), *Disability and Political Theory*. Cambridge: Cambridge University Press. 79–98.

Tribe, L. H. 1989. 'The Curvature of Constitutional Space: What Lawyers Can Learn from Modern Physics' *Harvard Law Review* 103(1), 1–39.

Tronto, J. 1993. *Moral Boundaries: A Political Argument for an Ethic of Care*. New York: Routledge.

Valverde, M. 2015. *Chronotopes of Law: Jurisdiction, Scale and Governance*. Oxon: Routledge.

Conclusion

As Massey argued, binary thinking has become "bound up with ways of spatio-temporalising the world which are so seemingly 'natural', so habitual, that we have almost forgotten to think about them" (Massey et al., 1999, 8). This book has been a reminder to challenge these habits. It has traced the spaces and parameters of current thinking and debate in mental capacity law, exploring and exposing the ways that these parameters are created and sustained, as well as their productive effects. Central to this is a number of mutually reinforcing binaries, which are embedded in broader logics of liberalism and which signal the primacy of boundedness within these logics. The relational and spatial dynamics engaged with in this book offer both an analytical approach through which to expose and understand these binaries and the broader frameworks that they are entangled in, but also offer alternative onto-epistemological starting points from which to rethink and reconfigure our approach to legal subjectivity and the form and possibilities of legal responses.

As a critical lens for mental capacity law, this attentiveness to spatial and relational dynamics has enabled a careful exploration of the binary framework that draws the boundaries of mental capacity law. Going beyond current theoretical debates on relational autonomy and vulnerability, these conceptual tools have drawn attention to the broader, mutually reinforcing boundaries that ideas of autonomy and capacity are entangled with. It has highlighted the need to not just focus attention at the individual level, and to avoid reinforcing problematic binary frameworks in attempts to move beyond them. Instead, a spatial and relational perspective has enabled deeper understanding of the historical contingencies and processes that have led to the current framework, and critical junctures within these processes. Rather than being seen as natural, pre-determined, or necessary, the framework, through this lens, becomes open to contention. In this way, distinctions drawn between capacity/incapacity, empowerment/protection, disability/non-disability, freedom/restraint, and public/private become less compelling, opening up new ways to approach questions arising in the context of mental capacity law. As well as unsettling the static legal subject inhabiting liberal legal approaches, new ways of conceptualising responses and responsibility have emerged. Dismantling the boundaries drawn around the individual, state, and communities, through complicating scale and temporality in the assemblage, opens up ways to rethink when, how, and where 'interventions' ought to take place, and their form. This acknowledgement of the processes of boundary making, following Barad and new materialist thought, is an important lens through which to open up ways of reconfiguring. Rather than just offering a lens for critique, the conceptual tools offered throughout the book are focused on sites for change.

In reflecting upon the potentiality in reconfiguring, it is important to "braid the strands" (Delaney, 2010, 23) and attend to the various implications of this relational and spatial turn. How can the myriad insights around subjectivity, responsibility, boundedness, processes, and dynamics feed into transformative legal projects? Delaney suggests that such projects entail respatialisation and resignification. The chapters have offered ways both to dismantle problematic logics and conceptualisations, as well as ways to reconceptualise them, through their dynamic relations and entanglements, in order to modify their legal significance, and in turn, alter the spaces (both discursive and material) they inhabit. Through mapping the webs that these logics are situated in, and their boundaries, I have also sought to traverse these in order to produce alternative spatial and relational dynamics.

As seen in the Introduction, this rethinking has been prompted both by the challenges posed by the Convention on the Rights of Persons with Disabilities (CRPD) and by a dissatisfaction with the stagnant and often narrow boundaries of debate in mental capacity scholarship. Rather than taking these boundaries as a natural, pre-given starting point within which reforms must be situated, instead I have highlighted the importance of tracing their roots, exposing the underpinning ideals and effects of these, and in turn, challenging their legitimacy. At a time when the problematic underpinnings and effects of our current legal framework are becoming more apparent, we need to be mindful of the tendency, as Rose warns, that "the old theories reappear as solutions to their own failure" (Rose, 1987, 61). It is hoped that some of the ideas here will catalyse new thinking around the CRPD, as well as interdisciplinary engagements with mental capacity law to further deepen our understanding of its role and effects.

It might be questioned why *law*, via the CRPD, is seen as providing the answer or catalyst for this shift, particularly given the role law has played in producing the problematic relations and norms that are illuminated throughout the preceding chapters. It is now trite to acknowledge that law alone cannot solve all of society's problems, yet such statements betray a lack of understanding of the role that law has played in the creation of such problems, and can play as part of broader legal and political reconfigurations. As discussed throughout the book, law (in various guises) does play an important role in the shaping of institutional relations and intra-actions. It is implicated in everyday, mundane spaces despite its purported absence. Moving away from a particularly positivist understanding of the role of law, and instead recognising its (sometimes absent) presence in the creation of particular boundaries and relations is central to this project. Drawing attention to the legal processes involved as part of broader assemblages, the ways such processes draw particular boundaries through legal concepts such as jurisdiction and state obligations, how legal responses are presented through a scalar and topographical lens, and also recognising the way that law *creates* rather than responds to, represents, or discovers difference enables us to get a firmer grasp on how legal dynamics and relations can be reconfigured, as well as how law manifests resistance to such change through sedimenting particular practices and presenting them as natural or objective. As Krieger argues, and as perhaps is starkly evident in the current debates as to implementing the CRPD,

> entrenched norms and institutionalized practices, operating as taken-for-granted background rules, systematically skew the interpretations of transformative legal rules so that those rules increasingly come to resemble the normative and institutional systems they were intended to displace.
>
> (Krieger, 2003, 349)

Deeping our understanding of how this happens and examining "the link between substantive norms and institutional powers and decision making" (Sheppard, 2010, 266) helps to resist such capture.

It is important to reflect briefly on what might be the challenges in taking such a project forward, particularly in relation to the CRPD. At one level, it could legitimately be asked whether the CRPD is an appropriate vehicle for significant legal upheaval in the first place. Whilst this book has been critical of legal liberalism and its underpinning ideals, it could be argued that the CRPD is itself a product of this very system and so must necessarily be built on said ideals and logics. This is certainly true to a degree, and it is undoubtedly constrained by this in relation to the structural processes and rules of engagement that it is embedded in as part of the UN legal system. Moreover, the residue of liberal legal ideals is present across the Articles of the Convention in terms of the language used and a focus on autonomy. On the other hand, the process through which the CRPD came into being, and the heavy involvement of disabled people in this and in the framing of the Convention offers a different perspective and signals at least a potential for a shift despite the broader landscape it is situated in. Moreover, it must also be recognised that despite the familiar shape and form of the Convention, it does impose a number of positive obligations on States Parties and has been widely recognised as melding social and economic rights into what are otherwise seen as traditional civil and political rights. As such, whilst the Convention may ultimately be constrained by its location in a broader liberal legal system, at the same time it seems to unsettle the traditional boundaries of this.

Despite this – and ultimately, the extent to which the CRPD can break out of a liberal legal mould will of course remain to be seen – the Convention does at the very least provide a crucial opportunity for mental capacity law. It has provoked something of an existential crisis for ideas of capacity and autonomy. In responding to this, we may want, and need, to go beyond mere compliance with the CRPD. This book has not been about providing a blueprint for CRPD compliance; it has been about tracing and exposing the logics which currently constrain our legal analysis and debates and offering ways to move beyond them. Whilst scholars and practitioners have been struggling to fit the requirements of the Convention into our legal framework, what becomes apparent is that the problems may not lie in the CRPD but in the binary framework that they are trying to understand it through.

In transgressing these boundaries, what then emerges in their wake? As has been seen, this active process of critique and dismantling has productive effects, and shifts in certain nodes of these binary logics will facilitate (and necessitate) shifts elsewhere. At the same time, we need to be aware of the effects of such shifts, and be "responsive to the borders it may leave in place and create, even as it works to critique, dismantle, and move beyond other borders" (Hall, 2015, 1; also see Mohanty, 2003). Attentiveness to this requires a deeper, interdisciplinary engagement with law's processes and effects, grappling with the possibilities of law which is not built upon and constrained by binary framings, and it is hoped that this book has opened up the space for this engagement for mental capacity law.

Beyond mental capacity law, the insights developed in the book also have the potential to feed into socio-legal scholarship more broadly, offering new ways to conceptualise and think through legal problematisations which are similarly constrained by binary frameworks. The discussion has also sought to add to disciplinary debates beyond law, such as in political theory, political and human geography, and disability studies. It is hoped that by opening up this dynamic conversation between mental capacity law, law more broadly, and these other disciplines, new research agendas, interdisciplinary approaches, and solutions may emerge.

References

Delaney, D. 2010. *Nomospheric Investigations: The Spatial, The Legal and The Pragmatics of World Making*. Oxfordshire: Routledge.

Hall, K. Q. 2015. 'New Conversations in Feminist Disability Studies: Feminism, Philosophy, and Borders' *Hypatia* 30(1), 1–12.

Krieger, L. H. 2003. 'Sociolegal Backlash' in L. H. Krieger (Ed), *Backlash Against the ADA: Reinterpreting Disability Rights*. Michigan: University of Michigan Press. 340–95.

Massey, D. with the collective. 1999. 'Issues and Debates' in D. Massey, J. Allen and P. Sarre (Eds), *Human Geography Today*. Cambridge: Polity Press. 3–21.

Mohanty, C. 2003. *Feminism without Borders*. Durham: Duke University Press.

Rose, N. 1987. 'Beyond the Public/Private Division: Law, Power and the Family' *Journal of Law & Society* 14(1), 61–76.

Sheppard, C. 2010. *Inclusive Equality: The Relational Dimensions of Systemic Discrimination in Canada*. Montreal: McGill-Queen's University Press.

Index

Note: Page numbers followed by 'n' refer to footnotes.

For Product Safety Concerns and Information please contact our EU
representative GPSR@taylorandfrancis.com
Taylor & Francis Verlag GmbH, Kaufingerstraße 24, 80331 München, Germany

www.ingramcontent.com/pod-product-compliance
Ingram Content Group UK Ltd.
Pitfield, Milton Keynes, MK11 3LW, UK
UKHW020005200926
475702UK00015B/2490

* 9 7 8 1 0 3 2 1 1 5 7 7 1 *